the
Vegetarian
Slow Cooker

the Vegetarian Slow Cooker

Over 200 delicious recipes

Judith Finlayson

Robert
ROSE

For complete cataloguing information, see page 304.

Disclaimer

The recipes in this book have been carefully tested by our kitchen and our tasters. To the best of our knowledge, they are safe and nutritious for ordinary use and users. For those people with food or other allergies, or who have special food requirements or health issues, please read the suggested contents of each recipe carefully and determine whether or not they may create a problem for you. All recipes are used at the risk of the consumer.

We cannot be responsible for any hazards, loss or damage that may occur as a result of any recipe use.

For those with special needs, allergies, requirements or health problems, in the event of any doubt, please contact your medical adviser prior to the use of any recipe.

Design and Production: Daniella Zanchetta/PageWave Graphics Inc.
Editor: Carol Sherman
Recipe Editor: Jennifer MacKenzie
Proofreader: Karen Campbell-Sheviak
Photography: Colin Erricson and Mark T. Shapiro
Food Styling: Kathryn Robertson and Kate Bush
Prop Styling: Charlene Erricson

Cover image: Potato and Pea Coconut Curry (page 132)

We acknowledge the financial support of the Government of Canada through the Book Publishing Industry Development Program (BPIDP) for our publishing activities.

Published by Robert Rose Inc.
120 Eglinton Avenue East, Suite 800, Toronto, Ontario, Canada M4P 1E2
Tel: (416) 322-6552 Fax: (416) 322-6936

Printed and bound in Canada

1 2 3 4 5 6 7 8 9 TCP 18 17 16 15 14 13 12 11 10

Contents

Acknowledgments

A cookbook is never just a one-person production. There are so many facts (consider the lines of recipe ingredients alone) and components (photographs and food styling among them) that it requires a community of people working together to create a book that will meet the demanding criteria of today's marketplace. Basically, I've been working with the same terrific team for almost 10 years. They are consummate professionals with whom I enjoy working, and I feel very fortunate to have their support.

First and foremost is my husband, Bob Dees, who said, "You should think about revising your vegetarian slow cooker book." As usual, he was right. I'd also like to thank Marian Jarkovich at Robert Rose, for her support of this and all my projects.

The dramatic difference between a manuscript (the typed copy an author works on) and a finished cookbook depends upon the work of designers, photographers and stylists. Thanks to the team at PageWave Graphics, especially Daniella Zanchetta, who designed this book. As always, Colin Erricson and Mark Shapiro took fabulous photographs, food stylists Kathryn Robertson and Kate Bush made my recipes look delicious and prop stylist Charlene Erricson provided a perfect setting for her preparations.

I take pride in the quality of my recipes. Recipe testers Audrey King and Jennifer MacKenzie help to ensure that my standards are maintained, often making helpful suggestions for improvement.

No matter how diligent I am, the sheer volume of detail ensures that errors will creep in. Thanks to copy editor Karen Campbell-Sheviak, who catches things the rest of us miss. And last, but certainly not least, my editor, Carol Sherman, whose eagle eye, patient demeanor and great sense of humor always make the editorial process a pleasure.

Introduction

In 2004, my book *125 Best Vegetarian Slow Cooker Recipes* was published. Its success, coupled with the increased interest in all forms of vegetarianism, inspired me to produce a follow-up volume. Today, more and more people — even those who are not vegetarians — are eating less meat. There are many reasons for this trend, not the least of which is the growing body of evidence that a diet high in vegetables, legumes, whole grains and fruit can provide much more than daily sustenance. Not only are plant foods lower in calories and saturated fat than meat, but they also have disease-fighting properties. Consuming adequate amounts of these foods appears to have the power to prevent and possibly even cure many illnesses, from Type-2 diabetes to cardiovascular disease.

In the past few years, we have also become more aware of the moral issues surrounding meat consumption, which range from a large carbon footprint to the unethical treatment of animals. One result is the identification of a new species of eater, the "flexitarian," a sometime vegetarian who consciously monitors their consumption of meat, with a view toward improving not only their own health status but also that of the planet.

So perhaps not surprisingly, vegetarianism, once unusual, is now becoming mainstream. The same can be said for slow cookers. Recently, I heard a presentation from an executive of a major food company who said her firm now assumes that their customers own a slow cooker. This makes perfect sense to me simply because the appliance is one of the most effective time-management tools any cook can have. With its help, even the busiest people can arrive home after a hectic day to an old-fashioned home-cooked meal that is ready to serve.

In this book, like those I've previously published, I've tried to include a wide range of recipes that will appeal to many tastes and requirements — from great family food to more sophisticated recipes for entertaining, including desserts. There are more than 130 "vegan friendly" recipes in this volume, which have been identified as such for easy access. And many recipes that contain eggs or dairy can be easily substituted with egg substitutes and/or non-diary ingredients that suit your taste.

As enjoyable as it is to recreate many of the more traditional dishes that were a meaningful part of the past, such as baked beans and cobblers, in developing this book I've also had great fun experimenting with more exotic dishes that reflect the expanding horizons of cooking in our global world. Eggplant Lentil Ragoût and Parsnip and Coconut Curry with Crispy Shallots are two favorites that represent Mediterranean and Southeast Asian cultures, respectively. I particularly enjoy using herbs and spices in such dishes as Turkish-Style Barley Soup and Vegetable Biriyani. And I love updating old standards such as Classic French Onion Soup or transforming dishes such as Chicken Paprikash into a vegetarian version — Tempeh Paprikash.

There's more to using a slow cooker than putting food on the table. In my opinion, the meals it allows you to prepare nourish both body and soul. Made from fresh and wholesome ingredients, with levels of fat and salt controlled by the home cook, slow cooker dishes are certainly nutritious. But more than that, they offer a reassuring antidote to the stresses of our fast-paced, high-tech age. There are few experiences more pleasurable than arriving home to be greeted by the appetizing aroma of a simmering soup or stew, the kinds of dishes that the slow cooker excels at producing. With the slow cooker's help, anyone can prepare delicious food with a minimum of attention and maximum certainty of success. I sincerely hope you will try these recipes and that you will enjoy them and make the slow cooker a regular part of your life.

– Judith Finlayson

Using Your Slow Cooker

An Effective Time Manager

In addition to producing great-tasting food, a slow cooker is one of the most effective time-management tools any cook can have. Basically, it allows you to be in the kitchen when it suits your schedule. If you prefer, you can do most of the prep work in advance, when it's most convenient for you, and once the appliance is turned on there is little or nothing left for you to do. The slow cooker performs unattended while you carry on with your workaday life. You can be away from the kitchen all day and return to a hot, delicious meal.

Slow Cooker Basics

A Low-Tech Appliance

Slow cookers are amazingly low-tech. The appliance usually consists of a metal casing and a stoneware insert with a tight-fitting lid. For convenience, you should be able to remove the insert from the metal casing. This makes it easier to clean and increases its versatility, not only as a vessel for refrigerating dishes that have been prepared to the Make Ahead stage, but also as a serving dish. The casing contains the heat source, electrical coils that usually surround the stoneware insert. These coils do their work using the energy it takes to power a 100-watt light bulb. Because the slow cooker operates on such a small amount of electricity, you can safely leave it turned on while you are away from home.

Shapes, Sizes and Configurations

Slow cookers are generally round or oval in shape and range in size from $1\frac{1}{2}$ to $8\frac{1}{2}$ quarts. The small round ones are ideal for dips and fondues, as well as some soups, main courses and desserts. The smaller oval ones (approximately $1\frac{1}{2}$ to 4 quarts) are extremely versatile because they are tiny enough to work well with limited quantities but also have enough volume to accommodate some full-batch recipes. The larger sizes (5 to $8\frac{1}{2}$ quarts), usually oval in shape, are necessary to cook big-batch dishes and those that need to be cooked in a separate dish or pan that can fit into the stoneware.

I have recommended slow cooker sizes for all my recipes. However, please be aware that so many new models are coming onto the market that I have not been able to test all the configurations myself. Use your common sense. The stoneware should be at least one-third to three-quarters full. Dishes that contain an abundance of vegetables and liquid will likely need a model that can accommodate greater volume. Because I use my slow cookers a lot for entertaining, I feel there is a benefit to having at least two: a smaller ($1\frac{1}{2}$ to 4 quart) size which is ideal for preparing dips, roasting nuts or making recipes with smaller yields, and a larger (5 to 6 quart) oval one, which I use most of the time to cook recipes with larger yields as well as those calling for a baking dish or pan set inside the stoneware. Once you begin using your slow cooker, you will get a sense of what suits your needs.

Your slow cooker should come with a booklet that explains how to use the appliance. I recommend that you read this carefully and/or visit the manufacturer's website for specific information on the model you purchased. There are now so many models, shapes and sizes of slow cookers on the market that it is impossible to give one-size-fits-all instructions for using them.

Cooking Times

Over the years I've cooked in a wide variety of slow cookers and have found that cooking times can vary substantially from one to another. This is true even among different models sold under the same brand. The quality control on some of the lower-priced models may not be as rigorous as it should be, which accounts for some of the difference. That said, I've also found that some of the newer slow cookers tend to cook much more quickly than those that are a few years old. Please bear these discrepancies in mind if you follow my recipes and find that your food is overcooked. Although it may not seem particularly helpful if you're just starting out, the only firm advice I can give is: Know your slow cooker. After trying a few of these recipes, you will get a sense of whether your slow cooker is faster or slower than the ones I use, and you will be able to adjust the cooking times accordingly. Other variables that can affect cooking time are extreme humidity, power fluctuations and high altitude. Be extra vigilant if any of these circumstances affect you.

Cooking Great-Tasting Food

The slow cooker's less-is-better approach is, in many ways, the secret of its success. The appliance does its work by cooking foods very slowly — from about 200°F (100°C) on the Low setting to 300°F (150°C) on High. This slow, moist cooking environment brings the best out of long-cooking whole grains such as wheat berries and barley, as well as legumes, for which it is best-known. It also helps to ensure success with delicate puddings and custards, among other dishes. I also love to make cheesecakes in my slow cooker because they emerge from this damp cocoon perfectly cooked every time. They have a beautifully creamy texture and don't dry out or crack, which happens all too easily in the oven.

Some benefits of long, slow cooking:
- it allows the seasoning in complex sauces to intermingle without scorching;
- it makes succulent chilies and stews that don't dry out or stick to the bottom of the pot; and
- it ensures success with delicate dishes such as puddings and custards.

Entertaining Worthy

I often use my slow cookers to help prepare the meal when I entertain, and as you use this book, you'll notice recipes that have been identified as "Entertaining Worthy." Some of these are clearly special occasion dishes, but many may strike you as pretty down home, particularly if you're trying to impress guests. All of which is to say, my selections are entirely subjective and very much reflect my approach to entertaining. While every now and again I like to pull out the stops and do a bang up elegant dinner party, most of the time I prefer to have one or two couples over for a casual Friday night meal. And on those evenings the kinds of dishes everyone prefers tend to be classic low-key comfort foods, which in my opinion are truly "entertaining worthy."

Understanding Your Slow Cooker

Like all appliances, the slow cooker has its unique way of doing things, so you need to understand how it works and adapt your cooking style accordingly. When friends learned I was writing my first slow cooker cookbook, many had the same response: "Oh, you mean that appliance that allows you to throw the ingredients in and return home to a cooked meal!"

"Well, sort of," was my response. Over the years I've learned to think of my slow cooker as an indispensable helpmate and I can hardly imagine living without its assistance. But I also know that it can't work miracles. Off the top of my head, I can't think of any great dish that results when ingredients are merely "thrown together." Success in the slow cooker, like success in the oven or on top of the stove, depends upon using proper cooking techniques. The slow cooker saves you time because it allows you to forget about the food once it is in the stoneware. But you still must pay attention to the advance preparation. Here are a few tips that will help to ensure slow cooker success.

Soften Vegetables

Although it requires an extra pan, I am committed to softening most vegetables before adding them to the slow cooker. In my experience this is not the most time-consuming part of preparing a slow cooker dish — it usually takes longer to peel and chop the vegetables, which you have to do anyway. But it dramatically improves the quality of the dish for two reasons. Not only does browning add color, it begins the process of caramelization, which breaks down the natural sugars in foods and releases their flavor. It also extracts the fat-soluble components of foods, which further enriches the taste. Moreover, tossing herbs and spices in with the softened vegetables helps to produce a sauce in which the flavors are better integrated than they would be if this step were skipped.

Reduce the Quantity of Liquid

As you use your slow cooker, one of the first things you will notice is that it generates liquid. Because slow cookers cook at a low heat, tightly covered, liquid doesn't evaporate as it does in the oven or on top of the stove. As a result, food made from traditional recipes will be watery. So the second rule of successful slow cooking is to reduce the amount of liquid. Because I don't want to reduce the flavor, I prefer to cook with broth rather than water.

Cut Root Vegetables into Thin Slices or Small Pieces

Perhaps surprisingly, root vegetables — carrots, parsnips and particularly potatoes — cook even more slowly than meat in the slow cooker. Root vegetables should be thinly sliced or cut into small pieces: no larger than 1-inch (2.5 cm) cubes.

Pay Attention to Cooking Temperature

Many desserts such as those containing milk, cream or some leavening agents need to be cooked on High. In these recipes, a Low setting is not suggested as an option. For recipes that aren't dependent upon cooking at a particular temperature, the rule of thumb is that 1 hour of cooking on High equals 2 to 2½ hours on Low.

Don't Overcook

Although slow cooking reduces your chances of overcooking food, it is still not a "one size fits all" solution to meal preparation. Many vegetables such as legumes and root vegetables need a good 8 hour cooking span on Low and may even benefit from a longer cooking time. But most others are cooked in about 6 hours on Low. If you're away from the house all day, it makes sense to have a slow cooker that automatically switches to Warm after the food is cooked. One solution (which is not possible if you are cooking meat because of food safety concerns) is to extend the cooking time by assembling the dish ahead of time, then refrigerating it overnight in the stoneware. Because the mixture and the stoneware are chilled, the vegetables will take longer to cook. (Be sure to use the Low setting and don't preheat the casing before adding the insert. Otherwise, your stoneware might crack.)

Use Ingredients Appropriately

Some ingredients do not respond well to long, slow cooking and should be added during the last 30 minutes after the temperature has been increased to High. These include zucchini, peas, snow peas, leafy greens, milk and cream (which will curdle if cooked too long).

I love to cook with peppers, but I've learned that most become bitter if cooked for too long. The same holds true for cayenne pepper or hot pepper sauces such as Tabasco, and large quantities of spicy curry powder. (Small quantities of curry powder seem to fare well, possibly because natural sugars in the vegetables counter any bitterness.) The solution to this problem is to add pepper(s) to a recipe during the last 30 minutes of cooking. All the recipes in this book address these concerns in the instructions.

Since I am not a vegan, many of my recipes contain dairy products. In some cases, where I am comfortable with the solution, I have suggested non-dairy alternatives. But I have also assumed that if you do not eat dairy, you will be well aware of the alternatives and will have sourced the products that work for you. Try a few of the recipes using non-dairy alternatives, for example olive oil for butter, egg replacement products for eggs, soft tofu

or soy yogurt for yogurt, rice, nut or soy milk for milk or cream, the many varieties of soy cheese for those made from milk and ices or soy ice cream for whipped cream or ice cream. You will soon get a feel for those that produce satisfactory results.

Whole-Leaf Herbs and Spices

For best results use whole rather than ground herbs and spices in the slow cooker. Whole spices such as cinnamon sticks and cloves and whole-leaf herbs such as dried thyme and oregano leaves release their flavors slowly throughout the long cooking period, unlike ground spices and herbs, which tend to lose flavor during slow cooking. If you're using fresh herbs, add them finely chopped, during the last hour of cooking, unless you include the whole stem (this works best with thyme and rosemary).

I recommend the use of cracked black peppercorns rather than ground pepper in many of my recipes because they release flavor slowly during the long cooking process. "Cracked pepper" can be purchased in the spice sections of supermarkets, but I like to make my own with a mortar and pestle. A rolling pin or even a heavy can on its side will also break up the peppercorns for use in slow-cooked dishes. If you prefer to use ground black pepper, use one-quarter to one-half the amount of cracked black peppercorns called for in the recipe.

Cooking Oils

There is a great deal of conflicting information surrounding the safety of oils for cooking, and those you choose to use will likely reflect the perspective you accept. That's why most of my recipes just call for "oil." You are free to use the kind of cooking oil you prefer, for instance, canola, peanut, safflower, sunflower or corn. However, I should point out that I shy away from using refined oils because I don't think they are healthy. Olive oil is my cooking oil of choice. It has been in use for thousands of years and, in my opinion, has passed the test of time. It is a relatively stable oil (unlike flax or walnut oil), which means it can tolerate temperatures that are suitable for most cooking tasks (approximately 350°F/180°C), which makes it a good choice for softening vegetables and browning meat. In some recipes with an Asian flavor profile, I have suggested coconut oil, which adds pleasant flavor to the dish, and in others that have Mediterranean overtones, I have specified olive oil, but in the end, the choice is yours.

Using Dishes and Pans in the Slow Cooker

Some dishes, notably puddings and custards, need to be cooked in an extra dish that is placed in the slow cooker stoneware. Not only will you need a large oval slow cooker for this purpose, finding a dish or pan that fits into the stoneware can be a challenge. I've found that standard 7-inch (18 cm) square, 4-cup (1 L) and 6-cup (1.5 L) ovenproof baking dishes or soufflé dishes are the best all-round pans for this purpose, and I've used them to cook most of the custard-like recipes in this book. A 7-inch (18 cm) springform pan, which fits into a large oval slow cooker, is also a useful item for making cheesecakes.

Before you decide to make a recipe requiring a baking dish, ensure that you have a container that will fit into your stoneware. I've noted the size and dimensions of the containers used in all relevant recipes. Be aware that varying the size and shape of the dish is likely to affect cooking times.

Making Smaller Quantities

Over the years many people have asked me for slow cooker recipes that make smaller quantities, suitable for one or two people. Since most recipes reheat well or can be frozen for future use, making a big-batch recipe can be an efficient strategy for having a delicious, nutritious meal on hand for those nights when there is no time to cook. However, since more and more households comprise single people or couples who want to enjoy the benefits of using a slow cooker, I have noted those recipes that are suitable for being halved. Since slow cookers depend on volume to operate efficiently, it is important to use a small slow cooker (approximately $1\frac{1}{2}$ to $3\frac{1}{2}$ quarts) when cutting a recipe in half.

Making Ahead

Most of the recipes in this book can be at least partially prepared ahead of time and held for up to two days in the refrigerator, which is a great time saver for busy days. (Look for the Make Ahead instructions accompanying appropriate recipes.)

Maximize Slow Cooker Convenience

To get the most out of your slow cooker, consider the following:
- Prepare a recipe up to two days before you intend to cook — when it suits your schedule best. Cook a recipe overnight and refrigerate until ready to serve.
- Make a big-batch recipe and freeze a portion for a second or even a third meal.

Food Safety in the Slow Cooker

Because it cooks at a very low temperature for long periods of time, cooking with a slow cooker requires a bit more vigilance about food safety than does cooking at higher temperatures. The slow cooker needs to strike a delicate balance between cooking slowly enough that it doesn't require your attention and fast enough to ensure that food reaches temperatures that are appropriate to inhibit bacterial growth. Bacteria grow rapidly at temperatures higher than 40°F (4°C) and lower than 140°F (60°C). Once the temperature reaches 165°F (74°C), bacteria are killed. That's why it is so important to leave the lid on when you're slow cooking, particularly

during the early stages. This helps to ensure that bacteria-killing temperatures are reached in the appropriate amount of time.

Slow cooker manufacturers have designed the appliance to ensure that bacterial growth is not a concern. So long as the lid is left on and the food is cooked for the appropriate length of time, that crucial temperature will be reached quickly enough to ensure food safety.

The following tips will help to ensure that utmost food safety standards are met:
- Keep any foods containing dairy or eggs refrigerated until you are ready to cook. Bacteria multiply quickly at room temperature. Do not allow ingredients to rise to room temperature before cooking.
- Limit the number of times you lift the lid while food is cooking. Each time the lid is removed it takes approximately 20 minutes to recover the lost heat. This increases the time it takes for the food to reach the "safe zone."
- If the power goes out while you are away discard the food if it has not finished cooking. If the food has cooked completely, it should be safe for up to 2 hours.
- Refrigerate leftovers as quickly as possible.
- Do not reheat food in the slow cooker.

Testing for Safety

If you are concerned that your slow cooker isn't cooking quickly enough to ensure food safety, try this simple test. Fill the stoneware insert with 8 cups (2 L) of cold water or until three-quarters full if smaller than 2 quarts. Set temperature to Low and let heat for 8 hours. Using an accurate thermometer and checking quickly (because the temperature drops when the lid is removed), check to ensure that the temperature is 185°F (85°C). If the slow cooker has not reached that temperature, it's not heating food fast enough to avoid food safety problems. If the temperature is significantly higher than that, the appliance is not cooking slowly enough to be used as a slow cooker.

Keeping Food Warm

Many slow cookers have a Warm setting, which holds the food at 165°F (74°C). Programmable models will automatically switch to Warm when the time is up. Cooked food can be kept warm in the slow cooker for up to two hours. At that point it should be transferred to small containers so it cools as rapidly as possible and then be refrigerated or frozen. Because the appliance heats up so slowly, food should never be reheated in a slow cooker.

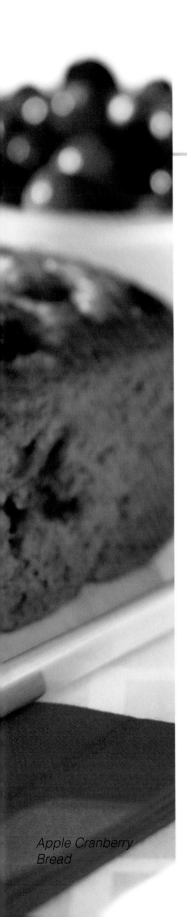

Bread and Breakfast

Apple Cranberry Bread

Apple Cranberry Bread

This bread, like the others in this book, can be made in almost any kind of baking dish that will fit into your slow cooker. I have a variety of baking pans that work well: a small loaf pan (about 8 by 4 inches/20 by 10 cm) makes a traditionally shaped bread; a round (6 cup/1.5 L) soufflé dish or a square (7 inch/18 cm) baking dish produces slices of different shapes. All taste equally good.

I like to use evaporated cane sugar because it contains some nutrients, but if you don't have it, substitute packed brown sugar.

I love the combination of flavors in this delicious bread — a hint of orange combined with tart cranberries. It makes a great snack, a nutritious dessert and can even be eaten for breakfast.

- **8- by 4-inch (20 by 10 cm) approx. loaf pan or 6-cup (1.5 L) soufflé or baking dish, greased (see Tips, left)**
- **Large (minimum 5 quart) oval slow cooker**

1 cup	all-purpose flour	250 mL
1 cup	whole wheat flour	250 mL
¼ cup	milled flax seeds	50 mL
2 tsp	baking powder	10 mL
½ tsp	salt	2 mL
½ tsp	ground cinnamon	2 mL
¾ cup	raw cane sugar, such as Demerara or other evaporated cane juice sugar (see Tips, left)	175 mL
¼ cup	olive oil	50 mL
1	egg	1
2 tbsp	finely grated orange zest (2 oranges)	25 mL
¾ cup	orange juice (1 large navel orange)	175 mL
1 tsp	vanilla extract	5 mL
1 cup	finely chopped peeled cored apple (about 1 apple)	250 mL
1 cup	fresh or frozen cranberries	250 mL

1. In a bowl or on a sheet of waxed paper, combine all-purpose and whole wheat flours, flax seeds, baking powder, salt and cinnamon. Mix well.

2. In a separate bowl, beat sugar, oil, egg, orange zest and juice and vanilla until thoroughly blended. Add dry ingredients, stirring just until blended. Fold in apple and cranberries.

3. Spoon batter into prepared pan. Cover pan tightly with foil and secure with a string. Place pan in slow cooker stoneware and pour in enough boiling water to come 1 inch (2.5 cm) up the sides of the dish. Cover and cook on High for 4 hours, until a tester inserted in the center comes out clean. Unmold and serve warm or let cool.

Banana Walnut Oat Bread

This moist and flavorful bread makes a delicious snack. You can also serve it as a dessert or for a breakfast on the run.

- **Large (minimum 5 quart) oval slow cooker**
- **8- by 4-inch (20 by 10 cm) approx. loaf pan or 6-cup (1.5 L) soufflé or baking dish, greased (see Tip, left)**

1/3 cup	butter, softened	75 mL
2/3 cup	raw cane sugar, such as Demerara or other evaporated cane juice sugar (see Tips, left)	150 mL
2	eggs	2
3	ripe bananas, mashed (about 1 1/4 cups/ 300 mL)	3
3/4 cup	all-purpose flour, unbleached if possible	175 mL
3/4 cup	rolled oats (not quick-cooking)	175 mL
2 tbsp	milled flax seeds	25 mL
2 tsp	baking powder	10 mL
1/2 tsp	salt	2 mL
1/4 tsp	baking soda	1 mL
1/2 cup	finely chopped walnuts	125 mL

1. In a bowl, beat butter and sugar until light and creamy. Add eggs, one at a time, beating until incorporated. Beat in bananas.

2. In a separate bowl or on a sheet of waxed paper, combine flour, oats, flax seeds, baking powder, salt and baking soda. Add to banana mixture, stirring just until combined. Fold in walnuts.

3. Spoon batter into prepared pan. Cover pan tightly with foil and secure with a string. Place pan in slow cooker stoneware and pour in enough boiling water to come 1 inch (2.5 cm) up the sides of the dish. Cover and cook on High for 3 hours, until a tester inserted in the center comes out clean. Unmold and serve warm or let cool.

Makes 1 large loaf or
up to 3 small loaves
Serves 10 to 12

Tip

If your slow cooker will accommodate a 9- by 5-inch (2 L) loaf pan, by all means use it to make this bread. Cooking time will be 3 hours or more.

Steamed Brown Bread

Served warm, this slightly sweet bread is a delicious accompaniment to baked beans. It also goes well with wedges of Cheddar cheese.

- Three 19-oz (540 mL) vegetable tins, washed, dried and sprayed with vegetable oil spray, or one 8-cup (2 L) soufflé or baking dish, lightly greased
- Large (minimum 5 quart) oval slow cooker

1 cup	all-purpose flour	250 mL
1 cup	whole wheat flour	250 mL
½ cup	rye flour	125 mL
½ cup	cornmeal	125 mL
2 tbsp	granulated sugar	25 mL
1 tsp	salt	5 mL
1 tsp	baking soda	5 mL
1½ cups	buttermilk	375 mL
½ cup	molasses	125 mL
2 tbsp	olive oil	25 mL

1. In a bowl or on a sheet of waxed paper, combine all-purpose, whole wheat and rye flours, cornmeal, sugar, salt and baking soda. Mix well and make a well in the center.

2. In a separate bowl, mix together buttermilk, molasses and olive oil. Pour into well and mix until blended.

3. Spoon batter into prepared cans (in equal amounts) or single baking dish. Cover top(s) with foil and secure with a string. Place in slow cooker stoneware and pour in enough boiling water to come 1 inch (2.5 cm) up the sides of the dish. Cover and cook on High for 2 hours, if using cans, or 3 hours, if using a baking dish, until a tester inserted in the center comes out clean. Unmold and serve warm.

Tip

When making whole-grain cereals in the slow cooker, be aware that stirring encourages creaminess. Obviously, for convenience, I don't suggest that you wake up during the night to stir the cereal while it's cooking. However, if you have time, let it sit on Warm for at least 15 minutes before serving and stir it several times, if possible.

Hot Oatmeal

Rolled oats, often called porridge when cooked, are the most popular hot cereal in North America. Less toothsome than steel-cut oats (see intro, below), these are whole oat kernels that have been softened by steaming then rolled.

- **Small to medium (1½ to 3½ quart) slow cooker**
- **Lightly greased slow cooker stoneware**

1¼ cups	rolled oats	300 mL
½ tsp	salt	2 mL
4 cups	water	1 L
	Milk or non-dairy alternative, optional	
	Maple syrup, honey or raw cane sugar, optional	

1. In prepared slow cooker stoneware, combine oats, salt and water. Stir well. Place a clean tea towel, folded in half (so you will have two layers), over top of the stoneware to absorb moisture. Cover and cook on Low for 8 hours or overnight or on High for 4 hours. Stir well and serve with milk or non-dairy alternative and maple syrup, if using.

Tips

Using your slow cooker makes it quite convenient to prepare long-cooking whole grains such as steel-cut oats and whole barley. Cook a big batch overnight on Sundays, cover and refrigerate any leftovers. You can enjoy them throughout much of the week. When you're ready to serve, add a little water and cover. Reheat on the stovetop or in a microwave oven.

If you're halving this recipe, be sure to use a small (1½ to 2 quart) slow cooker.

Irish Oatmeal

Although rolled oats are very tasty, my favorite oat cereal is steel-cut oats, which are often sold under the name "Irish Oatmeal." They have more flavor than rolled oats and an appealingly crunchy texture.

- **Small to medium (1½ to 3½ quart) slow cooker**
- **Lightly greased slow cooker stoneware**

1 cup	steel-cut oats	250 mL
½ tsp	salt	2 mL
4 cups	water	1 L
	Raisins, chopped bananas or pitted dates, optional	
	Maple syrup, honey or raw cane sugar, optional	
	Toasted nuts and seeds, optional	
	Milk or non-dairy alternative, optional	

1. In prepared slow cooker stoneware, combine oats, salt and water. Stir well. Place a clean tea towel, folded in half (so you will have two layers), over top of stoneware to absorb moisture. Cover and cook on Low for 8 hours or overnight or on High for 4 hours. Stir well. Serve with raisins, maple syrup, nuts and milk or non-dairy alternative, if using.

Vegan Friendly

Can Be Halved

Tips

Like lentils, some millet may contain bits of dirt or discolored grains. If your millet looks grimy, rinse it thoroughly in a pot of water before using. Swish it around and remove any offending particles, then rinse under cold running water.

The addition of salt adds a bit of depth to this cereal. If you're watching your sodium intake, feel free to omit it.

This cereal has a tendency to get dry and brown around the edges if cooked for longer than 8 hours. If you need to cook it for longer, add an additional ½ cup (125 mL) of water.

If you're not using Medjool dates, which are naturally soft, place the chopped dates in a microwave-safe dish, cover with water and microwave on High for 30 seconds to soften before adding to cereal.

If you're halving this recipe, be sure to use a small (1½ to 2 quart) slow cooker.

Homemade Multigrain Cereal with Fruit

A steaming bowl of this tasty cereal gets you off to a good start in the morning by providing a portion of the nutrients you'll need to remain energized and productive throughout the day.

- **Small to medium (1½ to 3½ quart) slow cooker**
- **Lightly greased slow cooker stoneware**

½ cup	brown rice	125 mL
½ cup	millet (see Tips, left)	125 mL
½ cup	wheat berries	125 mL
2	medium all-purpose apples, peeled, cored and thinly sliced	2
4 cups	water (see Tips, left)	1 L
½ tsp	vanilla extract	2 mL
¼ tsp	salt, optional	1 mL
½ cup	chopped pitted soft dates, preferably Medjool (see Tips, left)	125 mL
	Chopped toasted nuts, optional	
	Wheat germ, optional	

1. In prepared slow cooker stoneware, combine rice, millet, wheat berries and apples. Add water, vanilla, and salt, if using. Cover and cook on Low for up to 8 hours or overnight or on High for 4 hours. Add dates and stir well. Serve sprinkled with toasted nuts and/or wheat germ, if using.

Hot Multigrain Cereal

Hot cereal is one of my favorite ways to begin the day, and happily you can use your slow cooker to ensure that all family members get off to a nutritious start. Cook the cereal overnight and leave the slow cooker on Warm in the morning. Everyone can help themselves according to their schedules.

Tips

Multigrain cereals are one way of ensuring that you maximize the nutritional benefits of cereal grains. You can buy them pre-packaged, usually in 3-, 5- or 7-grain combinations or under a brand name. Or you can make your own by combining your favorite whole grains such as brown rice, wheat berries, Job's tears, millet or barley. Store multigrain cereal in an airtight container in a cool, dry place.

When making whole-grain cereals in the slow cooker, be aware that stirring encourages creaminess. Obviously, for convenience, I don't suggest that you wake up during the night and stir the cereal. However, if you have time let the cereal sit on Warm for at least 15 minutes before serving and stir it several times, if possible.

If you're halving this recipe, be sure to use a small (1½ to 2 quart) slow cooker.

- **Small to medium (1½ to 3½ quart) slow cooker**
- **Lightly greased slow cooker stoneware**

1 cup	multigrain cereal, or ½ cup (125 mL) multigrain cereal and ½ cup (125 mL) rolled or steel-cut oats	250 mL
¼ tsp	salt	1 mL
4 cups	water	1 L
2	medium all-purpose apples, peeled and thickly sliced	2
¼ to ⅓ cup	raisins, optional	50 to 75 mL
	Milk or non-dairy alternative	

1. In prepared stoneware, combine cereal, salt, water and apples. Stir well. Place a clean tea towel, folded in half (so you will have two layers), over top of stoneware to absorb moisture. Cover and cook on Low for 8 hours or overnight or on High for 4 hours. Stir well and set to Warm. Just before serving, place raisins, if using, in a microwave-safe bowl and cover with water. Microwave for 20 seconds to soften. Add to hot cereal. Stir well and serve with milk or non-dairy alternative.

Vegan Friendly

Can Be Halved

Tips

When making whole-grain cereals in the slow cooker, be aware that stirring encourages creaminess. Obviously, for convenience, I don't suggest that you wake up during the night to stir the cereal while it's cooking. However, if you have time, let it sit on Warm for at least 15 minutes before serving and stir it several times, if possible.

If you're halving this recipe, be sure to use a small ($1\frac{1}{2}$ to 2 quart) slow cooker.

Apple Oatmeal with Wheat Berries

This flavorful cereal is an adaptation of a recipe that appeared in Eat, Drink and Be Healthy: The Harvard Medical School Guide to Healthy Eating. *It makes a deliciously different start to the day, and the combination of whole grains expands the range of nutrients you would get from a single grain.*

- **Small to medium ($1\frac{1}{2}$ to $3\frac{1}{2}$ quart) slow cooker**
- **Lightly greased slow cooker stoneware**

$1\frac{1}{2}$ cups	steel-cut oats	375 mL
$\frac{1}{2}$ cup	wheat, spelt or Kamut berries	125 mL
2	apples, peeled, cored and chopped	2
$\frac{1}{2}$ tsp	ground cinnamon	2 mL
$\frac{1}{2}$ tsp	vanilla extract	2 mL
$3\frac{1}{2}$ cups	water	875 mL
1 cup	cranberry or apple juice	250 mL
	Evaporated cane juice sugar, optional	
	Toasted walnuts and wheat germ, optional	

1. In prepared slow cooker, combine steel-cut oats, wheat berries, apples, cinnamon and vanilla. Add water and cranberry juice. Stir well. Place a clean tea towel, folded in half (so you will have two layers), over top of stoneware to absorb moisture. Cover and cook on Low for 8 hours or overnight or on High for 4 hours. Stir well. Top with sugar, walnuts and/or wheat germ, if using.

**Makes about
3 cups (750 mL)
Serves 6**

Vegan Friendly

Tip

Made with this quantity of liquid, the rice will be a bit crunchy around the edges, which suits my taste. If you prefer a softer version or will be cooking it longer than 8 hours, add $\frac{1}{2}$ cup (125 mL) of water or rice milk to the recipe.

Variation

Use half rice and half wheat, spelt or Kamut berries.

Breakfast Rice

Simple yet delicious, this tasty combination couldn't be easier to make. Also, because rice is a gluten-free grain, it makes a perfect breakfast for people who cannot tolerate that ingredient.

- **Small to medium ($1\frac{1}{2}$ to $3\frac{1}{2}$ quart) slow cooker**
- **Lightly greased slow cooker stoneware**

1 cup	brown rice	250 mL
4 cups	vanilla-flavored enriched rice milk	1 L
$\frac{1}{2}$ cup	dried cherries or cranberries	125 mL

1. In prepared slow cooker stoneware, combine rice, rice milk and cherries. Stir well. Place a clean tea towel, folded in half (so you will have two layers), over top of stoneware to absorb moisture. Cover and cook on Low for up to 8 hours or overnight or on High for 4 hours. Stir well and serve.

Vegan Friendly

Can Be Halved

Tips

When making whole-grain cereals in the slow cooker, be aware that stirring encourages creaminess. Obviously, for convenience, I don't suggest that you wake up during the night to stir the cereal while it's cooking. However, if you have time, let it sit on Warm for at least 15 minutes before serving and stir it several times, if possible.

I recommend the use of whole (hulled) barley because it is the most nutritious form of the grain, but if you prefer you can use pot or pearled barley, instead.

If you're halving this recipe, be sure to use a small ($1\frac{1}{2}$ to 2 quart) slow cooker.

Orange-Flavored Breakfast Barley with Cranberries and Pecans

Although it's extremely nutritious, whole barley takes a long time to cook. Fortunately, this isn't a problem if you're making it overnight in a slow cooker. Wake up to a delicious, nutritious breakfast and enjoy.

- **Small to medium ($1\frac{1}{2}$ to $3\frac{1}{2}$ quart) slow cooker**
- **Lightly greased slow cooker stoneware**

3 cups	water	750 mL
$\frac{1}{2}$ cup	whole (hulled) barley, rinsed and drained (see Tips, left)	125 mL
$\frac{1}{2}$ cup	dried cranberries	125 mL
1 tbsp	finely grated orange zest	15 mL
Pinch	salt	Pinch
$\frac{1}{4}$ cup	toasted chopped pecans	50 mL
	Milk or non-dairy alternative, optional	
	Raw cane sugar, honey or maple syrup, optional	

1. In prepared slow cooker stoneware, combine water, barley, cranberries, orange zest and salt. Stir well. Place a clean tea towel, folded in half (so you will have two layers), over top of stoneware to absorb moisture. Cover and cook on Low for 8 hours or overnight or on High for 4 hours. Stir well. Garnish with pecans. Serve with milk or non-dairy alternative and/or sugar, if using.

Starters and Snacks

*Sun-Dried Tomato
and Dill Cheesecake*

Tip

If using a springform pan, ensure that water doesn't seep into the cheesecake by wrapping the bottom of the pan in one large seamless piece of foil that extends up the sides and over the top. Cover the top with a single piece of foil that extends down the sides and secure with a string.

Make Ahead

You'll achieve best results if you make this cheesecake the day before you intend to serve it and chill it overnight.

Sun-Dried Tomato and Dill Cheesecake

When biting into this tasty cheesecake, you'll be hit with an appealing burst of sun-dried tomato flavor. All it needs is simple crackers. It's also delicious on celery sticks.

- **Large (minimum 5 quart) oval slow cooker**
- **7-inch (18 cm) 6-cup (1.5 L) soufflé dish, lined with greased heavy-duty foil, or 7-inch (18 cm) well-greased springform pan (see Tip, left)**
- **Food processor**

Crust

1 cup	cracker crumbs, such as thin wheat crackers	250 mL
2 tbsp	melted butter	25 mL

Cheesecake

8 oz	cream cheese, softened	250 g
2	eggs	2
1/2 cup	coarsely chopped dill	125 mL
1/4 cup	chopped sun-dried tomatoes, packed in olive oil, drained	50 mL
2 tbsp	finely chopped green onions or chives	25 mL
	Salt	
	Freshly ground black pepper	
3/4 cup	shredded Emmenthal or Swiss cheese	175 mL

1. *Crust:* In a bowl, combine cracker crumbs and melted butter. Press mixture into the bottom of prepared dish. Place in freezer until ready to use.

2. *Cheesecake:* In a food processor fitted with a metal blade, combine cream cheese and eggs. Process until smooth. Add dill, sun-dried tomatoes and green onions. Season to taste with salt and pepper. Pulse until blended (do not overmix). Add cheese and pulse just until blended. Pour mixture over crust. Cover dish tightly with foil and secure with a string. (If using a springform pan, see Tip, left.) Place dish in slow cooker stoneware and pour in enough boiling water to come 1 inch (2.5 cm) up the sides of the dish.

3. Cover and cook on High for $2\frac{1}{2}$ to 3 hours or until edges are set and center is slightly jiggly. Remove from slow cooker and chill thoroughly, preferably overnight.

Serves 8

Entertaining Worthy

Tip

For the best flavor, toast and grind whole cumin seeds rather than buying ground cumin. *To toast cumin seeds:* Stir seeds in a dry skillet over medium heat until fragrant, about 3 minutes. Immediately transfer to a spice grinder or mortar and grind.

Make Ahead

You'll achieve best results if you make this cheesecake the day before you intend to serve it and chill it overnight.

Chile Cheesecake

This savory cheesecake is different and delicious. Although it is tasty on crackers, I like to spread it on tortilla chips, which complements the crust.

- **Large (minimum 5 quart) oval slow cooker**
- **7-inch (18 cm) 6-cup (1.5 L) soufflé dish, lined with greased heavy-duty foil, or 7-inch (18 cm) well-greased springform pan (see Tip, page 34)**
- **Food processor**

Crust

1 cup	ground tortilla chips, preferably corn	250 mL
2 tbsp	melted butter	25 mL

Cheesecake

8 oz	cream cheese, softened	250 g
2	eggs	2
1 cup	shredded Monterey Jack or Cheddar cheese	250 mL
1 tsp	ground cumin (see Tip, left)	5 mL
1 tsp	dried oregano	5 mL
1 tsp	pure chile powder, preferably ancho or New Mexico	5 mL
$\frac{1}{4}$ tsp	freshly ground black pepper	1 mL
2 tbsp	diced red bell pepper	25 mL
1	chile pepper, such as cayenne or jalapeño, seeded and diced	1
1	can ($4\frac{1}{2}$ oz/127 mL) diced mild green chiles, drained	1
	Salsa	

1. *Crust:* In a bowl, combine tortilla chips and melted butter. Press mixture into the bottom of prepared dish. Place in freezer until ready to use.

2. *Cheesecake:* In a food processor fitted with a metal blade, combine cream cheese and eggs and process until smooth. Add cumin, oregano, chile powder, shredded cheese and black pepper and pulse until blended. Stir in bell pepper, chile pepper and green chiles. Pour mixture over crust. Cover dish tightly with foil and secure with a string. (If using a springform pan, see Tip, page 34.) Place dish in slow cooker stoneware and pour in enough boiling water to come 1 inch (2.5 cm) up the sides of the dish.

3. Cover and cook on High for $2\frac{1}{2}$ to 3 hours or until edges are set and center is slightly jiggly. Remove from slow cooker and chill thoroughly, preferably overnight. Spread cake with a layer of salsa, just before serving.

Cheese 'n' Chiles

This old favorite is yummy and very forgiving. I like the flavor of poblano peppers, one of the mildest chile peppers, but if you can't find them use two sweet peppers (one each red and green adds a nice visual effect) and add a roasted jalapeño to compensate for the loss of spice. Serve with tortilla chips for dipping or over taco shells (see Variation, left) for a delicious snack.

Can Be Halved

Tip

To roast peppers: Preheat oven to 400°F (200°C). Place peppers on a baking sheet and roast, turning two or three times, until the skin on all sides is blackened. (This will take about 25 minutes.) Transfer peppers to a heatproof bowl. Cover with a plate and let stand until cool. Remove and, using a sharp knife, lift off skins. Discard skins, stem and core and slice according to recipe instructions.

If you're halving this recipe, be sure to use a small (1½ to 2 quart) slow cooker.

Variation

Cheesy Tacos: If you prefer, turn this into a snack. Warm 8 taco shells and fill with mixture. Garnish with any combination of salsa, chopped radishes, shredded lettuce or chopped tomato.

● **Small to medium (1½ to 3½ quart) slow cooker**

12 oz	Monterey Jack cheese, shredded	375 g
½ cup	full-fat sour cream	125 mL
4	green onions, finely chopped	4
2	roasted poblano peppers, peeled and diced (see Tip, left)	2
1	canned chipotle pepper in adobo sauce, minced	1
	Tortilla chips or tostadas	

1. In slow cooker stoneware, combine cheese and sour cream. Cover and cook on High for 30 minutes, until cheese is melted. Add green onions, roasted peppers and chipotle pepper and stir well. Cover and cook on High for 30 minutes, until hot and bubbly. Serve with tortilla chips or tostadas.

Tips

Although fresh tomatoes work well in this recipe, I've successfully made it using the same quantity of drained canned tomatoes. Use ones that are diced or chop whole ones.

For this quantity of beans, soak, cook and drain 1 cup (250 mL) dried cannellini beans (see Basic Beans, page 239) or drain and rinse 1 can (14 to 19 oz/398 to 540 mL) cannellini beans. Cannellini beans are also known as white kidney beans.

I like the chunky texture that using whole beans provides, but if you prefer, mash or purée the beans before adding them to the recipe.

Make Ahead

Complete Step 1. Cover and refrigerate mixture for up to 2 days. When you're ready to cook, complete the recipe.

Onion-Soused Beans

I've adapted this recipe from one developed by my friend Byron Ayanoglu, who says it is a Greek heirloom treatment for beans. He calls it "Yahni" and serves it as a side with Mediterranean dishes. I like to serve it as a starter. It's great on flatbread, sliced baguette or even celery sticks.

- **Small to medium (1½ to 3½ quart) slow cooker**
- **Large sheet of parchment paper**

2 tbsp	olive oil	25 mL
2	onions, thinly sliced on the vertical	2
1	stalk celery, diced	1
6	cloves garlic, minced	6
½ tsp	salt	2 mL
½ tsp	cracked black peppercorns	2 mL
2	bay leaves	2
1 tbsp	red wine vinegar	15 mL
1 tsp	granulated sugar	5 mL
½ cup	diced tomatoes (see Tips, left)	125 mL
2 cups	cooked cannellini beans (see Tips, left)	500 mL
	Extra virgin olive oil	
¼ cup	diced red or green onion	50 mL
¼ cup	finely chopped fresh parsley	50 mL

1. In a skillet, heat oil over medium heat. Add sliced onions and celery and cook, stirring, until softened, about 5 minutes. Add garlic, salt, peppercorns and bay leaves and cook, stirring, for 1 minute. Add vinegar, sugar and tomatoes and cook, stirring, until mixture boils.

2. Transfer to slow cooker stoneware. Stir in beans. Place a large piece of parchment over the beans, pressing it down to brush the food and extending up the sides of the stoneware so it overlaps the rim. Cover and cook on Low for 6 hours or High for 3 hours, until mixture is hot and bubbly. Lift out parchment and discard, being careful not to spill the accumulated liquid into the sauce.

3. Transfer to a serving dish. Drizzle with olive oil and garnish with red onion and parsley. Cover and set aside at room temperature for an hour to develop flavor. Serve at room temperature.

Tips

For this quantity of beans, soak, cook and drain 1 cup (250 mL) dried black beans (see Basic Beans, page 239) or drain and rinse 1 can (14 to 19 oz/398 to 540 mL) black beans.

For a smoother dip, purée the beans in a food processor or mash with a potato masher before adding to stoneware.

If you use a five-alarm salsa in this dip, you may want to omit the jalapeño pepper.

If you don't have time to roast your own pepper, use a bottled roasted red pepper.

To roast peppers: Preheat oven to 400°F (200°C). Place pepper(s) on a baking sheet and roast, turning two or three times, until the skin on all sides is blackened. (This will take about 25 minutes.) Transfer pepper(s) to a heatproof bowl. Cover with a plate and let stand until cool. Remove and, using a sharp knife, lift off skins. Discard skins and slice according to recipe instructions.

Black Bean and Salsa Dip

This tasty Cuban-inspired dip, which can be made from ingredients you're likely to have on hand, is nutritious and flavorful.

● **Small to medium (1½ to 3½ quart) slow cooker**

2 cups	cooked black beans (see Tips, left)	500 mL
8 oz	cream cheese, cubed	250 g
½ cup	tomato salsa	125 mL
¼ cup	sour cream	50 mL
1 tsp	chili powder	5 mL
1 tsp	ground cumin (see Tip, page 35)	5 mL
1 tsp	cracked black peppercorns	5 mL
1	jalapeño pepper, finely chopped, optional (see Tips, left)	1
1	roasted red bell pepper, finely chopped, optional (see Tips, left)	1
	Finely chopped green onion, optional	
	Finely chopped cilantro, optional	

1. In slow cooker stoneware, combine beans, cream cheese, salsa, sour cream, chili powder, cumin, peppercorns, and jalapeño pepper and bell pepper, if using. Cover and cook on High for 1 hour. Stir again and cook on High for an additional 30 minutes, until mixture is hot and bubbly.

2. Serve immediately or set temperature at Warm until ready to serve. Garnish with green onion and/or cilantro, if desired.

Vegan Friendly

Entertaining Worthy

Tip

For the best flavor, toast and grind whole cumin seeds rather than buying ground cumin. *To toast cumin seeds:* Simply stir seeds in a dry skillet over medium heat until fragrant, about 3 minutes. Immediately transfer to a spice grinder or mortar and grind.

Make Ahead

Complete Step 1. Cover and refrigerate for up to 2 days. When you're ready to cook, complete the recipe.

Spicy Black Bean Dip

Simple, yet delicious and nutritious to boot. What more could you want? I like to serve this with blue corn tortilla chips for a great starter or snack.

- **Small to medium (1½ to 3½ quart) slow cooker**
- **Food processor**

1	small red or sweet onion, coarsely chopped	1
2	cloves garlic, chopped	2
1 to 2	canned chipotle pepper(s) in adobo sauce	1 to 2
2 cups	cooked black beans (see Tips, page 38)	500 mL
2 tsp	ground cumin (see Tip, left)	10 mL
1 tsp	finely grated lime zest	5 mL
1 tsp	salt	5 mL
½ tsp	cracked black peppercorns	2 mL
2 cups	shredded Monterey Jack cheese or vegan alternative (about 8 oz/250 g)	500 mL
	Finely chopped cilantro	

1. In a food processor fitted with a metal blade, combine onion, garlic and chipotle pepper. Process until finely chopped. Add beans, cumin, lime zest, salt and peppercorns and process until desired consistency is achieved.

2. Transfer to slow cooker stoneware. Stir in cheese. Cover and cook on High for 1 hour. Stir well. Cover and cook on High for 30 minutes, until mixture is hot and bubbly. Garnish with cilantro. Serve immediately or set temperature at Warm until ready to serve.

Tip

I always use Italian flat-leaf parsley because it has much more flavor than the curly leaf variety.

Make Ahead

Complete Step 1. Cover and refrigerate for up to 2 days. When you're ready to serve, heat peas on the stovetop until bubbles form about the edges. Complete the recipe.

Santorini-Style Fava Spread

This spread, which is Greek in origin, is unusual and particularly delicious. Although fava beans do figure in Greek cuisine, for most Greek people fava is synonymous with yellow split peas, one of the major indigenous foods of the island of Santorini, from which they make many dishes, including this spread. Serve this with warm toasted pita and wait for the compliments.

- **Small (1½ to 2 quart) slow cooker**
- **Food processor**

½ cup	extra virgin olive oil, divided	125 mL
½ cup	diced shallots (about 2 large)	125 mL
2 tsp	dried oregano	10 mL
1 tsp	salt	5 mL
½ tsp	cracked black peppercorns	2 mL
1 cup	yellow split peas	250 mL
4 cups	water	1 L
6	oil-packed sun-dried tomato halves, drained and coarsely chopped	6
4	cloves garlic, chopped	4
¼ cup	coarsely chopped Italian flat-leaf parsley (see Tip, left)	50 mL
4	fresh basil leaves, hand-torn	4
3 tbsp	red wine vinegar	45 mL
	Salt and freshly ground black pepper	
	Toasted pita bread	

1. In a skillet, heat 1 tbsp (15 mL) of the oil over medium heat. Add shallots and cook, stirring, until softened, about 3 minutes. Add oregano, salt and peppercorns and cook, stirring, for 1 minute. Add split peas and cook, stirring, until coated. Add water and bring to a boil. Boil for 2 minutes.

2. Transfer to slow cooker stoneware. Cover and cook on Low for 8 hours or on High for 4 hours, until peas have virtually disintegrated. Drain off excess water, if necessary. Transfer solids to a food processor. Add sun-dried tomatoes, garlic, parsley, basil and red wine vinegar. Pulse 7 or 8 times to chop and blend ingredients. With motor running, add remaining olive oil in a steady stream through the feed tube. Season to taste with additional salt and pepper and drizzle with additional olive oil, if desired. Serve warm with toasted pita.

Vegan Friendly

Entertaining Worthy

Can Be Halved

Tips

To sweat eggplant: Place cubed eggplant in a colander, sprinkle liberally with salt, toss well and set aside for 30 minutes to 1 hour. If time is short, blanch the pieces for a minute or two in heavily salted water. In either case, rinse thoroughly in fresh cold water and, using your hands, squeeze out the excess moisture. Pat dry with paper towels and it's ready to cook.

If you are halving this recipe, be sure to use a small (1½ to 2 quart) slow cooker.

Make Ahead

You'll achieve maximum results if you make this a day ahead and chill thoroughly before serving, or cook overnight, purée in the morning and chill.

Chilly Dilly Eggplant

This is a versatile recipe, delicious as a dip with raw vegetables or on pita triangles, as well as a sandwich spread on crusty French bread. It also makes a wonderful addition to a mezes or tapas-style meal. Although it is tasty warm, the flavor dramatically improves if it is thoroughly chilled before serving.

- **Small to medium (1½ to 3½ quart) slow cooker**
- **Blender or food processor**

2	eggplants, peeled, cut into 1-inch (2.5 cm) cubes and drained of excess moisture (see Tips, left)	2
2 to 3 tbsp	olive oil	25 to 45 mL
2	medium onions, chopped	2
4	cloves garlic, chopped	4
1 tsp	dried oregano	5 mL
1 tsp	salt	5 mL
½ tsp	freshly ground black pepper	2 mL
1 tbsp	balsamic or red wine vinegar	15 mL
½ cup	chopped fresh dill	125 mL
	Dill sprigs, optional	
	Finely chopped black olives, optional	

1. In a skillet, heat 2 tbsp (25 mL) oil over medium-high heat. Add eggplant, in batches, and cook, stirring and tossing, until it begins to brown, about 3 minutes per batch, adding more oil, if necessary. Transfer to slow cooker stoneware.

2. In same pan, using more oil, if necessary, cook onions over medium heat, stirring, until softened, about 3 minutes. Add garlic, oregano, salt and pepper and cook for 1 minute. Transfer to slow cooker and stir to combine thoroughly. Cover and cook on Low for 7 to 8 hours or on High for 4 hours, until vegetables are tender.

3. Transfer contents of slow cooker (in batches, if necessary) to a blender or food processor fitted with a metal blade. Add vinegar and dill and process until smooth, scraping down sides of bowl at halfway point. Taste for seasoning and adjust. Spoon into a small serving bowl and chill thoroughly. Garnish with sprigs of dill and chopped black olives, if using.

Tips

For this quantity of beans, soak, cook and drain 1 cup (250 mL) dried cannellini beans (see Basic Beans, page 239) or drain and rinse 1 can (14 to 19 oz/398 to 540 mL) cannellini beans. Cannellini beans are also known as white kidney beans.

If you prefer, use frozen artichokes, thawed, to make this recipe. You will need 6 artichoke hearts.

To make crostini: Preheat broiler. Brush baguette slices on both sides with olive oil and toast under broiler, turning once.

Artichoke and White Bean Crostini

In addition to being delicious, this spread is very versatile. I like to serve it to guests on crostini, but leftovers make a great sandwich ingredient. Spread it thickly over whole-grain bread and top with sliced tomatoes and arugula for a great lunchtime treat, or use a thin layer as a substitute for butter or mayo in your favorite sandwich.

- **Small (approx. 2 quart) slow cooker**
- **Food processor**

½	medium red onion, finely chopped	½
2	cloves garlic, minced	2
¼ cup	extra virgin olive oil, divided	50 mL
2 cups	drained cooked cannellini beans (see Tips, left)	500 mL
1	can (14 oz/398 mL) artichoke hearts, drained and coarsely chopped (see Tips, left)	1
½ cup	freshly grated Parmesan or vegan alternative	125 mL
1 tsp	paprika	5 mL
½ tsp	salt	2 mL
¼ tsp	freshly ground black pepper	1 mL
¼ cup	finely chopped fresh parsley	50 mL
24	crostini (see Tips, left)	24

1. In slow cooker stoneware, combine onion, garlic and 2 tbsp (25 mL) of the olive oil. Place a clean tea towel, folded in half (so you will have two layers), over top of stoneware to absorb moisture. Cover and cook on High for 30 minutes, until onions are softened.

2. Meanwhile, in a food processor fitted with a metal blade, in batches, if necessary, pulse beans and artichokes until desired consistency is achieved. After onions have softened, add bean mixture to stoneware along with Parmesan, paprika, salt, pepper and remaining olive oil. Replace tea towel. Cover and cook on Low for 4 hours or on High for 2 hours, until hot and bubbly. Add parsley and stir well. Serve on crostini.

Tip
If you prefer, use frozen artichokes, thawed, to make this recipe. You will need 6 artichoke hearts.

Make Ahead
Complete Step 1. Cover and refrigerate for up to 2 days. When you're ready to cook, complete the recipe.

Creamy Jalapeño-Spiked Mushroom and Artichoke Dip

If you're looking for something a little different but are still hankering for comfort food, try this. It's a great combination of flavors and textures. I like to serve it with whole-grain tortilla chips but sliced baguette works well, too.

- **Small (approx. 2 quart) slow cooker**
- **Food processor**

2 tbsp	olive oil, divided	25 mL
1 tbsp	butter	15 mL
4 oz	cremini mushrooms, stemmed and quartered	125 g
3 tbsp	diced onion	45 mL
3 tbsp	diced celery	45 mL
1 tbsp	minced garlic	15 mL
1/2 tsp	salt	2 mL
1/2 tsp	cracked black peppercorns	2 mL
1	can (14 oz/398 mL) artichoke hearts, drained (see Tip, left)	1
2	jalapeño peppers, seeded and diced	2
1 cup	shredded mozzarella cheese	250 mL
1/2 cup	mayonnaise	125 mL
1/2 cup	freshly grated Parmesan	125 mL

1. In a skillet, heat 1 tbsp (15 mL) of the oil and butter over medium-high heat. Add mushrooms and cook, stirring, until browned, about 5 minutes. Transfer to a food processor fitted with a metal blade and set aside. Reduce heat to medium. Add remaining olive oil, onion and celery to pan and cook, stirring, until softened, about 3 minutes. Add garlic, salt and peppercorns and cook, stirring, for 1 minute. Transfer to food processor, along with artichokes and jalapeño peppers. Pulse until desired consistency is achieved.

2. Transfer to slow cooker stoneware. Add mozzarella, mayonnaise and Parmesan. Stir well. Cover and cook on Low for 4 hours or on High for 2 hours, until hot and bubbly.

Tip

If you prefer a smoother dip, place spinach and artichokes in a food processor, in separate batches, and pulse until desired degree of fineness is achieved. Then combine with remaining ingredients in slow cooker stoneware.

Sumptuous Spinach and Artichoke Dip

Although spinach and artichoke dip has become a North American classic, its roots lie in Provençal cuisine, where the vegetables are usually baked with cheese and served as a gratin. This chunky dip, simplicity itself, always draws rave reviews and disappears to the last drop.

● **Small to medium (1½ to 3½ quart) slow cooker**

1 cup	shredded mozzarella cheese	250 mL
8 oz	cream cheese, cubed	250 g
¼ cup	freshly grated Parmesan	50 mL
1	clove garlic, minced	1
1	can (14 oz/398 mL) artichokes, drained and finely chopped	1
8 oz	trimmed fresh spinach leaves (about 8 cups/2 L)	250 g
¼ tsp	freshly ground black pepper	1 mL
	Tostadas or tortilla chips	

1. In slow cooker stoneware, combine mozzarella, cream cheese, Parmesan, garlic, artichokes, spinach and black pepper. Cover and cook on High for 2 hours, until hot and bubbly. Stir well and serve with tostadas or other tortilla chips.

Caper-Studded Caponata

This recipe differs from most caponata because it uses tomato paste rather than tomatoes and contains a sweet pepper and capers. I find it particularly delicious. If you don't feel like toasting bread, it is also great spread on crackers.

Vegan Friendly

Entertaining Worthy

Tips

I like to "sweat" eggplant and drain it of excess moisture because I find it doesn't soak up as much oil when browning. *To sweat eggplant:* Place the cubed eggplant in a colander and sprinkle liberally with salt. Leave for 30 minutes to 1 hour until the moisture comes to the surface. Rinse thoroughly in fresh cold water and, using your hands, squeeze out the excess moisture. If time is short, blanch the pieces for a minute or two in heavily salted water. In either case, rinse thoroughly in fresh cold water and, using your hands, squeeze out the excess moisture. Pat dry with paper towels and it's ready to cook.

You can also use salt-cured capers in this recipe, but they will need to soak in cold water for about 30 minutes, then thoroughly rinsed under cold running water before adding to the recipe.

Make Ahead

Complete Step 2. Cover and refrigerate for up to 2 days. When you're ready to cook, complete the recipe.

- **Small (approx. 2 quart) slow cooker**
- **Large sheet of parchment paper**

1	medium eggplant, peeled, cut into 1/2-inch (1 cm) cubes and drained of excess moisture (see Tips, left)	1
3 tbsp	red wine vinegar	45 mL
1 tsp	granulated sugar	5 mL
2 to 3 tbsp	olive oil	25 to 45 mL
4	cloves garlic, minced	4
1 tsp	cracked black peppercorns	5 mL
1/2 tsp	salt	2 mL
4 tbsp	tomato paste	60 mL
1/2	red bell pepper, seeded and diced	1/2
2 tbsp	drained capers (see Tips, left)	25 mL
1/4 cup	finely chopped fresh parsley	50 mL
	Country-style bread or 1 baguette, sliced and grilled or lightly toasted, optional	

1. In a small bowl, combine vinegar and sugar. Stir until sugar dissolves. Set aside.

2. In a skillet, heat 2 tbsp (25 mL) of the oil over medium-high heat. Add eggplant, in batches, if necessary, and cook, stirring and tossing, until it begins to brown, about 3 minutes per batch, adding more oil, if necessary. Transfer to slow cooker stoneware. Add garlic, peppercorns and salt to pan and cook, stirring, for 1 minute. Add tomato paste and vinegar mixture and stir to combine. Stir into stoneware.

3. Place a large piece of parchment over the eggplant mixture, pressing it down to brush the food and extending up the sides of the stoneware so it overlaps the rim. Cover and cook on Low for 6 hours or High for 3 hours, until mixture is hot and bubbly. Lift out parchment and discard, being careful not to spill the accumulated liquid into the mixture. Stir in bell pepper and capers. Cover and cook on High for 15 minutes, until bell pepper is soft and flavors blend. Transfer to a serving bowl and garnish with parsley. Serve warm or at room temperature, spooned onto grilled bread, if using.

Mushroom and Roasted Garlic Crostini

Tips

If you haven't planned ahead and roasted your garlic in the slow cooker, you can do it in the oven. Simply peel the cloves, remove the pith (the center part that often sprouts), then place the cloves on a piece of foil. Drizzle about ½ tsp (2 mL) olive oil over the garlic, then fold up the foil to make a tight packet. Bake in 400°F (200°C) oven for 20 minutes.

Leave small mushrooms whole. Cut larger ones into halves or quarters.

Keep a bottle of dry white vermouth on hand as it makes a satisfactory substitute for dry white wine. That way, you don't have to open a bottle of wine when you need only a small quantity.

Cover and refrigerate the mushroom cooking liquid. It is a great addition to soups, stews and gravies, along with or instead of broth.

If you are halving this recipe, be sure to use a small (1½ to 2 quart) slow cooker.

Make Ahead

Complete Steps 1 and 2. Cover and refrigerate mixture for up to 2 days. When you're ready to make the crostini, heat mushroom mixture almost to boiling point on the stovetop before spreading on crostini.

Everyone loves this tasty all-purpose hors d'oeuvre, which is both simple and elegant. It can be used as the first course to a dinner or as a party canapé.

- **Small to medium (1½ to 3½ quart) slow cooker**
- **Food processor**

8	cloves roasted garlic (see recipe, page 53 and Tips, left)	8
1 lb	white mushrooms, trimmed (see Tips, left)	500 g
2	large French shallots, finely chopped	2
2 tbsp	oil	25 mL
¼ cup	dry white wine or dry white vermouth	50 mL
2 tbsp	chopped fresh parsley	25 mL
2 tbsp	heavy or whipping (35%) cream, optional	25 mL
2 tsp	balsamic vinegar	10 mL
	Salt and freshly ground black pepper	
28	crostini (see Tips, page 44)	28
	Crumbled soft goat cheese	

1. In slow cooker stoneware, combine garlic, mushrooms, shallots, oil and wine. Cover and cook on Low for 8 hours or on High for 4 hours, until mushrooms are soft. Drain off liquid (see Tips, left).

2. Place mushroom mixture and parsley in a food processor fitted with a metal blade and pulse until ingredients are very finely chopped but not puréed. Add cream, if using, vinegar, salt and black pepper to taste and pulse two or three times to combine.

3. Preheat oven to 375°F (190°C). Spread mushroom mixture over crostini. Sprinkle goat cheese on top. Place on baking sheet and bake until cheese begins to brown and melt. Serve hot.

Tip

The amount of salt you'll need to add depends upon the accompaniment. If you're serving this with salty potato chips, err on the side of caution.

Variation

For a more herbal flavor, add 2 tbsp (25 mL) fresh thyme leaves along with the cream cheese.

Caramelized Onion Dip

This dip is one of life's guilty pleasures. I like to serve it with good potato chips while I'm preparing dinner for guests. It always disappears to the very last drop.

- **Small (approx. 2 quart) slow cooker**
- **Food processor**

2	onions, thinly sliced on the vertical	2
4	cloves garlic, chopped	4
1 tbsp	melted butter	15 mL
4 oz	cream cheese, cubed and softened	125 g
¹/₂ cup	sour cream	125 mL
1 tbsp	dark miso	15 mL
	Salt and freshly ground black pepper (see Tip, left)	
	Finely snipped chives	
	Natural potato chips, optional	
	Belgian endive, optional	

1. In slow cooker stoneware, combine onions, garlic and butter. Toss well to ensure onions are thoroughly coated. Place a clean tea towel, folded in half (so you will have two layers), over top of stoneware to absorb moisture. Cover and cook on High for 5 hours, stirring two or three times to ensure onions are browning evenly, replacing towel each time, until onions are nicely caramelized.

2. Transfer mixture to a food processor fitted with a metal blade. Add cream cheese, sour cream, miso, and salt and black pepper, to taste. Process until well blended. Transfer to a serving dish and garnish with chives. Serve with potato chips or leaves of Belgian endive, if using.

Tips

If you prefer, season with freshly ground black pepper, to taste, after the onions have finished cooking.

If you don't have fresh thyme, use 2 tbsp (25 mL) finely chopped fresh parsley, instead.

To make crostini: Preheat broiler. Brush baguette slices on both sides with olive oil and toast under broiler, turning once.

Make Ahead

Complete Steps 1 and 2. Cover and refrigerate for up to 2 days. When you're ready to cook, gently reheat the onion mixture. Complete the recipe.

Caramelized Onion Crostini

Surprise your guests and serve this unusual combination as an hors d'oeuvre at your next dinner party. They'll never guess that you haven't been standing over the stove, patiently stirring the onions and coaxing them to caramelize for this delicious treat.

● **Small (approx. 2 quart) slow cooker**

6	onions, thinly sliced on the vertical (about 3 lbs/1.5 kg)	6
3 tbsp	melted butter	45 mL
1 tbsp	granulated sugar	15 mL
1 tsp	salt	5 mL
1 tsp	cracked black peppercorns (see Tips, left)	5 mL
1 tbsp	fresh thyme (see Tips, left)	15 mL
1 tsp	balsamic vinegar	5 mL
16	crostini (see Tips, left)	16
2 cups	shredded Swiss or Gruyère cheese	500 mL

1. In slow cooker stoneware, combine onions and butter. Stir well to coat onions thoroughly. Cover and cook on High for 30 minutes to 1 hour, until onions are softened.

2. Add sugar, salt and peppercorns and stir well. Place a clean tea towel, folded in half (so you will have two layers), over top of stoneware to absorb moisture. Cover and cook on High for 4 hours, stirring two or three times to ensure the onions are browning evenly, replacing towel each time, until onions are nicely caramelized. Turn off slow cooker. Stir in thyme and balsamic vinegar.

3. Preheat broiler. Spread onions evenly over crostini and sprinkle cheese evenly over top. Place on baking sheet and broil until cheese is melted and brown, 2 to 3 minutes. Serve immediately.

Braised Tomato Bruschetta

Make Ahead

Complete the recipe. Cover and refrigerate bruschetta mixture for up to 3 days. Bring to room temperature before serving.

Variation

If you prefer, spread the warm toasted bread with a thin layer of soft goat cheese before topping with the bruschetta.

When they are in season, there are few things I enjoy eating more than bruschetta overflowing with fresh chopped tomatoes, seasoned with fleur de sel, *a hint of garlic and some fresh basil. Some time ago, I came across a recipe from Seattle's Café Lago, which suggested that a braised version of this summertime treat could be made using canned tomatoes, so I played with the idea and produced this result. It is simply delicious and a wonderful treat in the midst of winter, when succulent local field tomatoes are only a faint memory.*

- **Small to medium (1½ to 3½ quart) slow cooker**
- **Large sheet of parchment paper**

¼ cup	extra virgin olive oil, divided	50 mL
1	can (28 oz/796 mL) diced tomatoes, drained	1
2	cloves garlic, minced	2
2 tsp	dried oregano	10 mL
1 tsp	granulated sugar	5 mL
1 tsp	salt	5 mL
2 tbsp	finely chopped fresh parsley	25 mL
	Freshly ground black pepper	
6	slices of country-style bread or 12 slices of baguette, grilled or lightly toasted	6

1. In slow cooker stoneware, place 2 tbsp (25 mL) of the olive oil and swirl to coat bottom. Add tomatoes and sprinkle with garlic, oregano, sugar and salt. Drizzle with remaining olive oil. Place a large piece of parchment over the tomatoes, pressing it down to brush the food and extending up the sides of the stoneware so it overlaps the rim.

2. Cover and cook on Low for 6 hours or High for 3 hours, until mixture is hot and bubbly. Lift out parchment and discard, being careful not to spill the accumulated liquid into the tomato mixture. Stir in parsley and season to taste with pepper. Transfer to a serving dish and let cool to room temperature. To serve, spoon onto toasted or grilled bread.

Vegan Friendly

Can Be Halved

Tips

Double or triple this recipe to suit your needs.

There are many different ways to use roasted garlic. It's an easy way to enhance the flavor of simple soups, gravy or vinaigrette. Just whisk in the desired quantity. It also makes a delicious addition to mashed potatoes, a great topping for grilled vegetables and can be stirred into mayonnaise to make a roasted garlic *aïoli*. Spread it over crostini and top with fresh goat cheese for a delicious hors d'oeuvre. Mash into softened butter or margarine, add some finely chopped fresh herbs and make garlic bread or perhaps simplest of all, spread it on crackers or bread.

Slow-Roasted Garlic

If you like to have roasted garlic on hand to use as a condiment or in recipes such as Mushroom and Roasted Garlic Crostini (see recipe, page 48) here is a very easy way to make it. The garlic cooks away in the slow cooker, and you can forget about it while you do other things. Store for up to 2 days tightly covered in the refrigerator or frozen in small portions for up to 3 months.

- **Small (approx. 2 quart) slow cooker**
- **Food processor**
- **Large sheet of parchment paper**

30	cloves peeled garlic (about 2 heads)	30
2 tbsp	olive oil	25 mL

1. Lay parchment on a flat work surface and mound garlic in the middle. Spoon olive oil over garlic. Lift 2 opposite sides of parchment to meet in the middle, then fold them over to form a seal. Continue folding until flush with garlic. Fold remaining sides over to form a package. Place in stoneware, seam side down. Cover and cook on High for 4 hours, until garlic is nicely caramelized.

Tip

I recommend using a small to medium slow cooker for these recipes so the nuts are less likely to burn. You can make them in a larger slow cooker (approx. 5 quarts) but watch carefully and stir every 15 minutes, because the nuts will cook quite quickly (in just over an hour).

Variation

Curried Buttery Peanuts:
In a small bowl, combine sea salt with 2 tsp (10 mL) curry powder and a pinch of cayenne pepper. Substitute for plain salt.

Hot Roasted Nuts

● **Small to medium (1½ to 3½ quart) slow cooker (see Tip, left)**

Salty Almonds with Thyme

When entertaining in winter, I like to light a fire and place small bowls full of these tasty nibblers where they are easily accessible to guests.

2 cups	unblanched almonds	500 mL
½ tsp	ground white pepper	2 mL
1 tbsp	fine sea salt, or more to taste	15 mL
2 tbsp	extra virgin olive oil	25 mL
2 tbsp	fresh thyme	25 mL

1. In slow cooker stoneware, combine almonds and white pepper. Cover and cook on High for 1½ to 2 hours, stirring every 30 minutes, until nuts are nicely toasted.

2. In a mixing bowl, combine salt, olive oil and thyme. Add to hot almonds in stoneware and stir thoroughly to combine. Spoon mixture into a small serving bowl and serve hot or let cool.

Buttery Peanuts

Everyone loves these hot buttery peanuts — even me, and I'm usually not a fan of this Southern legume. Use peanuts with skins on or buy them peeled, depending upon your preference. Both work well in this recipe.

2 cups	raw peanuts	500 mL
¼ cup	melted butter or butter substitute	50 mL
2 tsp	fine sea salt	10 mL

1. In slow cooker stoneware, combine peanuts and butter. Cover and cook on High for 2 to 2½ hours, stirring occasionally, until peanuts are nicely roasted. Drain on paper towels. Place in a bowl, sprinkle with salt and stir to combine.

Soups

Double Tomato Soup with Arugula-Walnut Pesto

Tips

I like to use Italian San Marzano tomatoes, which are particularly rich. If you're using domestic tomatoes, you may want to add an additional sun-dried tomato to increase the tomato flavor.

If you are halving this recipe, be sure to use a small (approx. 2 quart) slow cooker.

Make Ahead

Complete Step 1. Cover and refrigerate for up to 2 days. When you're ready to cook, continue with the recipe.

Double Tomato Soup with Arugula-Walnut Pesto

If tomato soup is one of your favorites, I think you'll particularly enjoy this version. The deep tomato flavor finished with a fresh arugula-based pesto is a luscious combination. Serve this with whole-grain bread for a light dinner or lunch.

- **Medium (approx. 4 quart) slow cooker**
- **Food processor**

1 tbsp	olive oil	15 mL
1	onion, finely chopped	1
2	stalks celery, diced	2
4	cloves garlic, minced	4
1 tsp	dried Italian seasoning	5 mL
1 tsp	salt	5 mL
1/2 tsp	cracked black peppercorns	2 mL
1 tsp	granulated sugar	5 mL
1	can (28 oz/796 mL) tomatoes with juice	1
2	reconstituted sun-dried tomatoes, chopped (see Tips, left)	2
4 cups	vegetable broth	1 L
Pesto		
4 cups	packed stemmed arugula leaves	1 L
2	cloves garlic, minced	2
3/4 cup	freshly grated Parmesan or vegan alternative	175 mL
1/2 cup	walnuts	125 mL
1/2 cup	extra virgin olive oil	125 mL
1/2 tsp	salt	2 mL
	Freshly ground black pepper	

1. In a skillet, heat oil over medium heat. Add onion and celery and cook, stirring, until softened, about 4 minutes. Add garlic, Italian seasoning, salt and peppercorns and cook, stirring, for 1 minute. Stir in sugar. Add tomatoes with juice and sun-dried tomatoes and bring to a boil. Transfer to slow cooker stoneware. Stir in vegetable broth.

2. Cover and cook on Low for 6 hours or on High for 3 hours. Purée using an immersion blender. (You can also do this in batches in a food processor or stand blender.)

3. *Pesto:* In a food processor fitted with a metal blade, combine arugula, garlic, Parmesan and walnuts. Pulse until chopped. With motor running, add oil in a steady stream through the feed tube, being careful not to overprocess. Add salt, and pepper, to taste, and pulse to blend. To serve, ladle soup into bowls and top each serving with a generous dollop of pesto.

Tips

If you are halving this recipe, be sure to use a small (approx. 2 quart) slow cooker.

I always use Italian flat-leaf parsley because it has much more flavor than the curly leaf variety.

Make Ahead

Complete Step 1. Cover and refrigerate for up to 2 days. When you're ready to cook, complete the recipe.

Smoky Tomato Soup with Cheesy Crostini

This is a simple tomato soup with attitude. The smoked paprika adds interesting complexity, and the wonderfully unctuous melted Fontina completes the transformation by adding a lusciously creamy finish. I served this to a friend who doesn't like tomato soup and it made her a convert.

● **Medium (approx. 4 quart) slow cooker**

1 tbsp	olive oil	15 mL
2	onions, chopped	2
2	stalks celery, diced	2
4	cloves garlic, minced	4
1 tsp	salt	5 mL
1/2 tsp	cracked black peppercorns	2 mL
1/2 tsp	ground allspice	2 mL
1	can (28 oz/796 mL) diced tomatoes with juice	1
5 cups	vegetable broth	1.25 L
1/4 cup	heavy or whipping (35%) cream or soy creamer, divided	50 mL
2 tsp	smoked paprika (hot or sweet)	10 mL
12	slices baguette	12
	Thinly sliced Fontina or vegan melting cheese alternative	
	Finely chopped fresh parsley or snipped chives	

1. In a skillet, heat oil over medium heat. Add onions and celery and cook, stirring, until softened, about 5 minutes. Add garlic, salt, peppercorns and allspice and cook, stirring, for 1 minute. Add tomatoes with juice and bring to a boil. Transfer to slow cooker stoneware.

2. Stir in broth. Cover and cook on Low for 6 hours or on High for 3 hours. Purée using an immersion blender. (If you don't have an immersion blender, do this in a stand blender or food processor, in batches, and return to stoneware.)

3. In a small bowl, combine 2 tbsp (25 mL) of the cream and smoked paprika. Mix until blended. Add remaining cream and stir well. Add to stoneware and stir well. Cover and cook on High for 10 minutes to meld flavors.

4. Meanwhile, preheat broiler. Place baguette slices on a baking sheet and toast under broiler, turning once. Lay cheese slices over top of each and broil until melted. To serve, ladle soup into bowls and float 2 crostini on each serving. Garnish with parsley.

Vegan Friendly

Can Be Halved

Tips

Toasting fennel seeds intensifies their flavor. *To toast fennel seeds:* Stir seeds in a dry skillet over medium heat until fragrant, about 3 minutes. Immediately transfer to a mortar or spice grinder and grind finely.

To prepare bulb fennel: Before removing the core, chop off the top shoots (which resemble celery) and discard. If desired, save the feathery green fronds to use as a garnish. If the outer sections of the bulb seem old and dry, peel them with a vegetable peeler before using.

Whether you use salt, and the quantity you use, will depend on the sodium content of your broth. Prepared versions are generally much higher in sodium than those that are homemade.

For a slightly different tomato flavor, substitute 2 cans (each 14 oz/398 mL) fire-roasted tomatoes with juice for the crushed tomatoes.

If you are halving this recipe, be sure to use a small (approx. 2 quart) slow cooker.

Make Ahead

Complete Steps 1 and 2. Cover and refrigerate for up to 2 days. When you're ready to cook, complete the recipe.

Fennel-Scented Tomato and Wild Rice Soup

If, like me, you get cravings for tomatoes, this soup is for you. Made with fire-roasted tomatoes (see Tips, left), it provides a real tomato hit. The fennel brings intriguing licorice flavor, and the wild rice adds texture to make this soup particularly enjoyable.

● **Medium to large (3 1/2 to 5 quart) slow cooker**

1 tbsp	oil	15 mL
2	leeks, white part with just a bit of green, cleaned and sliced (see Tips, page 94)	2
1	bulb fennel, cored and thinly sliced on the vertical	1
3	cloves garlic, sliced	3
1 tsp	fennel seeds, toasted and ground (see Tips, left)	5 mL
1/2 tsp	salt, optional	2 mL
1/2 tsp	freshly ground black pepper	2 mL
1	can (28 oz/796 mL) crushed tomatoes	1
4 cups	vegetable broth, divided	1 L
3/4 cup	wild rice, rinsed and drained	175 mL
	Heavy or whipping (35%) cream or non-dairy alternative, optional	
	Finely chopped fennel fronds or Italian flat-leaf parsley	

1. In a large skillet, heat oil over medium heat. Add leeks and fennel bulb and cook, stirring, until softened, about 7 minutes. Add garlic, fennel seeds, salt, if using, and pepper and cook, stirring, for 1 minute. Stir in tomatoes and 2 cups (500 mL) of the broth. Remove from heat.

2. Purée using an immersion blender. (You can also do this in batches in a food processor or stand blender.) Transfer to slow cooker stoneware.

3. Add remaining 2 cups (500 mL) of broth and wild rice. Cover and cook on Low for 6 hours or on High for 3 hours, until rice is tender and grains have begun to split. Ladle into bowls, drizzle with cream, if using, and garnish with fennel fronds.

Vegan Friendly

Can Be Halved

Tips

To make garlic croutons:
Combine 1 cup (250 mL) crustless bread cubes (about 1 inch/2.5 cm) with 1 tbsp (15 mL) extra virgin olive oil and 1 clove of minced garlic. Toss well and season to taste with salt and freshly ground black pepper. Spread out on a baking sheet and bake in a preheated oven (325°F/160°C), tossing several times, until golden, about 8 minutes.

Use prepared ready-to-use broth or make your own (see pages 102 and 103). If you prefer, use half vegetable and half mushroom broth.

Use your favorite type of miso or whatever you have on hand. All work well in this recipe.

If you are halving this recipe, be sure to use a small (approx. 2 quart) slow cooker.

Make Ahead

Complete Steps 1 and 2. Cover and refrigerate for up to 2 days. When you're ready to cook, complete the recipe.

Variation

Wild Mushroom Soup with Miso and Ancient Grains:
To make this soup a little more substantial add ½ cup (125 mL) rinsed whole barley or wheat, spelt or Kamut berries along with the broth.

Wild Mushroom Soup with Miso

Not only is this hearty soup the perfect antidote to a bone-chilling day but mushrooms, particularly shiitake, are also great immune system boosters. A steaming mug will help you beat off lurking winter viruses, and I can't imagine anything more satisfying after coming in from the cold.

● **Large (approx. 5 quart) slow cooker**

1	package (½ oz/14 g) dried porcini mushrooms	1
1 cup	hot water	250 mL
1 tbsp	olive oil	15 mL
2	leeks, white part with just a bit of green, thinly sliced (see Tips, page 94)	2
1	carrot, peeled and diced	1
1	stalk celery, diced	1
2	cloves garlic, minced	2
1 tsp	salt	5 mL
½ tsp	cracked black peppercorns	2 mL
1	bay leaf	1
8 oz	fresh shiitake mushrooms, stems discarded and caps thinly sliced	250 g
8 oz	cremini mushrooms, trimmed and quartered	250 g
6 cups	vegetable or mushroom broth (see Tips, left)	1.5 L
1 cup	water	250 mL
¼ cup	miso (see Tips, left)	50 mL
	Finely snipped chives	
	Garlic croutons, optional (see Tips, left)	

1 In a bowl, combine porcini mushrooms and hot water. Let stand for 30 minutes. Drain through a fine sieve, reserving liquid. Pat mushrooms dry with paper towel and chop finely. Set aside.

2. In a skillet, heat oil over medium heat. Add leeks, carrot and celery and cook, stirring, until softened, about 7 minutes. Add garlic, salt, peppercorns, bay leaf and reserved reconstituted porcini mushrooms and cook, stirring, for 1 minute. Stir in reserved mushroom soaking liquid. Transfer to slow cooker stoneware.

3. Add shiitake and cremini mushrooms. Stir in broth and water. Cover and cook on Low for 6 hours or on High for 3 hours. Stir in miso. Cover and cook on High for 15 minutes to meld flavors. Discard bay leaf. Ladle soup into bowls and garnish with chives, and croutons, if using.

Vegan Friendly

Can Be Halved

Tips

Use the type of barley you prefer — pearled, pot or whole. Whole (also known as hulled) barley is the most nutritious form of the grain.

Barley, like all whole grains, really soaks up liquid. If you've refrigerated this soup and are reheating it, you'll need to add water to ensure an appropriate consistency.

Use prepared ready-to-use mushroom broth or make your own (page 102).

If you are halving this recipe, be sure to use a small (approx. 2 quart) slow cooker.

Make Ahead

Complete Step 1. Cover and refrigerate for up to 2 days. When you're ready to cook, complete the recipe. Because the barley soaks up liquid on sitting, add an extra $1/2$ cup (125 mL) of broth or water before cooking.

Mushroom Barley Soup with Miso

Served with whole-grain bread, this hearty and nutritious soup is a delicious meal in a bowl. If you feel the need for something more substantial, add a green salad or some Cheddar cheese.

● **Medium (approx. 4 quart) slow cooker**

2 tbsp	oil or butter	25 mL
2	onions, finely chopped	2
4	stalks celery, diced	4
4	cloves garlic, minced	4
1 tsp	dried thyme	5 mL
1 tsp	salt	5 mL
$1/2$ tsp	cracked black peppercorns	2 mL
1	bay leaf	1
$1/2$ cup	barley (see Tips, left)	125 mL
6 cups	mushroom broth (see Tips, left)	1.5 L
1 lb	cremini mushrooms, trimmed and quartered	500 g
$1/4$ cup	white miso	50 mL
	Finely chopped green onions or parsley	

1. In a skillet, heat oil over medium heat. Add onions and celery and cook, stirring, until softened, about 5 minutes. Add garlic, thyme, salt, peppercorns and bay leaf and cook, stirring, for 1 minute. Add barley and toss until coated. Transfer to slow cooker stoneware. Add mushroom broth.

2. Stir in mushrooms. Cover and cook on Low for 6 hours or on High for 3 hours. Stir in miso. Cover and cook on High for 15 minutes to meld flavors. Discard bay leaf. Ladle soup into bowls and garnish with green onions.

Vegan Friendly

Can Be Halved

Tips

Use the variety of barley you prefer— pearled, pot or whole. Whole (also known as hulled) barley is the most nutritious form of the grain.

Barley, like all whole grains, really soaks up liquid. If you've refrigerated this soup and are reheating it, you'll need to add water to ensure an appropriate consistency.

If you are halving this recipe, be sure to use a small (approx. 2 quart) slow cooker.

Make Ahead

Complete Step 1. Cover and refrigerate for up to 2 days. When you're ready to cook, continue with the recipe. Because the barley soaks up liquid on sitting, add an extra 1/2 cup (125 mL) of broth or water before cooking.

Variation

Miso-Spiked Vegetable Soup with Wheat Berries: Substitute an equal quantity of wheat, spelt or Kamut berries for the barley.

Miso-Spiked Vegetable Soup with Barley

Here's a hearty vegetable soup that's the perfect antidote to a blustery day. The addition of miso adds robustness and a hint of complexity that is often lacking in simple vegetable soups. Serve this with your favorite sandwich for a delicious soup and sandwich meal.

- **Large (approx. 5 quart) slow cooker**

1 tbsp	olive oil	15 mL
2	onions, finely chopped	2
4	carrots, peeled and diced	4
4	stalks celery, diced	4
1 tsp	dried thyme	5 mL
1/2 tsp	cracked black peppercorns	2 mL
1 cup	barley, rinsed and drained (see Tips, left)	250 mL
7 cups	vegetable broth, divided	1.75 L
2 cups	sliced green beans	500 mL
1/4 cup	dark miso	50 mL
1/2 cup	finely chopped fresh parsley	125 mL
	Freshly grated Parmesan or vegan alternative, optional	

1. In a skillet, heat oil over medium heat for 30 seconds. Add onions, carrots and celery and cook, stirring, until softened, about 7 minutes. Add thyme and peppercorns and cook, stirring, for 1 minute. Add barley and toss to coat. Add 2 cups (500 mL) of the broth and bring to a boil. Transfer to slow cooker stoneware.

2. Stir in remaining 5 cups (1.25 L) of broth. Cover and cook on Low for 8 hours or on High for 4 hours, until barley is tender. Set slow cooker on High, if necessary. Add green beans and miso. Cover and cook for 15 minutes, until beans are tender. Stir in parsley. Ladle into bowls and garnish with Parmesan, if using.

Vegan Friendly

Can Be Halved

Tips

After adding the yogurt, cooking on Low ensures that the soup doesn't boil, in which case the yogurt would curdle.

Use the type of barley you prefer — pearled, pot or whole. Whole (also known as hulled) barley is the most nutritious form of the grain.

Barley, like all whole grains, really soaks up liquid. If you've refrigerated this soup and are reheating it, you'll need to add water to ensure an appropriate consistency.

If you are halving this recipe, be sure to use a small (approx. 2 quart) slow cooker.

Make Ahead

Complete Step 1. Cover and refrigerate for up to 2 days. When you're ready to cook, complete the recipe. Because the barley soaks up liquid on sitting, add an extra ½ cup (125 mL) of broth or water before cooking.

Turkish-Style Barley Soup

If you're looking for something delightfully different but delicious, look no further. This simple soup is an exquisite combination of textures and flavors. Serve it as a light main course or in small quantities as a prelude to dinner.

● **Medium to large (3½ to 5 quart) slow cooker**

1 tbsp	olive oil	15 mL
1	onion, finely chopped	1
3	leeks, white part with just a bit of green, cleaned and thinly sliced (see Tips, page 94)	3
4	cloves garlic	4
1 tsp	salt	5 mL
½ tsp	cracked black peppercorns	2 mL
1	piece (2 inches/5 cm) cinnamon stick	1
2 tbsp	all-purpose flour	25 mL
½ cup	barley (see Tips, left)	125 mL
6 cups	vegetable broth, divided	1.5 L
2 tsp	sweet paprika, dissolved in 2 tbsp (25 mL) freshly squeezed lemon juice	10 mL
2	long green or red chiles, minced	2
¾ cup	full-fat yogurt or vegan alternative	175 mL
2 tbsp	finely chopped fresh mint	25 mL

1. In a skillet, heat oil over medium heat. Add onion and leeks and cook, stirring, until softened, about 4 minutes. Add garlic, salt, peppercorns, cinnamon stick and flour and cook, stirring, for 1 minute. Add barley and toss to coat. Add 2 cups (500 mL) of the broth and bring to a boil. Boil for 2 minutes. Transfer to slow cooker stoneware.

2. Stir in remaining 4 cups (1 L) of broth. Cover and cook on Low for 6 to 8 hours or on High for 3 to 4 hours, until barley is tender. Discard cinnamon stick.

3. Add paprika solution to slow cooker along with chile peppers, yogurt and mint. Cover and cook on Low for 15 minutes to meld flavors.

Vegan Friendly

Can Be Halved

Tips

This quantity of rice, combined with the okra, produces a dense soup, which condenses even more when refrigerated overnight. If you prefer a more soup-like consistency, add an additional cup (250 mL) of broth.

I like to use brown rice because it is the most nutritious form of the grain, but you may substitute an equal quantity of white rice, if you prefer.

If you are halving this recipe, be sure to use a small (approx. 2 quart) slow cooker.

Okra is a great thickener for broths but be sure not to overcook it because it will become unpleasantly sticky. Choose young okra pods 2 to 4 inches (5 to 10 cm) long that don't feel sticky to the touch, in which case they are too ripe. Gently scrub the pods, cut off the top and tail and slice.

Make Ahead

Complete Step 1. Cover and refrigerate for up to 2 days. When you're ready to cook, complete the recipe.

Vegetable Gumbo

This tasty vegetable soup reminds me of a delicious version of one of my favorite canned soups when I was a kid. Served with whole-grain bread, it makes an excellent lunch. If you're feeling indulgent and longing for comfort food that dredges up childhood memories, add a grilled cheese sandwich made with Cheddar cheese and whole wheat bread. Yum.

● **Medium to large (3½ to 5 quart) slow cooker**

1 tbsp	olive oil	15 mL
2	onions, finely chopped	2
6	stalks celery, diced	6
4	cloves garlic, minced	4
2 tsp	dried thyme, crumbled	10 mL
½ tsp	cracked black peppercorns	2 mL
1	bay leaf	1
1	can (28 oz/796 mL) diced tomatoes with juice	1
½ cup	brown rice (see Tips, left)	125 mL
4 cups	vegetable broth	1 L
2 tsp	paprika, dissolved in 4 tsp (20 mL) freshly squeezed lemon juice	10 mL
	Salt, optional	
2 cups	sliced okra (¼-inch/0.5 cm slices) (see Tips, left)	500 mL
1	green bell pepper, diced	1

1. In a skillet, heat oil over medium heat. Add onions and celery and cook, stirring, until softened, about 5 minutes. Add garlic, thyme, peppercorns and bay leaf and cook, stirring, for 1 minute. Add tomatoes with juice and bring to a boil. Transfer to slow cooker stoneware.

2. Add brown rice and broth. Cover and cook on Low for 6 hours or on High for 3 hours, until rice is tender. Discard bay leaf. Add paprika solution and stir well. Season to taste with salt, if using. Stir in okra and green pepper. Cover and cook on High for 20 minutes, until pepper is tender.

Vegan Friendly

Can Be Halved

Tips

Use 1 cup (250 mL) dried chickpeas, soaked, cooked and drained (see Basic Beans, page 239) for this quantity. If you prefer, substitute 1 can (14 to 19 oz/398 to 540 mL) chickpeas, drained and rinsed.

You can make your own harissa or use a prepared version, which is available in specialty grocery stores.

If you are halving this recipe, be sure to use a small (approx. 2 quart) slow cooker.

Make Ahead

Complete Step 1. Cover and refrigerate for up to 2 days. When you're ready to cook, continue with the recipe.

Harira

This traditional Moroccan soup, often made with lamb, is usually served during Ramadan at the end of a day of fasting. This vegetarian version is finished with a dollop of harissa, a spicy North African sauce, which adds flavor and punch. Served with whole-grain bread, harira makes a great light meal. A salad of shredded carrots topped with a sprinkling of currants adds color to the meal and complements the Middle Eastern flavors.

● **Medium to large (3½ to 5 quart) slow cooker**

2 cups	drained cooked chickpeas (see Tips, left)	500 mL
1 tbsp	oil	15 mL
2	onions, coarsely chopped	2
4	stalks celery, diced	4
2	cloves garlic, minced	2
1 tbsp	ground turmeric	15 mL
1 tbsp	grated lemon zest	15 mL
½ tsp	cracked black peppercorns	2 mL
1	can (28 oz/796 mL) diced tomatoes with juice	1
4 cups	vegetable broth	1 L
1 cup	dried red lentils, rinsed	250 mL
½ cup	finely chopped fresh parsley	125 mL
	Harissa (see Tips, left and page 215)	

1. In a skillet, heat oil over medium heat. Add onions and celery and cook, stirring, until softened, about 5 minutes. Add garlic, turmeric, lemon zest and peppercorns and cook, stirring, for 1 minute. Add tomatoes with juice and bring to a boil. Transfer to slow cooker stoneware. Stir in broth.

2. Add chickpeas and lentils to stoneware and stir well. Cover and cook on Low for 6 to 8 hours or on High for 3 to 4 hours, until mixture is hot and bubbly and lentils are tender. Stir in parsley.

3. Ladle into bowls and pass the harissa at the table.

Vegan Friendly
Can Be Halved

Tips

I prefer a slightly creamy texture in this soup, which I achieve by using my immersion blender for about 30 seconds to coarsely purée it. You can achieve a similar result by scooping out a cup (250 mL) of the soup and puréeing it in a blender or food processor, then stirring it back into the stoneware before serving.

Use 1 cup (250 mL) dried chickpeas, soaked, cooked and drained (see Basic Beans, page 239) for this quantity. If you prefer, substitute 1 can (14 to 19 oz/398 to 540 mL) chickpeas, drained and rinsed.

If you are halving this recipe, be sure to use a small (approx. 2 quart) slow cooker.

Make Ahead

Complete Step 1. Cover and refrigerate for up to 2 days. When you're ready to cook, complete the recipe.

Cumin-Laced Chickpea Soup with Roasted Red Peppers

If you're looking for a hearty vegetable soup but are feeling the need for more stimulating flavors, try this. The combination of cumin, carrots, chickpeas, red pepper and yogurt is inspired by the Middle East, but the result is a robust soup — albeit one that is still clean tasting and refreshing.

● **Medium to large (4 to 5 quart) slow cooker**

2 cups	drained cooked chickpeas (see Tips, left)	500 mL
1 tbsp	olive oil	15 mL
2	onions, finely chopped	2
2	carrots, peeled and diced	2
2	cloves garlic, minced	2
2 tsp	ground cumin (see Tips, page 83)	10 mL
1 tsp	salt	5 mL
1 tsp	cracked black peppercorns	5 mL
4 cups	vegetable broth, divided	1 L
2	roasted red peppers, diced	2
1 to 2 tbsp	fresh squeezed lemon juice	15 to 25 mL
1/2 cup	finely chopped fresh parsley	125 mL
	Plain yogurt or vegan alternative	

1. In a skillet, heat oil over medium heat. Add onions and carrots and cook, stirring, until softened, about 7 minutes. Add garlic, cumin, salt and peppercorns and cook, stirring, for 1 minute. Add 2 cups (500 mL) of the broth and bring to a boil. Transfer to slow cooker stoneware.

2. Stir in remaining 2 cups (500 mL) of broth and chickpeas. Cover and cook on Low for 6 hours or on High for 3 hours. Add roasted peppers, lemon juice and parsley and adjust seasoning, if necessary. Cover and cook on High for 5 minutes to meld flavors. To serve, ladle into bowls and top with a dollop of yogurt.

Tips

To sweat eggplant: Place cubed eggplant in a colander, sprinkle liberally with salt, toss well and set aside for 30 minutes to 1 hour. If time is short, blanch the pieces for a minute or two in heavily salted water. In either case, rinse thoroughly in fresh cold water and, using your hands, squeeze out excess moisture. Pat dry with paper towels and it's ready for cooking.

If you are halving this recipe, be sure to use a small (approx. 2 quart) slow cooker.

Make Ahead

Complete Steps 1 and 2. Cover and refrigerate for up to 2 days. When you're ready to cook, complete the recipe.

Balsamic-Spiked Split Pea Soup with Eggplant

If your taste buds are desperately seeking inspiration, try this soup. Lusciously thick and soothing, it conveys a panoply of enticing flavors that are not easily identified but are extremely appealing. I like to serve this as the centerpiece of a soup and salad dinner, perhaps with some whole-grain bread. It's also great for lunch or, in smaller portions, as the starter to a meal.

● **Medium to large (4 to 5 quart) slow cooker**

1	eggplant (about 1 lb/500 g), peeled, cubed (2 inches/5 cm) and sweated (see Tips, left)	1
2 tbsp	olive oil, divided (approx.)	25 mL
2	onions, finely chopped	2
2	carrots, peeled and diced	2
2	stalks celery, diced	2
4	cloves garlic, minced	4
1 tbsp	dried Italian seasoning	15 mL
1 tsp	salt	5 mL
1 tsp	cracked black peppercorns	5 mL
1 cup	yellow split peas, rinsed and drained	250 mL
1	can (28 oz/796 mL) tomatoes with juice, coarsely chopped	1
4 cups	vegetable broth, divided	1 L
2 tbsp	balsamic vinegar	25 mL
1 cup	parsley leaves	250 mL

1 In a large skillet, heat 1 tbsp (15 mL) of the oil over medium heat. Add eggplant, in batches, and cook until browned, adding more oil, as necessary. Transfer to slow cooker stoneware.

2. Add onions, carrots and celery to pan, adding more oil, if necessary, and cook, stirring, until softened, about 7 minutes. Add garlic, Italian seasoning, salt and peppercorns and cook, stirring, for 1 minute. Add peas and toss until coated. Add tomatoes with juice and 1 cup (250 mL) of the broth and bring to a boil. Boil for 2 minutes. Transfer to slow cooker stoneware.

3. Add remaining 3 cups (750 mL) of broth. Cover and cook on Low for 8 hours or on High for 4 hours, until peas are tender. Add vinegar and parsley and purée using an immersion blender. (You can also do this in batches in a food processor or stand blender.) Serve hot.

Vegan Friendly

Can Be Halved

Tips

Traditional wisdom suggests that yellow split peas do not need to be soaked before cooking. However, I have found that without pre-soaking they are likely to be a bit tough, possibly because most are somewhat old by the time they are purchased. In any case, I find the safest strategy is to give them a quick soak as per Step 1.

I like to use Enhanced Vegetable Broth (see Variation, page 103) when making this recipe as the flavor is more intense.

If you are halving this recipe, be sure to use a small (approx. 2 quart) slow cooker.

Make Ahead

Complete Steps 1 and 2. Cover and refrigerate overnight or for up to 2 days. When you're ready to cook, complete the recipe.

Greek-Style Split Pea Soup

This is a soup version of the Greek appetizer fava, a purée of yellow split peas and other delectable delights (see my recipe, page 41). Here I've suggested the addition of a persillade made with red wine vinegar as a flavor enhancer, but you can also finish the soup with a dollop of warm tomato sauce. For a smoother result, purée the soup after it has finished cooking.

● **Medium to large (4 to 5 quart) slow cooker**

2 cups	yellow split peas (see Tips, left)	500 mL
1 tbsp	olive oil	15 mL
2	onions, finely chopped	2
4	stalks celery, diced	4
4	carrots, peeled and diced	4
4	cloves garlic, minced	4
1 tsp	dried oregano, crumbled	5 mL
½ tsp	cracked black peppercorns	2 mL
6 cups	vegetable broth (see Tips, left)	1.5 L
	Salt, optional	

Persillade, optional

1 cup	packed fresh parsley, finely chopped	250 mL
4	cloves garlic, minced	4
4 tsp	red wine vinegar	20 mL
	Extra virgin olive oil, optional	

1. In a large pot, combine split peas and 8 cups (2 L) cold water. Bring to a boil over medium-high heat and boil rapidly for 3 minutes. Turn off heat and set aside for 1 hour. Drain and rinse thoroughly. Set aside.

2. In a skillet, heat oil over medium heat. Add onions, celery and carrots and cook, stirring, until softened, about 7 minutes. Add garlic, oregano and peppercorns and cook, stirring, for 1 minute. Transfer to slow cooker stoneware. Add reserved split peas and broth and stir well.

3. Cover and cook on Low for 8 hours or on High for 4 hours, until peas are tender. Add salt to taste, if using.

4. *Persillade, optional:* In a bowl, combine parsley, garlic and vinegar. (You can also make this in a mini-chopper.) Set aside at room temperature for 30 minutes to allow flavors to develop. To serve, ladle soup into bowls, drizzle with extra virgin olive oil, if using, and garnish with persillade, if using.

Tips

Shred Swiss chard as if you were making a chiffonade of basil leaves. Remove the stems, including the thick vein that runs up the bottom of the leaf, and thoroughly wash the leaves by swishing them around in a basin full of warm water; drain well. On a cutting board, stack the leaves two or three at a time. Roll them into a cigar shape and slice as thinly as you can.

If you are halving this recipe, be sure to use a small (approx. 2 quart) slow cooker.

Make Ahead

Complete Step 1. Cover and refrigerate for up to 2 days. When you're ready to cook, complete the recipe.

Variation

If you like the sweet taste of parsnips, substitute two parsnips for two of the carrots.

Chard-Studded Root Vegetable and Lentil Soup

This hearty soup is very flavorful and makes a great main course. Serve with a salad for a light meal.

• **Medium to large (4 to 5 quart) slow cooker**

1 tbsp	olive oil	15 mL
2	onions, finely chopped	2
4	carrots, peeled and diced	4
2	stalks celery, diced	2
4	cloves garlic, minced	4
1 tsp	salt	5 mL
1/2 tsp	cracked black peppercorns	2 mL
1	bay leaf	1
1 cup	green or brown lentils, rinsed	250 mL
6 cups	vegetable broth	1.5 L
1	potato, peeled and shredded	1
1/4 tsp	cayenne pepper, dissolved in 1 tbsp (15 mL) freshly squeezed lemon juice	1 mL
4 cups	packed shredded Swiss chard (see Tips, left)	1 L

1. In a skillet, heat oil over medium heat. Add onions, carrots and celery and cook, stirring, until softened, about 7 minutes. Add garlic, salt, peppercorns and bay leaf and cook, stirring, for 1 minute. Add lentils and toss until coated. Transfer to slow cooker stoneware. Stir in vegetable broth.

2. Add potato and stir well. Cover and cook on Low for 6 hours or on High for 3 hours, until lentils are tender. Add cayenne solution and stir well.

3. Add chard, in batches, stirring after each to submerge before adding the next batch. Cover and cook on High for 20 minutes, until chard is tender.

Tips

You can use any kind of paprika in this recipe: regular or sweet; hot, which produces a nicely peppery version; or smoked, which adds a delicious note of smokiness to the soup. If you have regular paprika and would like a bit of heat, dissolve $\frac{1}{4}$ tsp (1 mL) cayenne pepper in the lemon juice along with the paprika.

If you are halving this recipe, be sure to use a small (approx. 2 quart) slow cooker.

Make Ahead

Complete Step 1. Cover and refrigerate for up to 2 days. When you're ready to cook, complete the recipe.

Creamy Onion Soup with Kale

There is no cream in this delicious soup — unless you decide to drizzle a bit over individual servings as a finishing touch. The creaminess is achieved with the addition of potatoes, which are puréed into the soup, providing it with a velvety texture.

- **Medium to large ($3\frac{1}{2}$ to 5 quart) slow cooker**

1 tbsp	olive oil	15 mL
4	onions, thinly sliced	4
2	cloves garlic, minced	2
4	whole allspice	4
1	bay leaf	1
1 tsp	grated lemon zest	5 mL
$\frac{1}{2}$ tsp	cracked black peppercorns	2 mL
4 cups	vegetable broth	1 L
3	potatoes, peeled and diced	3
1 tsp	paprika dissolved in 2 tbsp (25 mL) freshly squeezed lemon juice (see Tip, left)	5 mL
4 cups	chopped kale	1 L

1. In a skillet, heat oil over medium heat. Add onions and cook, stirring, until softened, about 5 minutes. Add garlic, allspice, bay leaf, lemon zest and peppercorns and cook, stirring, for 1 minute. Transfer to slow cooker stoneware. Stir in broth.

2. Add potatoes and stir well. Cover and cook on Low for 8 hours or on High for 4 hours, until potatoes are tender. Discard allspice and bay leaf. Stir in paprika solution and add kale, in batches, stirring after each to submerge the leaves in the liquid. Cover and cook on High for 20 minutes, until kale is tender.

3. Purée using an immersion blender. (You can also do this in batches in a food processor or stand blender.) Serve immediately.

Fasolatha

Tips

Dried beans can sometimes be temperamental in the slow cooker. I find that bringing them to a rapid boil and boiling for 2 minutes on the stovetop before adding to the stoneware helps to ensure that they will be meltingly tender.

Traditional wisdom is that dried beans should never be cooked with an acid such as tomatoes, which will toughen them. My own experience is that the texture of cooked beans has more to do with how old they are before being cooked. The older they are, the tougher they are likely to be. I recommend buying legumes in small quantities from a purveyor with rapid turnover to ensure maximum freshness.

If you are halving this recipe, be sure to use a small (approx. 2 quart) slow cooker.

Make Ahead

Complete Step 1. Cover and refrigerate for up to 2 days. When you're ready to cook, complete the recipe.

This tasty soup is a version of a Greek one that is traditionally served during Lent. I like to serve it as a main course with some whole-grain bread and a simple green salad.

● **Medium to large (4 to 5 quart) slow cooker**

1 cup	dried white beans, such as Great Northern, navy or cannellini, soaked, drained and rinsed (see Basic Beans, page 239)	250 mL
1 tbsp	extra virgin olive oil	15 mL
2	onions, finely chopped	2
2	carrots, peeled and diced	2
4	stalks celery, diced	4
4	cloves garlic, minced	4
1 tbsp	dried oregano	15 mL
1/2 tsp	salt or to taste	2 mL
1/2 tsp	cracked black peppercorns	2 mL
1	can (14 oz/398 mL) diced tomatoes with juice	1
5 cups	vegetable broth, divided	1.25 L
1 to 2 tbsp	red wine vinegar	15 to 25 mL
1/4 cup	finely chopped Italian flat-leaf parsley	50 mL
	Extra virgin olive oil	

1. In a skillet, heat oil over medium heat. Add onions, carrots and celery and cook, stirring, until softened, about 7 minutes. Add garlic, oregano, salt and peppercorns and cook, stirring, for 1 minute. Add tomatoes with juice, beans and 2 cups (500 mL) of the broth. Bring to a boil and boil for 2 minutes. Stir well. Transfer to slow cooker stoneware.

2. Stir in remaining 3 cups (750 mL) of broth. Cover and cook on Low for 8 hours or on High for 4 hours, until beans are very tender. Stir in vinegar. To serve, ladle into bowls. Garnish with parsley and drizzle with olive oil.

Vegan Friendly

Can Be Halved

Tips

For best results, toast and grind cumin and coriander seeds yourself. *To toast cumin and coriander seeds:* Place in a dry skillet over medium heat, and cook, stirring, until fragrant, about 3 minutes. Immediately transfer to a spice grinder or mortar and grind finely.

I like to use frozen diced squash when making this soup because it is so convenient.

If you don't have fresh chile peppers, stir in your favorite hot pepper sauce, to taste, just before serving.

If you are halving this recipe, be sure to use a small (approx. 2 quart) slow cooker.

Make Ahead

Complete Step 1. Cover and refrigerate for up to 2 days. When you're ready to cook, complete the recipe.

Curried Squash and Red Lentil Soup with Coconut

Delicious, slightly exotic and hearty enough to anchor a soup and salad dinner, this soup has everything going for it. I like to cook it long enough so that the red lentils dissolve into the broth, but if you prefer your lentils to be firmer, reduce the cooking time to about 6 hours on Low.

● **Medium to large (4 to 5 quart) slow cooker**

1 tbsp	olive or coconut oil	15 mL
2	onions, finely chopped	2
4	cloves garlic, minced	4
2 tsp	minced gingerroot	10 mL
1 tbsp	ground cumin (see Tips, left)	15 mL
2 tsp	ground coriander	10 mL
1 tsp	salt	5 mL
1 tsp	cracked black peppercorns	5 mL
1 cup	red lentils, rinsed	250 mL
1	can (28 oz/796 mL) diced tomatoes with juice	1
4 cups	vegetable broth	1 L
2 cups	diced winter squash, such as butternut (see Tips, left)	500 mL
2 tsp	curry powder, dissolved in 2 tbsp (25 mL) freshly squeezed lemon juice	10 mL
1	can (14 oz/400 mL) coconut milk, divided	1
1	long red chile pepper or 2 Thai chile peppers, seeded and minced (see Tips, left)	1
	Thin lemon slices, optional	
	Finely chopped cilantro, optional	

1. In a skillet, heat oil over medium heat. Add onions and cook, stirring, until softened, about 3 minutes. Add garlic, ginger, cumin, coriander, salt and peppercorns and cook, stirring, for 1 minute. Add lentils and toss to coat. Stir in tomatoes with juice. Transfer to slow cooker stoneware.

2. Add broth and squash. Cover and cook on Low for 8 hours or on High for 4 hours, until lentils are tender.

3. In a small bowl, combine curry powder solution and about $1/4$ cup (50 mL) of the coconut milk. Stir until curry powder dissolves. Add to soup. Add remaining coconut milk and chile pepper and stir well. Cover and cook on High for 15 minutes, until heated through. When ready to serve, ladle into bowls and top with lemon slices and cilantro, if using.

Vegan Friendly

Entertaining Worthy

Can Be Halved

Tips

If you prefer, substitute 3 cups (750 mL) frozen lima beans for the dried ones and skip Step 1.

Parsnips and parsley root have a tendency to oxidize if exposed to air. If you are preparing these vegetables ahead of time, place them in an acidulated solution (8 cups/2 L water combined with 3 tbsp/45 mL lemon juice.) Drain well before adding to the slow cooker.

Some prepared vegetable broths have very strong flavor, which may overpower the ingredients in this soup. If you are using one of these, I suggest you reduce the quantity to 4 cups (1 L) and add 2 cups (500 mL) water.

If you are halving this recipe, be sure to use a small (approx. 2 quart) slow cooker.

Make Ahead

Complete Steps 1 and 2. Cover and refrigerate for up to 2 days. When you're ready to cook, complete the recipe.

Creamy Parsnip, Parsley Root and Butterbean Soup

The creaminess in this delicious soup comes from the puréed butterbeans, but a drizzle of real cream adds a very pleasant finish to the result. It's a wonderful winter soup, full of highly nutritious vegetables. Serve it in small portions as the prelude to an elegant meal or for supper with a salad, whole-grain bread and perhaps some good Cheddar.

● **Medium to large (4 to 5 quart) slow cooker**

1¼ cups	dried butterbeans or lima beans (see Tips, left)	300 mL
1 tbsp	olive oil	15 mL
1	onion, finely chopped	1
2 tbsp	minced shallots (about 2 small)	25 mL
2	stalks celery, diced	2
2 cups	cubed (1 inch/2.5 cm) peeled parsnips (about 3 medium) (see Tips, left)	500 mL
1 cup	cubed (1 inch/2.5 cm) peeled parsley root (4 medium)	250 mL
	Salt	
½ tsp	cracked black peppercorns	2 mL
2	bay leaves	2
6 cups	vegetable broth, divided (see Tips, left)	1.5 L
	Cayenne pepper, optional	
	Finely chopped parsley leaves	
	Heavy or whipping (35%) cream or soy creamer, optional	

1. In a large pot of water, bring beans to a boil over medium heat. Boil rapidly for 3 minutes. Cover, turn off heat and let stand for 1 hour. Drain in a colander placed over a sink and rinse thoroughly under cold running water. Using your hands, pop the beans out of their skins. Discard skins. Set beans aside.

2. In a skillet, heat oil over medium heat. Add onion, shallots, celery, parsnips and parsley root and cook, stirring, until softened, about 5 minutes. Add ½ tsp (2 mL) salt, peppercorns and bay leaves and cook, stirring, for 1 minute. Stir in skinned beans and 2 cups (500 mL) of the broth. Bring to a boil and boil for 1 minute. Transfer to slow cooker stoneware.

3. Add remaining 4 cups (1 L) of broth and stir well. Cover and cook on Low for 6 hours or on High for 3 hours, until vegetables are very tender.

4. Discard bay leaves. Purée using an immersion blender. (You can also do this in batches in a food processor or stand blender.) Add cayenne, to taste, if using, and season with salt, to taste. To serve, ladle into bowls and garnish with parsley. Drizzle with cream, if using.

Risi e Bisi

Tips

Using a rice that is high in starch, such as Arborio, imbues this soup with a creamy finish. If you prefer a more nutritious option, use short-grain brown rice, which is starchier than longer-grain varieties.

If you want to make this vegan, omit the butter and drizzle the soup with extra virgin olive oil after it is ladled into bowls.

If you are halving this recipe, be sure to use a small (approx. 2 quart) slow cooker.

Make Ahead

Complete Step 1. Cover and refrigerate for up to 2 days. When you're ready to cook, complete the recipe.

This Venetian take on rice and peas takes a variety of forms, from soup to more concentrated versions resembling liquidy risotto. I particularly enjoy this simple but delicious adaptation, which is mild and creamy. Just be sure to use glutinous rice such as Arborio. When the starch cooks, it thickens the broth, producing a luscious texture. This is a perfect soup for those who are feeling under the weather — mildly flavorful and very restorative.

● **Medium to large (4 to 5 quart) slow cooker**

1 tbsp	olive oil	15 mL
2	onions, finely chopped	2
4	cloves garlic, minced	4
1 tsp	dried thyme	5 mL
1/2 tsp	salt	2 mL
1/2 tsp	cracked black peppercorns	2 mL
2	bay leaves	2
1/2 cup	short-grain white or brown rice, such as Arborio (see Tips, left)	125 mL
6 cups	vegetable broth, divided	1.5 L
2 cups	green peas, thawed if frozen	500 mL
1/2 cup	freshly grated Parmesan or vegan alternative	125 mL
1/4 cup	finely chopped parsley	50 mL
1 tbsp	butter, optional (see Tips, left)	15 mL

1. In a skillet, heat oil over medium heat. Add onions and cook, stirring, until softened, about 3 minutes. Add garlic, thyme, salt, peppercorns and bay leaves and cook, stirring, for 1 minute. Add rice and 2 cups (500 mL) of the vegetable broth and bring to a boil. Boil rapidly for 2 minutes. Transfer to slow cooker stoneware.

2. Add remaining 4 cups (1 L) of broth and stir well. Cover and cook on Low for 6 hours or on High for 3 hours, until rice is tender. Stir in peas, Parmesan, parsley, and butter, if using. Stir well. Cover and cook on High for 15 minutes, until peas are tender. Discard bay leaves.

Entertaining Worthy
Can Be Halved

Tips

To save time, you can use pre-cut squash (often available in the produce section) or frozen diced squash. You will need 2 lbs (1 kg) or 7 cups (1.75 L).

If you are halving this recipe, be sure to use a small (approx. 2 quart) slow cooker.

Make Ahead

Complete Step 1. Cover and refrigerate for up to 2 days. When you're ready to cook, complete the recipe.

Butternut Apple Soup with Swiss Cheese

Topped with melted cheese, this creamy and delicious soup makes a light main course, accompanied by a green salad. It can also be served as a starter to a more substantial meal.

- **Medium to large (3½ to 5 quart) slow cooker**
- **6 to 8 ovenproof bowls**

1 tbsp	olive oil	15 mL
2	onions, chopped	2
4	cloves garlic, minced	4
2 tsp	dried rosemary, crumbled, or 1 tbsp (15 mL) chopped fresh	10 mL
½ tsp	cracked black peppercorns	2 mL
5 cups	vegetable broth	1.25 L
2	tart apples (such as Granny Smith), peeled and coarsely chopped	2
1	butternut squash (about 2½ lbs/1.25 kg), peeled and cubed (1 inch/2.5 cm) (see Tip, left)	1
	Salt, optional	
1 cup	shredded Swiss cheese	250 mL
½ cup	finely chopped walnuts, optional	125 mL

1. In a skillet, heat oil over medium heat. Add onions and cook, stirring, until softened, about 3 minutes. Add garlic, rosemary and peppercorns and cook, stirring, for 1 minute. Transfer to slow cooker stoneware. Stir in broth.

2. Add apples and squash and stir well. Cover and cook on Low for 6 hours or on High for 3 hours, until squash is tender. Preheat broiler.

3. Purée soup using an immersion blender. (You can also do this in batches in a food processor or stand blender.) Season to taste with salt, if using.

4. Preheat broiler. Ladle into ovenproof bowls. Sprinkle with cheese and broil until cheese melts, about 2 minutes. (You can also do this in batches in a microwave oven on High, about 1 minute per batch.) Sprinkle with walnuts, if using. Serve immediately.

Vegan Friendly
Entertaining Worthy
Can Be Halved

Tips

If you're using prepared vegetable broth, be aware that some brands are extremely strong, resembling vegetable juice more than broth. If this is the case, dilute your broth with up to 3 cups (750 mL) water, to suit your taste. Otherwise, the flavor of the broth will overpower the recipe.

If you are halving this recipe, be sure to use a small (approx. 2 quart) slow cooker.

Make Ahead

Complete Step 1. Cover and refrigerate for up to 2 days. When you're ready to cook, complete the recipe.

Indian-Spiced Spinach Soup

This luscious soup is inherently creamy because of the puréed lentils and potatoes, which basically dissolve into the broth. It makes a delicious starter for any meal and a great dish for a multi-dish Indian-themed dinner. I also enjoy it for lunch with whole-grain bread.

● **Medium to large (3½ to 5 quart) slow cooker**

1 tbsp	olive oil	15 mL
2	leeks, white and light green parts or white part with just a bit of green, cleaned and sliced (see Tips, page 94)	2
2	cloves garlic, minced	2
1 tsp	minced gingerroot	5 mL
2 tsp	ground cumin (see Tips, page 84)	10 mL
½ tsp	ground coriander	2 mL
½ tsp	ground turmeric	2 mL
½ tsp	cracked black peppercorns	2 mL
½ tsp	salt	2 mL
½ cup	green or brown lentils, rinsed	125 mL
6 cups	vegetable broth, divided	1.5 L
2	potatoes, peeled and shredded	2
¼ tsp	cayenne pepper, dissolved in 2 tbsp (25 mL) freshly squeezed lemon juice	1 mL
6 cups	packed spinach leaves (about 2 bunches) Heavy or whipping (35%) cream or soy creamer	1.5 L

1. In a skillet, heat oil over medium heat. Add leeks and cook, stirring, until softened, about 5 minutes. Add garlic, ginger, cumin, coriander, turmeric, peppercorns and salt and cook, stirring, for 1 minute. Add lentils and toss to coat. Add 2 cups (500 mL) of the broth and bring to a boil. Transfer to slow cooker stoneware.

2. Add remaining 4 cups (1 L) of broth and potatoes. Stir well. Cover and cook on Low for 6 hours or on High for 3 hours, until potatoes and lentils are tender.

3. Add cayenne pepper solution to stoneware and stir well. Add spinach, in batches, stirring after each to submerge the leaves in the liquid. Cover and cook on High for 15 minutes, until spinach is wilted and flavors meld. Purée using an immersion blender. (You can also do this in batches in a food processor or stand blender.) Ladle into bowls and drizzle with cream.

Tips

For the best flavor, toast cumin seeds and grind them yourself. *To toast cumin seeds:* Place in a dry skillet over medium heat, and cook, stirring, until fragrant, about 3 minutes. Immediately transfer to a spice grinder or mortar and grind finely.

You may need to adjust the quantity of salt depending upon the saltiness of the broth you're using.

If you like heat, increase the quantity of cayenne to $1/2$ tsp (2 mL).

If you are halving this recipe, be sure to use a small (approx. 2 quart) slow cooker.

Make Ahead

Complete Step 1. Cover and refrigerate for up to 2 days. When you're ready to cook, complete the recipe.

Coconut-Spiked Pumpkin Soup with Cumin and Ginger

Here's a hearty soup with Asian flavors that makes a nice centerpiece for lunch or a light supper or an elegant starter to a more substantial dinner.

● **Medium to large (4 to 6 quart) slow cooker**

1 tbsp	oil	15 mL
2	onions, finely chopped	2
2	carrots, peeled and diced	2
2	stalks celery, diced	2
4	cloves garlic, minced	4
2 tbsp	minced gingerroot	25 mL
1 tbsp	ground cumin (see Tips, left)	15 mL
$1/2$ tsp	salt (see Tips, left)	2 mL
$1/2$ tsp	cracked black peppercorns	2 mL
5 cups	vegetable broth, divided	1.25 L
6 cups	cubed ($1/2$ inch/1 cm) peeled pumpkin or orange squash, such as butternut	1.5 L
$1/4$ tsp	cayenne pepper (see Tips, left)	1 mL
2 tbsp	freshly squeezed lime juice	25 mL
1 cup	coconut milk	250 mL

1. In a skillet, heat oil over medium heat. Add onions, carrots and celery and cook, stirring, until softened, about 7 minutes. Add garlic, ginger, cumin, salt and peppercorns and cook, stirring for 1 minute. Add 1 cup (250 mL) of the broth and bring to a boil. Transfer to slow cooker stoneware.

2. Add remaining 4 cups (1 L) of broth and pumpkin. Cover and cook on Low for 6 hours, until pumpkin is tender. Purée using an immersion blender. (If you don't have an immersion blender, do this in a stand blender or food processor, in batches, and return to stoneware.)

3. In a small bowl, combine cayenne and lime juice, stirring until cayenne dissolves. Add to slow cooker along with coconut milk. Stir well. Cover and cook on High for 15 minutes to meld flavors.

Tips

For the best flavor, toast cumin and coriander seeds and grind them yourself. *To toast cumin and coriander seeds:* Place in a dry skillet over medium heat and cook, stirring, until fragrant, about 3 minutes. Immediately transfer to a spice grinder or mortar and grind finely.

If you are using large parsnips in this recipe, cut away the woody core and discard.

To enhance the Asian flavors and expand the range of nutrients you consume, substitute extra virgin coconut oil for the olive oil. Its flavors blend very well with the others in this recipe.

If you are halving this recipe, be sure to use a small (approx. 2 quart) slow cooker.

Make Ahead

Complete Step 1. Cover and refrigerate for up to 2 days. When you're ready to cook, complete the recipe.

Curried Parsnip Soup with Green Peas

Flavorful and elegant, this soup makes a great introduction to a more substantial meal. Served with whole-grain bread, it is also a satisfying lunch. I like to complete this soup with a drizzle of heavy cream, which gives a smooth and sophisticated finish, but if you're averse to dairy, substitute coconut milk or soy creamer.

● **Medium to large ($3\frac{1}{2}$ to 5 quart) slow cooker**

1 tbsp	olive oil or extra virgin coconut oil	15 mL
2	onions, finely chopped	2
4	cloves garlic, minced	4
2 tsp	ground cumin (see Tips, left)	10 mL
1 tsp	ground coriander	5 mL
$\frac{1}{2}$ tsp	cracked black peppercorns	2 mL
1	piece (1 inch/2.5 cm) cinnamon stick	1
1	bay leaf	1
6 cups	vegetable broth	1.5 L
4 cups	sliced peeled parsnips (about 1 lb/500 g) (see Tips, left)	1 L
2 tsp	curry powder, dissolved in 4 tsp (20 mL) freshly squeezed lemon juice	10 mL
2 cups	sweet green peas, thawed if frozen	500 mL
$\frac{1}{3}$ cup	heavy or whipping (35%) cream, coconut milk or soy creamer plus additional for drizzling	75 mL

1. In a skillet, heat oil over medium heat. Add onions and cook, stirring, until softened, about 3 minutes. Add garlic, cumin, coriander, peppercorns, cinnamon stick and bay leaf and cook, stirring, for 1 minute. Transfer to slow cooker stoneware. Add vegetable broth.

2. Add parsnips and stir well. Cover and cook on Low for 6 hours or on High for 3 hours, until parsnips are tender. Discard cinnamon stick and bay leaf. Purée using an immersion blender. (If you don't have an immersion blender, do this in a stand blender or food processor, in batches, and return to stoneware.) Add curry powder solution, green peas and cream. Cover and cook on High for 20 minutes, until peas are tender and cream is heated through. Ladle into bowls and drizzle with additional cream.

Tips

Some prepared vegetable broths have a very strong flavor, which may overpower the celery in this soup. If you are using one of these, I suggest you reduce the quantity to 4 cups (1 L) and add 2 cups (500 mL) water.

Although it tastes like celery, celery root, or celeriac, is actually a member of the parsley family. This vegetable oxidizes quickly on contact with air. To prevent browning, I recommend that after dicing, you place both the celery root and the potatoes in a large bowl of acidulated water (8 cups/2 L water combined with 3 tbsp/45 mL lemon juice.) Drain well before adding to the slow cooker.

Use the kind of cheese you prefer when making the toasts. I have made this using Stilton and freshly grated Parmesan but almost any good cheese or vegan alternative that melts well will work. Slice thinly, crumble, shred or grate depending upon the texture of the cheese.

If you are halving this recipe, be sure to use a small (approx. 2 quart) slow cooker.

Make Ahead

Compete Step 1. Cover and refrigerate for up to 2 days. When you're ready to cook, complete the recipe.

Creamy Double Celery Soup with Cheesy Toasts

Using two kinds of celery, regular stalks plus celery root, intensifies the celery flavor in this robust soup. It makes a nice prelude to a meal, drizzled with additional cream. I also like to serve it as the centerpiece of a soup and salad dinner. With two toasts per person it's more than enough.

● **Medium to large (4 to 5 quart) slow cooker**

1 tbsp	butter or olive oil	15 mL
1 tbsp	olive oil	15 mL
2	onions, finely chopped	2
4	stalks celery, peeled and diced	4
4	cloves garlic, minced	4
1 tsp	salt	5 mL
1 tsp	cracked black peppercorns	5 mL
$1/2$ tsp	freshly grated nutmeg	2 mL
6 cups	vegetable broth, divided (see Tips, left)	1.5 L
1	large celery root (about $1\frac{1}{2}$ lbs/750 g), peeled and diced (see Tips, left)	1
1	potato, peeled and diced	1
$1/2$ cup	heavy or whipping (35%) cream or soy milk	125 mL
Pinch	cayenne pepper	Pinch

Toasts

6 to 12	slices ($1/4$ inch/0.5 cm) baguette	6 to 12
	Olive oil	
	Cheese or vegan alternative (see Tips, left)	

1. In a skillet, melt butter with oil over medium heat. Add onions and celery and cook, stirring, until softened, about 5 minutes. Add garlic, salt, peppercorns and nutmeg and cook, stirring, for 1 minute. Add 2 cups (500 mL) of the vegetable broth. Transfer to slow cooker stoneware.

2. Add remaining 4 cups (1 L) of vegetable broth, celery root and potato. Stir well. Cover and cook on Low for 6 hours or on High for 3 hours. Purée using an immersion blender. (If you don't have an immersion bender, do this in a food processor or stand blender, in batches, and return to stoneware.) Stir in cream and cayenne.

3. *Toasts:* Preheat broiler. Brush baguette slices with olive oil on both sides. Toast under preheated broiler, turning once, until golden, about 2 minutes per side. Spread one side with cheese and return to broiler until melted. To serve, ladle soup into bowls and top with toasts.

Entertaining Worthy

Tip

If you are pressed for time, skip Step 1 and soften the onions on the stovetop. Heat the butter in a large skillet over medium heat. Add the onions and cook, stirring, until they soften, about 10 minutes. Transfer to stoneware and continue with Step 2.

Make Ahead

Complete Steps 1 and 2. Cover and refrigerate onions for up to 2 days. When you're ready to cook, complete the recipe, adding 1 hour to the cooking time in Step 3.

Classic French Onion Soup

On a chilly day, there's nothing more appetizing than a bowl of steaming onion soup, bubbling away under a blanket of browned cheese. Normally, caramelizing the onions for this masterpiece is a laborious process that can easily involve an hour of almost constant stirring. Fortunately, your slow cooker can now do most of this tiresome work for you.

- **Medium to large (3½ to 5 quart) slow cooker**
- **6 ovenproof soup bowls**

10	onions, thinly sliced on the vertical	10
2 tbsp	melted butter	25 mL
1 tbsp	granulated sugar	15 mL
8 cups	Enhanced Vegetable Broth (see Variation, page 103)	2 L
2 tbsp	brandy or cognac	25 mL
1 tsp	salt	5 mL
1 tsp	cracked black peppercorns	5 mL
12	slices baguette, about ½-inch (1 cm) thick	12
2 cups	shredded Swiss or Gruyère cheese	500 mL

1. In slow cooker stoneware, combine onions and butter. Toss well to ensure onions are thoroughly coated. Cover and cook on High for 1 hour, until onions are softened.

2. Add sugar and stir well. Place a clean tea towel, folded in half (so you will have two layers), over top of stoneware to absorb moisture. Cover and cook on High for 4 hours, stirring two or three times to ensure that onions are browning evenly, replacing towels each time.

3. Add broth, brandy, salt and peppercorns and stir well. Remove towels, cover and cook on High for 2 hours.

4. Preheat broiler. Ladle soup into ovenproof bowls. Place 2 baguette slices in each bowl. Sprinkle liberally with cheese and broil until top is bubbly and brown, 2 to 3 minutes. Serve immediately.

Vegan Friendly

Entertaining Worthy

Can Be Halved

Tips

If you're using prepared vegetable broth, be aware that some brands are extremely strong, resembling vegetable juice more than broth. If this is the case, dilute your broth with up to 3 cups (750 mL) water, to suit your taste. Otherwise, the flavor of the broth will overpower the recipe.

If you are halving this recipe, be sure to use a small (approx. 2 quart) slow cooker.

Make Ahead

Complete Step 1. Cover and refrigerate for up to 2 days. When you're ready to cook, complete the recipe.

Fennel-Laced Celery Soup

The hint of fennel adds a delightfully different accent to this almost-classic cream of celery soup. The potato disappears after the ingredients are puréed and acts as a thickener so you don't need to add the cream unless you prefer a mellow finish. Serve this as a prelude to an elegant meal or as the centerpiece to a light soup and salad dinner.

● **Medium (approx. 4 quart) slow cooker**

1 tbsp	oil	15 mL
4 cups	diced celery (about 12 stalks)	1 L
2	onions, finely chopped	2
1	bulb fennel, trimmed, cored and chopped	1
4	cloves garlic, minced	4
1 tsp	dried thyme	5 mL
1 tsp	salt	5 mL
1/2 tsp	cracked black peppercorns	2 mL
6 cups	vegetable broth, divided (see Tip, left)	1.5 L
1	potato, peeled and shredded	1
1/2 cup	heavy or whipping (35%) cream or soy creamer, optional	125 mL
	Finely chopped chives	

1. In a skillet, heat oil over medium heat. Add celery, onions and fennel and cook, stirring, until softened, about 5 minutes. Add garlic, thyme, salt and peppercorns and cook, stirring, for 1 minute. Add 2 cups (500 mL) of the vegetable broth. Transfer to slow cooker stoneware.

2. Add remaining 4 cups (1 L) of vegetable broth and potato. Cover and cook on Low for 6 hours or on High for 3 hours, until vegetables are tender. Purée using an immersion blender. (If you don't have an immersion blender, do this in a food processor or stand blender, in batches, and return to slow cooker.) Stir in cream, if using. To serve, ladle into bowls and garnish with chives.

Creamy Sunchoke Soup

Tips

Jerusalem artichokes oxidize quickly on contact with air. To prevent browning, place them in a large bowl of acidulated water (6 cups/1.5 L water combined with 2 tbsp/25 mL lemon juice.) Drain well before adding to the slow cooker.

If you are halving this recipe, be sure to use a small (approx. 2 quart) slow cooker.

Make Ahead

Complete Step 1. Cover and refrigerate for up to 2 days. When you're ready to cook, complete the recipe.

If you live in northern regions where they grow wild, sunchokes, which are also known as Jerusalem artichokes, start coming into farmers' markets in the fall. This relative of the sunflower has a lovely crispy texture and a mild nutty flavor and makes a beautifully creamy soup with a uniquely delicate taste.

● **Medium to large (4 to 5 quart) slow cooker**

2 tbsp	butter or olive oil	25 mL
2	leeks, white part only with just a bit of green, cleaned and sliced (see Tips, page 94)	2
2	stalks celery, diced	2
2	cloves garlic, minced	2
1 tsp	salt	5 mL
1/2 tsp	cracked black peppercorns	2 mL
1/2 tsp	dried thyme	2 mL
1	bay leaf	1
4 cups	vegetable broth	1 L
3 cups	peeled, sliced (1 inch/2.5 cm) Jerusalem artichokes (see Tip, left)	750 mL
1	potato, peeled and shredded	1
	Finely chopped parsley or snipped chives	
	Heavy or whipping (35%) cream or soy creamer, optional	

1. In a skillet, melt butter over medium heat. Add leeks and celery and cook, stirring, until softened, about 5 minutes. Add garlic, salt, peppercorns, thyme and bay leaf and cook, stirring, for 1 minute. Add broth and bring to a boil. Transfer to slow cooker stoneware.

2. Add Jerusalem artichokes and potato. Cover and cook on Low for 6 hours or on High for 3 hours, until chokes and potatoes are tender. Discard bay leaf. Purée using an immersion blender. (You can also do this in batches in a food processor or stand blender.) To serve, ladle into bowls, garnish liberally with parsley, and drizzle with cream, if using.

Smoked Tofu Gumbo

Tips

Cajun seasoning is a prepared blend and its spiciness varies from brand to brand. If yours is hot, use a smaller quantity.

Use any kind of chile pepper here, but taste the broth before adding and adjust the quantity to ensure the spiciness meets your taste. For instance, if you're using a habanero pepper, I'd recommend no more than half of one.

Look for smoked tofu in well-stocked natural foods stores. If you can't find it, substitute the same quantity of seasoned extra-firm tofu. *To make seasoned tofu:* On a plate, combine ¼ cup (50 mL) all-purpose flour and 2 tsp (10 mL) smoked paprika. Roll cubed tofu in mixture until lightly coated. Discard any excess flour. In a skillet, heat oil over medium-high heat. Add dredged tofu and sauté, stirring, until nicely browned on all sides.

Filé powder is ground sassafras leaves. It is a traditional Cajun seasoning used to thicken and add flavor to gumbo.

Make Ahead

Complete Step 1. Cover and refrigerate for up to 2 days. When you're ready to cook, continue with the recipe.

If, like me, you periodically get cravings for smoked food, here's a recipe that will provide satisfaction and save you the trouble of heating up the smoker. I like to enjoy this for lunch with chunky whole-grain rolls.

● **Medium to large (4 to 5 quart) slow cooker**

1 tbsp	oil	15 mL
2	onions, finely chopped	2
4	stalks celery, diced	4
2	carrots, peeled and diced	2
4	cloves garlic, minced	4
1 to 2 tsp	Cajun seasoning	5 to 10 mL
1 tsp	salt	5 mL
1 tsp	cracked black peppercorns	5 mL
1 tsp	dried thyme	5 mL
2	bay leaves	2
¼ cup	short-grain brown rice (see Tips, page 92)	50 mL
5 cups	vegetable broth, divided	1.25 L
2 cups	cubed (½ inch/1 cm) smoked tofu (about 8 oz/250 g) (see Tips, left)	500 mL
1	red bell pepper, seeded and diced	1
1	fresh chile pepper, seeded and diced (see Tips, left)	1
1 tsp	filé powder, optional	5 mL
	Finely chopped green onions	
	Hot pepper sauce	

1. In a skillet, heat oil over medium heat. Add onions, celery and carrots and cook, stirring, until softened, about 7 minutes. Add garlic, Cajun seasoning, salt, peppercorns, thyme and bay leaves and cook, stirring, for 1 minute. Add rice and toss to coat. Add 2 cups (500 mL) of the broth and bring to a boil. Boil for 2 minutes. Transfer to slow cooker stoneware

2. Add remaining 3 cups (750 mL) of broth. Cover and cook on Low for 6 hours or High for 3 hours, until rice is tender.

3. Add smoked tofu, bell pepper, and chile pepper, if using. Cover and cook on High for 20 minutes, until pepper is tender and tofu is heated through. Discard bay leaves. Stir in filé powder, if using. Ladle into bowls and garnish with green onions. Pass the hot pepper sauce at the table.

Vegan Friendly

Entertaining Worthy

Can Be Halved

Tips

I like to use equal quantities of sweet and hot paprika in this soup, which adds a pleasant bit of zest. If you like a smoky flavor, use 1 tsp (5 mL) of smoked paprika along with the sweet.

If you prefer, use frozen artichokes, thawed, to make this recipe. You'll need 12 artichoke hearts.

If you are halving this recipe, be sure to use a small (approx. 2 quart) slow cooker.

Make Ahead

Complete Step 1. Cover and refrigerate for up to 2 days. When you're ready to cook, complete the recipe.

Creamy Artichoke Soup

If you're looking for a soup that is traditionally comforting but with a twist, try this deliciously different variation on old-fashioned leek and potato soup. The artichokes add flavor and texture, and the lemon-Parmesan finish, with just a hint of paprika, will appeal to jaded taste buds.

● **Medium to large (4 to 5 quart) slow cooker**

1 tbsp	oil	15 mL
3	leeks, white part only with just a bit of green, cleaned and sliced (see Tip, page 94)	3
4	cloves garlic, minced	4
1 tsp	salt	5 mL
1/2 tsp	cracked black peppercorns	2 mL
6 cups	vegetable or mushroom broth, divided	1.5 L
2	cans (each 14 oz/398 mL) artichoke hearts, drained (see Tips, left)	2
2	potatoes, peeled and shredded	2
2 tsp	paprika, dissolved in 2 tbsp (25 mL) freshly squeezed lemon juice (see Tips, left)	10 mL
1 cup	freshly grated Parmesan or vegan alternative	250 mL
	Finely chopped parsley or chives	

1. In a skillet, heat oil over medium heat. Add leeks and cook, stirring, until softened, about 5 minutes. Add garlic, salt and peppercorns and cook, stirring, for 1 minute. Add 2 cups (500 mL) of the broth and stir well. Transfer to slow cooker stoneware.

2. Add remaining 4 cups (1 L) of broth, artichokes and potatoes. Stir well. Cover and cook on Low for 6 hours or on High for 3 hours. Purée using an immersion blender. (If you don't have an immersion blender, do this in a food processor or stand blender, in batches, and return to slow cooker.)

3. Add paprika solution to slow cooker along with Parmesan and stir well. To serve, ladle into bowls and garnish with parsley.

Tips

Store brown rice in the refrigerator or use it within a few weeks of purchase. The bran layer contains oil, which although healthy, becomes rancid when kept at room temperature for a long period.

I like to use brown rice because it is the most nutritious form of the grain, but if you prefer you can substitute an equal quantity of white rice.

To make garlic croutons: Combine 1 cup (250 mL) crustless bread cubes (about 1 inch/2.5 cm) with 1 tbsp (15 mL) extra virgin olive oil and 1 clove of minced garlic. Toss well and season to taste with salt and freshly ground black pepper. Spread out on a baking sheet and bake in a preheated (325°F/160°C) oven, tossing several times, until golden, about 8 minutes.

If you are halving this recipe, be sure to use a small (approx. 2 quart) slow cooker.

Make Ahead

Complete Step 1. Cover and refrigerate for up to 2 days. When you're ready to cook, complete the recipe.

Soup à la Crécy

In French cooking, crécy is a term for certain dishes containing carrots. In my books, this soup, which may be thickened with potatoes or rice, is one of the tastiest. This classic soup makes a nice centerpiece for a light soup and salad dinner accompanied with dark rye bread. It also makes an elegant first course for a more sophisticated meal.

● **Medium to large (3½ to 5 quart) slow cooker**

1 tbsp	olive oil	15 mL
2	leeks, white part with just a bit of green, cleaned and thinly sliced (see Tips, page 94)	2
4 cups	thinly sliced, peeled carrots (about 1 lb/500 g)	1 L
2 tsp	dried thyme, crumbled	10 mL
1 tsp	cracked black peppercorns	5 mL
2	bay leaves	2
6 cups	vegetable broth	1.5 L
½ cup	brown rice (see Tips, left)	125 mL
	Salt, optional	
	Heavy or whipping (35%) cream or non-dairy alternative, optional	
½ cup	finely chopped parsley or snipped chives	125 mL
½ cup	garlic croutons (see Tips, left)	125 mL

1. In a large skillet, heat oil over medium heat. Add leeks and carrots and cook, stirring, until softened, about 7 minutes. Add thyme, peppercorns and bay leaves and cook, stirring, for 1 minute. Transfer to slow cooker stoneware. Add broth and stir well.

2. Stir in rice. Cover and cook on Low for 8 hours or on High for 4 hours, until carrots are tender. Discard bay leaves.

3. Purée using an immersion blender. (You can also do this in batches in a food processor or stand blender.) Season to taste with salt, if using. Ladle into bowls and drizzle with cream, if using. Garnish with parsley and croutons.

Tips

To clean leeks: Fill a basin full of lukewarm water. Split the leeks in half lengthwise and submerge them in the water, swishing them around to remove all traces of dirt. Transfer to a colander and rinse thoroughly under cold water.

Since celery root oxidizes quickly on contact with air, be sure to use it as soon as you have peeled and chopped it, or toss it with 1 tbsp (15 mL) lemon juice to prevent discoloration.

If you are halving this recipe, be sure to use a small (approx. 2 quart) slow cooker.

Make Ahead

Complete Step 1. Cover and refrigerate for up to 2 days. When you're ready to cook, complete the recipe.

Vichyssoise with Celery Root and Watercress

This refreshing soup is delicious and easy to make, and can be a prelude to the most sophisticated meal. More nutritious than traditional vichyssoise, it has a pleasing nutty flavor that may be enhanced with a garnish of chopped toasted walnuts. In the summer, I aim to have leftovers in the refrigerator and treat myself to a small bowl for a yummy afternoon snack.

• **Medium to large (3½ to 5 quart) slow cooker**

1 tbsp	olive oil	15 mL
3	leeks, white and light green parts only or white part with just a bit of green, cleaned and coarsely chopped (see Tips, left)	3
2	cloves garlic, minced	2
½ tsp	cracked black peppercorns	2 mL
6 cups	vegetable broth	1.5 L
1	large celery root (celeriac), peeled and sliced	1
2	bunches (each about 4 oz/125 g) watercress, tough parts of the stems removed	2
	Salt, optional	
½ cup	heavy or whipping (35%) cream or soy milk	125 mL
	Toasted chopped walnuts, optional	
	Watercress sprigs, optional	

1. In a skillet, heat oil over medium heat. Add leeks and cook, stirring, until softened, about 5 minutes. Add garlic and peppercorns and cook, stirring, for 1 minute. Transfer to slow cooker stoneware. Stir in broth.

2. Add celery root and stir well. Cover and cook on Low for 6 hours or on High for 3 hours, until celery root is tender. Add watercress, in batches, stirring after each to submerge the leaves in the liquid.

3. Purée using an immersion blender. (You can also do this in batches in a food processor or stand blender.) Transfer to a large bowl. Season to taste with salt, if using. Stir in cream. Cover and refrigerate until thoroughly chilled, about 4 hours.

4. Ladle into bowls and garnish with walnuts and/or watercress, if using.

Entertaining Worthy

Can Be Halved

Tip

Be sure to use Enhanced Vegetable Broth in this soup to ensure the most flavorful result.

If you are halving this recipe, be sure to use a small (approx. 2 quart) slow cooker.

Make Ahead

Complete Step 1. Cover and refrigerate for up to 2 days. When you're ready to cook, complete the recipe.

Savory Cheddar Cheese Soup

This hearty meal-in-a-bowl, which is deliciously rich, is a real show-stopper. It makes a great weeknight dinner with salad or doubles as a starter to a traditional meal. My family likes to scoop up the vegetables on thick slices of country bread, but if you're serving this to guests, puréeing the mixture before adding the cream and cheese produces a more polished result.

● **Medium to large (3½ to 5 quart) slow cooker**

1 tbsp	butter	15 mL
2	leeks, white part with just a bit of green, cleaned and finely chopped (See Tips, page 94)	2
2	carrots, peeled and finely chopped	2
3	stalks celery, peeled and finely chopped	3
2 tbsp	all-purpose flour	25 mL
1 tsp	dry mustard	5 mL
½ tsp	salt	2 mL
½ tsp	freshly ground black pepper	2 mL
5 cups	Enhanced Vegetable Broth (page 103)	1.25 L
1 tbsp	tomato paste	15 mL
1	bay leaf	1
½ cup	heavy or whipping (35%) cream	125 mL
3 cups	shredded Cheddar cheese	750 mL
	Hot pepper sauce to taste, optional	

1. In a large skillet, melt butter over medium heat. Add leeks, carrots and celery. Reduce heat to low. Cover and cook until vegetables are softened, about 10 minutes. Add flour, dry mustard, salt and pepper to pan and cook, stirring, for 1 minute. Add broth, tomato paste and bay leaf and cook until slightly thickened. Transfer to slow cooker stoneware.

2. Cover and cook on Low for 6 hours or on High for 3 hours. Discard bay leaf. If desired, purée using an immersion blender. (You can also do this by transferring the solids plus 1 cup/250 mL liquid to a food processor or stand blender and processing until smooth, then returning mixture to slow cooker.)

3. Add cream and cheese, cover and cook on High for 15 minutes, until cheese is melted and mixture is bubbly. Ladle into individual serving bowls and pass the hot pepper sauce, if desired.

Tips

For the best flavor, toast cumin seeds and grind them yourself. *To toast cumin seeds:* Place in a dry skillet over medium heat and cook, stirring, until fragrant, about 3 minutes. Immediately transfer to a spice grinder or mortar and grind finely.

If you prefer, use one red and one green bell pepper.

To clean leeks: Fill a sink full of lukewarm water. Split the leeks in half lengthwise and submerge them in the water, swishing them around to remove all traces of dirt. Transfer to a colander and rinse thoroughly under cold water.

If you are halving this recipe, be sure to use a small (approx. 2 quart) slow cooker.

Make Ahead

Complete Step 1. Cover and refrigerate for up to 2 days. When you're ready to cook, complete the recipe.

New World Leek and Potato Soup

I call this soup "new world" because it's a variation on the classic French leek and potato soup, using sweet potatoes and peppers, two ingredients that Christopher Columbus introduced to Europe during his explorations of the Americas. Serve small quantities as a prelude to a celebratory meal, or add whole-grain bread and a tossed green salad for a light supper.

- **Medium to large (3½ to 5 quart) slow cooker**

1 tbsp	olive oil	15 mL
4	large leeks, white part with just a bit of green, cleaned and thinly sliced (see Tips, left)	4
4	cloves garlic, minced	4
1 tbsp	ground cumin (see Tips, left)	15 mL
½ tsp	cracked black peppercorns	2 mL
6 cups	vegetable broth, divided	1.5 L
3	medium sweet potatoes (about 2 lbs/1 kg), peeled and cut into 1-inch (2.5 cm) cubes	3
2	green bell peppers, diced (see Tips, left)	2
1	long red chile pepper, minced, optional	1
	Salt, optional	
½ cup	heavy or whipping (35%) cream or soy milk	125 mL
	Roasted red pepper strips, optional	
	Finely snipped chives	

1. In a large skillet, heat oil over medium heat. Add leeks and cook, stirring, until softened, about 5 minutes. Add garlic, cumin and peppercorns and cook, stirring, for 1 minute. Add 2 cups (500 mL) of the vegetable broth and stir well. Transfer to slow cooker stoneware.

2. Add remaining 4 cups (1 L) of vegetable broth and sweet potatoes. Cover and cook on Low for 6 hours or on High for 3 hours, until potatoes are tender. Add green peppers, and chile pepper, if using. Cover and cook on High for 20 minutes, until peppers are tender. Season to taste with salt, if using.

3. Purée using an immersion blender. (You can also do this in batches using a food processor or stand blender.) To serve, ladle soup into bowls, drizzle with cream and garnish with roasted red pepper strips, if using, and chives.

Leafy Greens Soup

Tips

To clean leeks: Fill a sink full of lukewarm water. Split the leeks in half lengthwise and submerge them in the water, swishing them around to remove all traces of dirt. Transfer to a colander and rinse thoroughly under cold water.

If you are halving this recipe, be sure to use a small (approx. 2 quart) slow cooker.

Make Ahead

Complete Step 1. Cover and refrigerate for up to 2 days. When you're ready to cook, complete the recipe.

This delicious country-style soup is French in origin and based on the classic combination of leeks and potatoes, with the addition of healthful leafy greens. Sorrel, which has an intriguing but bitter taste, adds delightful depth to the flavor. Sorrel is available from specialty greengrocers or at farmers' markets during the summer, but if you're unsuccessful in locating it, arugula or parsley also work well in this recipe.

● **Medium to large (3½ to 5 quart) slow cooker**

2 tbsp	olive oil or butter	25 mL
6	small leeks, white and light green parts only or white part with a bit of green, cleaned and thinly sliced (see Tips, left)	6
4	cloves garlic, minced	4
1 tsp	salt	5 mL
1 tsp	dried tarragon	5 mL
½ tsp	cracked black peppercorns	2 mL
6 cups	vegetable broth, divided	1.5 L
3	medium potatoes, peeled and cut into ½-inch (1 cm) cubes	3
4 cups	packed torn Swiss chard leaves (about 1 bunch)	1 L
1 cup	packed torn sorrel, arugula or parsley leaves	250 mL
	Heavy or whipping (35%) cream or non-dairy alternative, optional	
	Garlic croutons, optional (see Tips, page 92)	

1. In a large skillet, heat oil over medium heat. Add leeks and cook, stirring, until softened, about 5 minutes. Add garlic, salt, tarragon and peppercorns and cook, stirring, for 1 minute. Add 2 cups (500 mL) of the broth and bring to a boil. Transfer to slow cooker stoneware.

2. Stir in remaining 4 cups (1 L) of broth and potatoes. Cover and cook on Low for 8 hours or on High for 4 hours, until potatoes are tender. Add Swiss chard and sorrel, in batches, stirring after each to submerge the leaves in the liquid. Cover and cook on High for 20 minutes, until greens are tender.

3. Purée using an immersion blender. (You can also do this in batches in a food processor or stand blender.) Spoon into individual serving bowls and drizzle with cream and/or top with croutons, if using.

Vegan Friendly

Can Be Halved

Tips

If you prefer a smoother soup, do not purée the vegetables in Step 2. Instead, wait until they have finished cooking, and purée the soup in the stoneware using an immersion blender before adding the vinegar and cabbage. Allow the soup time to reheat (cook on High for 10 or 15 minutes) before adding the cabbage to ensure that it cooks.

If you are halving this recipe, be sure to use a small (approx. 2 quart) slow cooker.

Make Ahead

Complete Steps 1 and 2. Cover and refrigerate for up to 2 days. When you're ready to cook, complete the recipe.

Cabbage Borscht

Served with dark rye bread this hearty soup makes a soul-satisfying meal, particularly in the dark days of winter. I like to make this using Enhanced Vegetable Broth, which intensifies the robust flavors.

- **Large (approx. 5 quart) slow cooker**
- **Food processor**

1 tbsp	olive oil	15 mL
2	onions, finely chopped	2
4	stalks celery, diced	4
2	carrots, peeled and diced	2
4	cloves garlic, minced	4
1 tsp	caraway seeds	5 mL
1 tsp	salt	5 mL
$\frac{1}{2}$ tsp	cracked black peppercorns	2 mL
1	can (28 oz/796 mL) tomatoes with juice, coarsely chopped	1
1 tbsp	brown sugar	15 mL
3	medium beets, peeled and diced	3
1	potato, peeled and diced	1
4 cups	Enhanced Vegetable Broth (page 103)	1 L
1 tbsp	red wine vinegar	15 mL
4 cups	finely shredded cabbage	1 L
	Sour cream, optional	
	Finely chopped dill	

1. In a skillet, heat oil over medium heat. Add onions, celery and carrots and cook, stirring, until softened, about 7 minutes. Add garlic, caraway seeds, salt and peppercorns and cook, stirring, for 1 minute.

2. Transfer to a stand blender or food processor fitted with a metal blade (see Tips, left). Add half the tomatoes with juice and process until smooth. Transfer to slow cooker stoneware.

3. Add remaining tomatoes, brown sugar, beets and potato to stoneware. Add vegetable broth.

4. Cover and cook on Low for 6 hours or on High for 3 hours, until vegetables are tender. Add vinegar and cabbage, in batches, stirring until each is submerged. Cover and cook on High for 20 to 30 minutes, until cabbage is tender. To serve, ladle into bowls, add a dollop of sour cream, if using, and garnish with dill.

Tips

I often use coconut oil when making this soup because its pleasantly nutty taste complements the Thai flavors.

If you are halving this recipe, be sure to use a small (approx. 2 quart) slow cooker.

Make Ahead

Ideally, make this soup the day before you intend to serve it so it can chill overnight in the refrigerator.

Beet Soup with Lemongrass and Lime

This Thai-inspired soup, which is served cold, is elegant and refreshing. Its jewel-like appearance and intriguing flavors make it a perfect prelude to any meal. I especially like to serve it at summer dinners in the garden.

● **Medium to large (3½ to 5 quart) slow cooker**

1 tbsp	olive oil or extra virgin coconut oil (see Tips, left)	15 mL
1	onion, chopped	1
4	cloves garlic, minced	4
2	stalks lemongrass, trimmed, smashed and cut in half crosswise	2
2 tbsp	minced gingerroot	25 mL
2 tsp	cracked black peppercorns	10 mL
6 cups	vegetable broth, divided	1.5 L
6	beets (about 2½ lbs/1.25 kg), peeled and chopped	6
1	red bell pepper, diced	1
1	long red chile pepper, seeded and diced, optional	1
	Grated zest and juice of 1 lime	
	Salt, optional	
	Coconut cream, optional	
	Finely chopped fresh cilantro	

1. In a skillet, heat oil over medium heat. Add onion and cook, stirring, until softened, about 3 minutes. Add garlic, lemongrass, ginger and peppercorns and cook, stirring, for 1 minute. Add 2 cups (500 mL) of the vegetable broth and stir well. Transfer to slow cooker stoneware.

2. Add remaining 4 cups (1 L) of vegetable broth and beets. Cover and cook on Low for 8 hours or on High for 4 hours, until beets are tender. Add red pepper, and chile pepper, if using. Cover and cook on High for 30 minutes, until peppers are tender. Discard lemongrass.

3. Purée using an immersion blender. (You can also do this in batches in a food processor or stand blender.) Transfer to a large bowl. Stir in lime zest and juice. Season to taste with salt, if using. Cover and refrigerate until thoroughly chilled, preferably overnight.

4. Ladle into bowls, drizzle with coconut cream, if using, and garnish with cilantro.

Vegan Friendly

Can Be Halved

Tips

If you have mushroom stems left over from another recipe, add them to the stoneware. However, make sure they are in good condition. When making broth of any kind you should never use vegetables that are passed their peak.

You can substitute the green part of leeks or scallions for all or part of the onions in this recipe. Use about 2 cups (500 mL) coarsely chopped and packed for each onion.

If you are halving this recipe, be sure to use a small (approx. 2 quart) slow cooker.

Homemade Mushroom Broth

The advantages to making your own mushroom broth are that you can control the quantity of salt and it is more economical than buying a prepared version. This makes a mildly flavored version, which I prefer. If a stronger mushroom flavor appeals to you, double the quantity of dried portobello mushrooms.

● **Large (minimum 5 quart) slow cooker**

1	package (½ oz/14 g) dried portobello mushrooms, crumbled	1
1 cup	hot water	250 mL
1 tbsp	oil	15 mL
2	onions, coarsely chopped	2
4	stalks celery, coarsely chopped	4
4	cloves garlic, coarsely chopped	4
1 tsp	salt	5 mL
1 tsp	dried thyme	5 mL
1 tsp	cracked black peppercorns	5 mL
8	sprigs parsley	8
12 cups	water	3 L

1. In a bowl, combine dried mushrooms and hot water, Stir well and let stand for 30 minutes. Drain liquid into stoneware. Set solids aside.

2. Meanwhile, in a skillet, heat oil over medium heat. Add onions and celery and cook, stirring, until softened, about 5 minutes. Add garlic, salt, thyme, peppercorns, parsley and reserved reconstituted mushrooms and cook, stirring, for 1 minute. Transfer to slow cooker stoneware. Add water. Cover and cook on High for 6 hours. Strain, discarding solids. Refrigerate for up to 5 days or freeze in portions in airtight containers.

Vegetable Broth

Tips

There are few firm rules about what vegetables to include in broth. Making broth is a good way to use up the parts of vegetables that are usually discarded, such as the green part of scallions or leeks, which can be substituted for onions, or mushroom stems, which add depth and flavor. However, the vegetables must be in good condition. Do not use any that have passed their peak. Moreover, vegetables from the cruciferous family, which includes broccoli, cabbage and turnip, should not be used as their pungency will overpower the other ingredients.

If you are halving this recipe, be sure to use a small (approx. 2 quart) slow cooker.

Variation

Roasted Vegetable Broth: Preheat oven to 425°F (220°C). In a bowl, toss celery, carrots, onions and garlic in 1 tbsp (15 mL) olive oil. Spread on a baking sheet and roast, turning 3 or 4 times, for 20 minutes, until nicely browned. Transfer to slow cooker stoneware, add remaining ingredients and proceed with recipe.

This recipe produces a mildly flavored broth that will not overpower the taste of most vegetable recipes. If you prefer a stronger-tasting broth, after straining off the liquid, transfer to a stockpot and simmer, uncovered, for 30 minutes until it is reduced by about one-third or use Roasted or Enhanced Vegetable Broth (see below).

● **Large (approx. 5 quart) slow cooker**

8 cups	water	2 L
4	stalks celery, coarsely chopped	4
4	carrots, scrubbed and coarsely chopped	4
2	onions, coarsely chopped	2
2	cloves garlic	2
4	sprigs parsley	4
2	bay leaves	2
½ tsp	salt	2 mL
8	black peppercorns	8

1. In slow cooker stoneware, combine water, celery, carrots, onions, garlic, parsley, bay leaves, salt and peppercorns. Cover and cook on Low for 8 hours or on High for 4 hours. Strain and discard solids. Cover and refrigerate for up to 5 days or freeze in an airtight container.

Enhanced Vegetable Broth

To enhance 8 cups (2 L) prepared or Vegetable Broth, combine in a large saucepan over medium heat with 2 carrots, peeled and coarsely chopped, 1 tbsp (15 mL) tomato paste, 1 tsp (5 mL) celery seed, 1 tsp (5 mL) cracked black peppercorns, ½ tsp (2 mL) dried thyme, 4 parsley sprigs, 1 bay leaf and 1 cup (250 mL) white wine. Bring to a boil. Reduce heat to low and simmer, covered, for 30 minutes, then strain and discard solids.

Fondues and Savories

Nippy Cheddar Rabbit

Tip

If you prefer, substitute 1 tbsp (15 mL) Dijon mustard for the dry mustard.

Variation

For a slightly different flavor, substitute 1 tbsp (15 mL) dark miso for the chili sauce.

Nippy Cheddar Rabbit

When I was growing up, my mother's Welsh rarebit was one of my favorite treats. Now that I'm a mother myself, I still think it's yummy, and so does my family. Made with beer, this slightly adult version is a great pre-dinner nibbler for guests. It also doubles as a light luncheon dish served, like mom's, over hot toast.

- **Small (maximum 3½ quart) slow cooker**
- **Fondue forks**

8 oz	old (aged) Cheddar cheese, shredded	250 g
1 cup	beer	250 mL
2	egg yolks, beaten	2
¼ tsp	dry mustard	1 mL
1 tbsp	tomato-based chili sauce	15 mL
1 tsp	packed brown sugar	5 mL
Pinch	cayenne pepper	Pinch
	White bread, crusts removed, cut into 1-inch (2.5 cm) cubes and lightly toasted under broiler	

1. In slow cooker stoneware, combine cheese and beer. Cover and cook on High for 30 minutes or until cheese melts.

2. In a bowl, whisk together egg yolks, mustard, chili sauce, brown sugar and cayenne. Pour mixture into slow cooker stoneware and stir until thickened.

3. Spear toasted bread with fondue forks and dip in cheese, ensuring that guests have napkins or plates to catch any dripping sauce.

Tips

I always use unsalted butter, not only because I prefer the taste, but also because it allows me more control over the quantity of salt I consume.

Because this fondue doesn't cook for a long time, I prefer to put the garlic through a press rather than mincing to ensure that the flavor is fully integrated into the cheese mixture. If you don't have a garlic press, a fine mince will do.

Creamy Italian Fondue

Although Swiss Fondue has become the standard against which others are measured, other countries have their own techniques for making delicious dips with hot melted cheese. One of my favorites is Fonduta, a particularly rich and creamy fondue that comes from the Piedmontese region of Italy. I like to serve this with chunks of focaccia, a crusty Italian bread, but any crusty white bread will do. Since the sauce is runny — part of its unctuous charm — pass napkins or small plates to catch any drips. You can also serve this as a sauce over slices of grilled polenta, which turns it into a plated appetizer eaten with forks.

- **Small (maximum 3½ quart) slow cooker**
- **Fondue forks**

3 cups	shredded Fontina cheese	750 mL
¾ cup	half-and-half (10%) cream	175 mL
1 tbsp	melted butter (see Tips, left)	15 mL
½	small clove garlic, put through a press (see Tips, left)	½
2	egg yolks	2
2 tbsp	hot milk	25 mL
¼ tsp	freshly ground black pepper	1 mL
	Chunks of crusty bread	

1. In slow cooker stoneware, combine cheese and cream. Cover and cook on Low for 1 hour. Increase heat to High.

2. In a small bowl, combine melted butter and garlic. Pour mixture into cheese mixture, stirring well, until thoroughly combined and the cheese is completely melted.

3. In a bowl, beat egg yolks with hot milk. Add to cheese mixture, stirring to thoroughly combine. Add pepper and stir.

4. Spear bread with fondue forks and dip in sauce, ensuring that guests have napkins or plates to catch any dripping sauce.

Kids' Favorite Fondue

Tips

If you're in a hurry, bring the tomatoes to a boil on top of the stove after they have been processed. Then transfer to the slow cooker.

Large cans of tomatoes come in 28 oz (796 mL) and 35 oz (980 mL) sizes. For convenience, I've called for the 28 oz (796 mL) size in my recipes. If you're using the 35 oz (980 mL) size, drain off 1 cup (250 mL) liquid before adding to recipe.

Thanks to my dear friend, Marilyn Linton, writer, editor and volunteer extraordinaire, for this oh-so-easy "fondue." Creamy and delicious, it is a great hit with adults as well as kids. Give everyone their own fondue fork and serve with thick slices of French baguette, quartered, celery sticks or slices of green pepper.

- **Small (maximum 3 ½ quart) slow cooker**
- **Fondue forks**

1	can (28 oz/796 mL) tomatoes with juice (see Tips, left)	1
1 tsp	dried oregano	5 mL
1 tsp	salt	5 mL
¼ tsp	freshly ground black pepper	1 mL
3 cups	shredded Cheddar cheese	750 mL
	Sliced baguette	
	Celery sticks	
	Sliced green bell pepper	

1. In a food processor or blender, process tomatoes with juice until relatively smooth. Transfer to slow cooker stoneware. Add oregano, salt and pepper and cook on High for 1 hour, until tomatoes are hot and bubbly.

2. Add cheese to slow cooker in handfuls, stirring to combine after each addition. Reduce heat to Low and serve, or cover and keep on Low until ready to serve. Using fondue forks, dip bread or vegetables into fondue.

Tip

I always use unsalted butter, not only because I prefer the taste, but also because it allows me more control over the quantity of salt I consume.

Make Ahead

Complete Steps 1 and 2. Cover and refrigerate onion mixture for up to 2 days. When you're ready to cook, complete the recipe.

Caramelized Onion Quiche

Caramelize the onions ahead of time and you can conveniently serve this tasty dish for Sunday brunch. A tossed green salad or sliced tomatoes make a perfect accompaniment.

- **6-cup (1.5 L) baking or soufflé dish, lined with greased heavy-duty foil**
- **Large (minimum 5 quart) oval slow cooker**

Crust

²/₃ cup	cheese-flavored cracker crumbs	150 mL
2 tbsp	melted butter (see Tip, left)	25 mL

Filling

4	onions, thinly sliced	4
2 tbsp	melted butter	25 mL
1 tsp	dried thyme	5 mL
1 tsp	cracked black peppercorns	5 mL
1 tsp	paprika or ¼ tsp (1 mL) cayenne pepper, optional	5 mL
½ tsp	salt	2 mL
3	eggs	3
1 cup	heavy or whipping (35%) cream	250 mL
½ cup	freshly grated Parmesan	125 mL

1. *Crust:* In a bowl, mix together crumbs and butter. Press mixture into bottom of prepared pan. Place in freezer until ready to use.

2. *Filling:* In slow cooker stoneware, combine onions and butter. Toss well to ensure onions are thoroughly coated. Place a clean tea towel, folded in half (so you will have two layers), over top of stoneware to absorb moisture. Cover and cook on High for 5 hours, stirring two or three times to ensure onions are browning evenly and replacing the towel each time, until onions are nicely caramelized. Stir in thyme, peppercorns, paprika, if using, and salt. Set aside.

3. In a bowl, whisk eggs. Add cream, whisking until smooth. Stir in Parmesan and onions. Pour into chilled crust. Cover entire pan tightly with foil and secure with a string. Place in clean slow cooker stoneware and pour in enough boiling water to reach 1 inch (2.5 cm) up the sides of the dish.

4. Cover and cook on High for 3 to 4 hours, until a tester inserted into the center of the custard comes out clean. Serve immediately.

Tip

I always use unsalted butter, not only because I prefer the taste, but also because it allows me more control over the quantity of salt I consume.

Make Ahead

Complete Step 1. Cover and freeze for up to 2 days. When you're ready to cook, complete the recipe.

Spinach and Tomato Quiche

Although this quiche is somewhat untraditional given the cracker crumb crust, the cream-based filling is easy to prepare and the results are very tasty. Serve this with a tossed green salad for brunch, lunch or a light supper.

- **6-cup (1.5 L) baking or soufflé dish, lined with greased heavy-duty foil**
- **Large (minimum 5 quart) oval slow cooker**
- **Food processor**

Crust

1 cup	cracker crumbs (about 20 crackers)	250 mL
2 tbsp	melted butter (see Tip, left)	25 mL

Filling

3	eggs	3
1 cup	heavy or whipping (35%) cream	250 mL
2 cups	packed baby spinach leaves	500 mL
1	can (14 oz/398 mL) diced tomatoes with juice	1
1/2 cup	finely grated Parmesan cheese	125 mL
1/3 cup	finely chopped shallots	75 mL

1. *Crust:* In a bowl, mix together crumbs and butter. Press mixture into bottom of prepared dish. Place in freezer until ready to use.

2. *Filling:* In a food processor, combine eggs and cream. Process until blended. Add spinach, tomatoes with juice, Parmesan and shallots and pulse until spinach is chopped and ingredients are blended. Pour into chilled crust. Cover dish tightly with foil and secure with a string. Place in slow cooker stoneware and pour in enough boiling water to reach 1 inch (2.5 cm) up the sides of the dish.

3. Cover and cook on High for 3 to 4 hours, until a tester inserted into the center of the custard comes out clean. Let cool slightly. Serve warm.

Tips

I prefer the more robust flavor of cremini mushrooms in this recipe but white mushrooms work well, too.

I like the combination of mushrooms and tarragon. If you don't have dried tarragon, substitute an equal quantity of dried thyme.

Mushroom Flan

If you like cream of mushroom soup (one of my favorites), you'll enjoy this dish, which tastes like a main course version of that old classic. To complete the meal, add a green salad or steamed spinach tossed with a little extra virgin olive oil and a splash of fresh lemon juice.

- **6-cup (1.5 L) soufflé or baking dish, lightly greased**
- **Large (minimum 5 quart) oval slow cooker**
- **Food processor**

1 tbsp	olive oil	15 mL
1 tbsp	butter	15 mL
8 oz	sliced mushrooms (see Tips, left)	250 g
1 tsp	dried tarragon (see Tips, left)	5 mL
	Salt and freshly ground black pepper	
3	eggs	3
2	egg yolks	2
½ tsp	salt	2 mL
2 cups	half-and-half (10%) cream	500 mL
	Freshly ground black pepper	

1. In a skillet, heat oil and butter over medium-high heat until butter melts. Add mushrooms and cook, stirring, until they begin to brown and release their liquid, about 5 minutes. Stir in tarragon. Remove from heat and season to taste with salt and pepper. Set aside.

2. In a food processor, combine eggs, egg yolks and salt. Pulse to blend. Add mushrooms and pulse until chopped. Add cream and pulse to blend. Transfer to prepared dish. Cover dish tightly with foil and secure with a string. Place in slow cooker stoneware and pour in enough boiling water to reach 1 inch (2.5 cm) up the sides of dish. Cover and cook on High for 3 hours, until a tester inserted in the center comes out clean. Let cool slightly. Remove foil from dish. Run a sharp knife around the outside of the dish and invert onto a serving plate. Season to taste with pepper. Serve warm.

Tips

If you don't have fresh rosemary, substitute 1 tbsp (15 mL) dried rosemary leaves.

If you prefer a stronger herbal flavor, increase the quantity of garlic to as much as 4 cloves.

If you like a bit of heat, add $\frac{1}{2}$ tsp (2 mL) each hot pepper flakes and dry mustard to the infusion in Step 1.

Herb-Infused Cheese Flan

This is a good lunch dish served with a green salad. The flavors improve if it cools slightly before serving, which also makes it a great dish for a buffet. Although it's not my favorite presentation, I know at least one person who loves eating it cold.

- **4-cup (1 L) baking dish, lightly greased**
- **Large (minimum 5 quart) oval slow cooker**

2 cups	half-and half (10%) cream	500 mL
2	bay leaves	2
2	cloves garlic, chopped	2
1	sprig rosemary	1
2	eggs	2
2	egg yolks	2
$\frac{1}{2}$ tsp	salt	2 mL
$\frac{1}{4}$ tsp	cayenne pepper	1 mL
1 cup	freshly grated Parmesan	250 mL
	Freshly ground black pepper	

1. In a saucepan over medium heat, combine cream, bay leaves, garlic and rosemary and heat until bubbles form around the edges. Remove from heat, cover and set aside until flavors infuse, about 15 minutes. Strain, reserving liquid and discarding solids.

2. In a bowl, whisk cream mixture with eggs and egg yolks until well integrated. Whisk in salt and cayenne. Stir in Parmesan and season to taste with black pepper. Transfer to prepared dish. Cover dish tightly with foil and secure with a string. Place in slow cooker stoneware and pour in enough boiling water to reach 1 inch (2.5 cm) up the sides of the dish. Cover and cook on High for 3 hours, until a tester inserted into the center comes out clean. Remove foil from dish. Run a sharp knife around the outside of the dish and invert onto a serving plate. Let cool slightly and serve warm.

Tips

I recommend soaking the bread mixture in a large mixing bowl because the bread condenses as it absorbs the liquid and is more likely to fit into the baking dish when transferred.

Use old (aged) or medium cheddar cheese when making this strata. The mild version is not robust enough to stand up to the hearty flavors of the spinach, onion and mustard.

Make Ahead

Complete Steps 1 and 2. Cover and refrigerate overnight. When you're ready to cook, complete the recipe.

Spinach and Cheddar Cheese Strata

This is an exceptionally delicious savory — how can you beat the combination of spinach and Cheddar cheese, with a hint of crunch that comes from sweet onion? This is perfect for brunch, lunch or dinner with the addition of a simple side salad.

- **8-cup (2 L) baking or soufflé dish, lightly greased**
- **Large (minimum 5 quart) oval slow cooker**

¼ cup	softened butter (approx.)	50 mL
3	thick (about 1 inch/2.5 cm) slices day-old bread, preferably whole wheat	3
4 cups	baby spinach	1 L
½	large sweet onion, such as Vidalia, thinly sliced on the vertical	½
2 cups	shredded Cheddar cheese, divided (see Tips, left)	500 mL
4	eggs, beaten	4
2 tbsp	Dijon mustard	25 mL
1 tsp	salt	5 mL
1 tsp	cracked black peppercorns	5 mL
¼ tsp	cayenne pepper	1 mL
1	can (12 oz/370 mL) evaporated milk	1

1. Butter the bread on both sides and cut into 1-inch (2.5 cm) cubes. Place in a large mixing bowl. Add baby spinach, onion and 1½ cups (375 mL) of the cheese. Toss well. Cover remaining cheese and refrigerate until ready to use.

2. In a separate bowl, whisk together eggs, Dijon mustard, salt, peppercorns and cayenne. Whisk in milk. Pour over bread mixture, stirring until well coated. Cover with plastic wrap and, using your hands, push the bread down so it is submerged in the liquid. Refrigerate for 2 hours or overnight, pushing the bread down into the liquid once or twice, if possible.

3. Transfer to prepared dish. Cover with foil, leaving room for the strata to expand, and secure with a string. Place dish in slow cooker stoneware and pour in enough boiling water to reach 1 inch (2.5 cm) up the sides of the dish. Cover and cook on High for 3 to 4 hours, until pudding is puffed.

4. Preheat broiler. Remove foil and sprinkle remaining ½ cup (125 mL) of the Cheddar evenly over top of pudding. Place under broiler until melted and nicely browned.

Tips

To toast bread cubes: Place on a rimmed baking sheet in a 325°F (160°C) oven for 5 to 7 minutes, stirring twice. If your bread is very fresh, it may not actually toast but just dry out, which is fine.

For best results use slightly stale bread. The quality of your bread also affects the volume of the pudding. The denser your bread (usually, a positive) the more volume you'll have. You may find you have just slightly too much to fit in your dish. In this case, discard the excess (it won't be much). Overnight soaking also helps because the bread condenses as it absorbs the liquid.

If you like the flavor of sun-dried tomatoes, you may wish to use the larger quantity.

Make Ahead

Complete Steps 1 and 2. Cover and refrigerate overnight. When you're ready to cook, complete the recipe.

Artichoke, Sun-Dried Tomato and Goat Cheese Strata

This is a great brunch dish, particularly because you can assemble it the night before, then put it in the slow cooker in the morning to be ready as your guests arrive. The flavor combinations are very appealing; the artichokes provide a pleasant hint of acid, which is complemented by the hint of tomato. I like to serve it with a green salad tossed in walnut oil vinaigrette and sprinkled with toasted walnuts to add healthy omega-3 fatty acids to the meal.

- **8-cup (2 L) baking or soufflé dish, lightly greased**
- **Large (minimum 5 quart) slow cooker**

8 cups	cubed (½ inch/1 cm) sourdough or whole wheat bread, toasted (see Tips, left)	2 L
1 cup	sliced green onions, white part with just a bit of green	250 mL
4 to 6	oil-packed sun-dried tomatoes, drained and finely chopped (see Tips, left)	4 to 6
1	can (14 oz/398 mL) artichoke hearts, drained and chopped	1
8 oz	soft goat cheese, crumbled, divided	250 g
4	eggs	4
2 cups	evaporated milk	500 mL
1 tsp	salt	5 mL
½ tsp	cracked black peppercorns	2 mL

1. In a large mixing bowl, combine bread, green onions, sun-dried tomatoes, to taste, artichokes and half of the goat cheese. Toss well. Cover remaining cheese and refrigerate until ready to use.

2. In a separate bowl, whisk together eggs, milk, salt and peppercorns. Pour over bread mixture and stir well. Cover with plastic wrap and, using your hands, push the bread down so it is submerged in the liquid. Refrigerate for at least 2 hours or overnight, pushing the bread down into the liquid once or twice, if possible.

3. Transfer to prepared dish. Cover with foil, leaving room for the strata to expand, and secure with a string. Place dish in slow cooker stoneware and pour in enough boiling water to reach 1 inch (2.5 cm) up the sides of the dish. Cover and cook on High for 3 hours, until pudding is puffed.

4. Preheat broiler. Sprinkle remaining goat cheese evenly over top of strata and broil until melted and nicely browned. Let cool slightly before serving.

Tips

Before adding the tomatoes, drain off ½ cup (125 mL) of the juice and save for another use.

If you can't find olive bread, use country-style bread and add ¼ cup (50 mL) chopped pitted black olives along with the sun-dried tomatoes. Reduce the quantity of salt to ½ tsp (2 mL).

For best results use slightly stale bread. If your bread is very fresh, the strata is likely to be a bit soggy. The quality of your bread also affects the volume of the pudding. The denser your bread (usually, a positive) the more volume you'll have. You may find you have just slightly too much to fit in your dish. In this case, discard the excess (it won't be much).

Make Ahead

Complete Steps 1 and 2. Refrigerate overnight. When you're ready to cook, complete the recipe.

Olive-Studded Strata with Tomatoes

Despite the Fontina cheese, the flavors in this delicious bread-based dish are very Provençal. Served with salad, it makes a delicious meal, from brunch to dinner.

- **8-cup (2 L) baking or soufflé dish, lightly greased**
- **Large (minimum 5 quart) oval slow cooker**

¼ cup	butter, softened (approx.)	50 mL
3	thick (1 inch/2.5 cm) slices olive bread (see Tips, left)	3
¼ cup	fresh thyme or finely chopped fresh parsley	50 mL
2 tbsp	finely chopped reconstituted sun-dried tomatoes	25 mL
3	eggs	3
2	egg yolks	2
1 cup	evaporated milk	250 mL
1 tsp	salt	5 mL
1 tsp	cracked black peppercorns	5 mL
1	can (28 oz/796 mL) diced tomatoes with all but ½ cup (125 mL) juice (see Tips, left)	1
2 cups	shredded Fontina cheese, divided	500 mL

1. Butter the bread on both sides and cut into 1-inch (2.5 cm) cubes. Place in a large mixing bowl (see Tips, page 114). Add thyme and sun-dried tomatoes and toss well.

2. In a separate bowl, whisk eggs, egg yolks, milk, salt and peppercorns until blended. Whisk in tomatoes and the appropriate amount of juice, then stir in 1½ cups (375 mL) of the Fontina. Cover remaining cheese and refrigerate until ready to use. Pour over bread mixture, stirring until well coated. Cover with plastic wrap and, using your hands, push the bread down so it is submerged in the liquid. Refrigerate for at least 2 hours or overnight, pushing the bread down into the liquid once or twice, if possible.

3. Transfer to prepared dish. Cover with foil, leaving room for the strata to expand, and secure with a string. Place dish in slow cooker stoneware and pour in enough boiling water to reach 1 inch (2.5 cm) up the sides of the dish. Cover and cook on High for 3 to 4 hours, until pudding is puffed.

4. Preheat broiler. Remove foil and sprinkle remaining ½ cup (125 mL) Fontina over top of pudding. Place under broiler until melted and nicely browned.

Tip

For best results when making bread puddings, use slightly stale bread. If your bread is very fresh, the pudding is likely to be a bit soggy. The quality of your bread also affects the volume of the pudding. The denser your bread (usually, a positive) the more volume you'll have. You may find you have just slightly too much to fit in your dish. In this case, discard the excess (it won't be much). Overnight soaking also helps because the bread condenses as it absorbs the liquid.

Mushroom and Onion Bread and Butter Pudding with Dill

Dill adds a refreshing hit to this mellow pudding. As with all bread-based puddings, allowing it to cool slightly before serving improves the flavors, which are muted when it is very hot.

- **8-cup (2 L) baking or soufflé dish, lightly greased**
- **Large (minimum 5 quart) oval slow cooker**

2 tbsp	butter (see Tip, opposite)	25 mL
8 oz	white mushrooms, trimmed and sliced	250 g
	Salt and freshly ground black pepper	
3	thick (about 1 inch/2.5 cm) slices day-old bread, cubed	3
1 tbsp	olive oil	15 mL
1	Spanish onion, thinly sliced on the vertical	1
2	stalks celery, diced	2
4	cloves garlic, minced	4
¼ cup	finely chopped fresh dill	50 mL
4	eggs	4
1 cup	evaporated milk	250 mL
1 tsp	salt	5 mL
1 tsp	cracked black peppercorns	5 mL
1	can (28 oz/796 mL) diced tomatoes with juice	1
¼ cup	freshly grated Parmesan	50 mL

1. In a skillet, melt butter over medium-high heat. Add mushrooms and cook, stirring, until they begin to brown and lose their liquid, about 7 minutes. Remove from heat and season to taste with salt and pepper. Transfer to a large mixing bowl. Add bread and toss well.

2. Return skillet to medium heat and add olive oil. Add onion and celery and cook, stirring, until softened, about 5 minutes. Add garlic and cook, stirring, for 1 minute. Add to bread mixture along with dill and toss well.

3. In a bowl, beat eggs, milk, salt and peppercorns. Add tomatoes with juice and mix well. Pour mixture over bread and stir well. Cover with plastic wrap and, using your hands, push the bread down so it is submerged in the liquid. Refrigerate for at least 2 hours or overnight, pushing the bread down into the liquid once or twice, if possible.

Tip

I always use unsalted butter, not only because I prefer the taste, but also because it allows me more control over the quantity of salt I consume.

Make Ahead

Complete Steps 1 and 2. Cover and refrigerate overnight. When you're ready to cook, complete the recipe.

4. Transfer to prepared dish. Cover with foil, leaving room for the pudding to expand, and secure with a string. Place dish in slow cooker stoneware and pour in enough boiling water to reach 1 inch (2.5 cm) up the sides of the dish. Cover and cook on High for 3 to 4 hours, until pudding is puffed.

5. Preheat broiler. Remove foil and sprinkle Parmesan evenly over top of pudding. Place under broiler until melted and nicely browned. Serve immediately.

Tips

For best results use slightly stale bread. If your bread is very fresh, the pudding is likely to be a bit soggy. The quality of your bread also affects the volume of the pudding. The denser your bread (usually, a positive) the more volume you'll have. You may find you have just slightly too much to fit in your dish. In this case, discard the excess (it won't be much). Overnight soaking also helps because the bread condenses as it absorbs the liquid.

Make Ahead

Complete Steps 1 and 2. Cover and refrigerate overnight. When you're ready to cook, complete the recipe.

Savory Bread Pudding with Mushrooms

A yummy combination of soft bread and mushrooms, held together by a cheese custard, this dish is the ultimate comfort food. Serve it warm from the slow cooker accompanied by a simple tossed salad. Leftovers are great, too.

- **8-cup (2 L) baking or soufflé dish, lightly greased**
- **Large (minimum 5 quart) oval slow cooker**

2 tbsp	butter	25 mL
8 oz	thinly sliced mushrooms	250 g
1 tsp	dried thyme	5 mL
1 cup	finely chopped green or red onions	250 mL
3	thick (about 1 inch/2.5 cm) slices day-old bread, cubed (see Tips, left)	3
2 cups	shredded Cheddar cheese, preferably old (aged), divided	500 mL
5	eggs	5
1 cup	evaporated milk	250 mL
1 tbsp	Dijon mustard	15 mL
1 tsp	salt	5 mL
1 tsp	cracked black peppercorns	5 mL

1. In a skillet, melt butter over medium-high heat. Add mushrooms and cook, stirring, until they begin to brown and lose their liquid, about 7 minutes. Remove from heat and stir in thyme and green onions. Transfer to a large mixing bowl. Add bread and 1 1/2 cups (375 mL) of the Cheddar cheese and toss well. Cover remaining cheese and refrigerate until ready to use.

2. In a separate bowl, whisk together eggs, milk, Dijon mustard, salt and peppercorns. Pour over bread mixture and stir well. Cover with plastic wrap and, using your hands, push the bread down so it is submerged in the liquid. Refrigerate for at least 2 hours or overnight, pushing the bread down into the liquid once or twice, if possible.

3. Transfer to prepared dish. Cover with foil, leaving room for the pudding to expand, and secure with a string. Place dish in slow cooker stoneware and pour in enough boiling water to reach 1 inch (2.5 cm) up the sides of the dish. Cover and cook on High for 3 to 4 hours, until pudding is puffed.

4. Preheat broiler. Remove foil and sprinkle remaining 1/2 cup (125 mL) Cheddar evenly over top of pudding. Broil until melted and nicely browned.

Tips
If using a springform pan, ensure that water doesn't seep into the cake by wrapping the bottom of the pan in one large seamless piece of foil that extends up the sides and over the top. Cover the top with a single piece of foil that extends down the sides and secure with a string.

I always use unsalted butter, not only because I prefer the taste, but also because it allows me more control over the quantity of salt I consume.

Go easy on the salt when seasoning as the cheese adds quite a bit to the mixture.

Make Ahead
Complete Step 1. Cover and freeze for up to 2 days. When you're ready to cook, complete the recipe.

Broccoli and Cheddar Cheesecake

Since I was a child, I've loved the combination of broccoli and Cheddar cheese. Usually, it shows up in a rich sauce smothering the vegetable or in a hearty meal-in-a-bowl soup. If you like these flavors but are looking for a different presentation, try this. In season, serve it with a salad of sliced tomatoes for a delightful dinner or lunch.

- **7-inch (18 cm) 6-cup (1.5 L) soufflé dish, lined with greased heavy-duty foil, or 7-inch (18 cm) well-greased springform pan.**
- **Large (minimum 5 quart) oval slow cooker**
- **Food processor**

Crust
1 cup	stone-ground cracker crumbs (about 16 crackers)	250 mL
3 tbsp	melted butter (see Tips, left)	45 mL

Cheesecake
5 cups	coarsely chopped broccoli florets (about 1 bunch), blanched and drained	1.25 L
2 cups	shredded Cheddar cheese	500 mL
2 oz	cream cheese, softened and cubed	60 g
2	eggs	2
1 tsp	Dijon mustard	5 mL
	Salt and freshly ground black pepper	

1. *Crust:* In a bowl, combine cracker crumbs and melted butter. Press mixture into bottom of prepared dish. Place in freezer until ready to use.

2. *Cheesecake:* In a food processor, combine Cheddar, cream cheeses, eggs and Dijon mustard. Process until smooth. Add broccoli and pulse to blend. Season to taste with salt and pepper. Spoon mixture over crust. Cover dish tightly with foil and secure with a string. (If using a springform pan, see Tips, left). Place dish in slow cooker stoneware and pour in enough boiling water to reach 1 inch (2.5 cm) up the sides of the dish. Cover and cook on High for about 3 hours, until a tester inserted in center comes out clean. Remove from stoneware. Let cool slightly, unmold and serve. Serve warm.

Tips

If using a springform pan, ensure that water doesn't seep into the cake by wrapping the bottom of the pan in one large seamless piece of foil that extends up the sides and over the top. Cover the top with a single piece of foil that extends down the sides and secure with a string.

I always use unsalted butter, not only because I prefer the taste, but also because it allows me more control over the quantity of salt I consume.

Make Ahead

Complete Step 1. Cover and freeze for up to 2 days. When you're ready to cook, complete the recipe.

Spinach, Sun-Dried Tomato and Cheddar Cheesecake

Rich, dense and delicious, you don't need much of this quiche-like dish to satisfy any longings for a cheese-flavored fix. Serve this with a lettuce and scallion salad topped with shredded carrots and chopped parsley to round out the nutrient mix.

- **7-inch (18 cm) well-greased springform pan, or 7-inch (18 cm) 6-cup (1.5 L) soufflé dish, lined with greased heavy-duty foil**
- **Large (minimum 5 quart) oval slow cooker**

Crust

1 cup	cheese-flavored cracker crumbs (about 24 crackers)	250 mL
2 tbsp	melted butter (see Tips, left)	25 mL

Filling

1 cup	evaporated milk	250 mL
3	eggs	3
1 tsp	paprika	5 mL
1/2 tsp	salt	2 mL
	Freshly ground black pepper	
1	package (10 oz/300 g) frozen spinach, thawed, squeezed dry and finely chopped	1
1/3 cup	finely chopped drained oil-packed sun-dried tomatoes	75 mL
1 cup	shredded Cheddar cheese	250 mL

1. *Crust:* In a bowl, mix together crumbs and butter. Press mixture into the bottom of prepared pan. Place in freezer until ready to use.

2. *Filling:* In a bowl, whisk together milk and eggs until blended. Whisk in paprika, salt, and black pepper to taste. Stir in spinach and tomatoes. Fold in cheese. Pour over chilled crust. Cover with foil, leaving room for the cheesecake to expand, and secure with a string. (If using a springform pan, see Tips, left.) Place in slow cooker stoneware and pour in enough boiling water to reach 1 inch (2.5 cm) up the sides of the dish.

3. Cover and cook on High for 3 to 4 hours, until a tester inserted in the center comes out clean. Serve immediately.

Tip

You can vary the flavor of this torta by adjusting the quantity and type of paprika you use. If you like the taste of paprika, use up to 2 tsp (10 mL). I've enjoyed combining half sweet paprika and half of the hot smoked variety.

Make Ahead

Complete Steps 1 and 2. Cover and refrigerate overnight. Expect to cook torta for about 3½ hours to accommodate the fact that the ingredients will be cold.

Shallot-Laced Torta

In Italian, torta means pie. In that country, there are many different versions of torta. This one is a spin on a crustless vegetable and cheese pie. It contains an abundance of shallots and a bit of thyme, which produces a mildly flavored but very tasty result. I like to serve it with a garden salad but sliced tomatoes in season would be very good, too.

- **6-cup (1.5) baking or soufflé dish, greased**
- **Large (minimum 5 quart) oval slow cooker**

1 tbsp	butter	15 mL
1 cup	finely chopped shallots	250 mL
2	cloves garlic, minced	2
1 tbsp	fresh thyme or ½ tsp (2 mL) dried thyme	15 mL
1 tsp	paprika (see Tips, left)	5 mL
½ tsp	salt	2 mL
½ tsp	cracked black peppercorns	2 mL
3	eggs	3
2 cups	fresh ricotta cheese	500 mL
1½ cups	freshly grated Parmesan	375 mL

1. In a skillet, melt butter over medium heat. Add shallots and cook, stirring, until softened, about 3 minutes. Add garlic, thyme, paprika, salt and peppercorns and cook, stirring for 1 minute. Remove from heat and set aside.

2. In a food processor fitted with a metal blade, pulse eggs until beaten. Add ricotta and Parmesan and process until mixture is well blended and the ricotta is smooth. Add reserved shallot mixture and pulse to blend. Spoon into prepared dish. Cover with foil, leaving room for the torta to expand, and secure with a string. Place dish in slow cooker stoneware and pour in enough boiling water to reach 1 inch (2.5 cm) up the sides of the dish.

3. Cover and cook on High for 2½ to 3 hours, until a knife inserted in the torta comes out clean. Let cool slightly, unmold and serve.

Tips

If you prefer, use frozen artichoke hearts, thawed, to make this recipe. You'll need 6 artichoke hearts.

If you aren't using packaged ricotta, you'll need 2 cups (500 mL) loosely packed.

Make Ahead

Complete Steps 1 and 2. Cover and refrigerate overnight. Expect to cook torta for about 3½ hours to accommodate the fact that the ingredients will be cold.

Cheese Torta with Artichokes and Sun-Dried Tomatoes

This tasty Italian-inspired torta is like a luscious airy cheesecake. Served with salad, it makes a great light supper and is a perfect dish to serve for brunch.

- **6-cup (1.5 L) baking or soufflé dish, greased**
- **Large (minimum 5 quart) oval slow cooker**
- **Food processor**

1	can (14 oz/398 mL) artichoke hearts, drained (see Tips, left)	1
½ cup	coarsely chopped drained oil-packed sun-dried tomatoes	125 mL
2 tbsp	snipped chives	25 mL
4	eggs	4
1	package (1 lb/500 g) ricotta cheese (see Tips, left)	1
1 cup	freshly grated Parmesan Salt and freshly ground black pepper	250 mL

1. In a food processor fitted with a metal blade, combine artichoke hearts, sun-dried tomatoes and chives. Pulse until artichokes are finely chopped. Transfer to a bowl and set aside.

2. Add eggs to food processor and pulse until beaten. Add ricotta and Parmesan and process until mixture is well blended and the ricotta is smooth. Add reserved artichoke mixture and pulse to blend. Season to taste with salt and pepper. Spoon into prepared dish. Cover with foil, leaving room for the torta to expand, and secure with a string.

3. Place dish in slow cooker stoneware and pour in enough boiling water to reach 1 inch (2.5 cm) up the sides of the dish. Cover and cook on High for 2½ to 3 hours, until a knife inserted in the torta comes out clean. Let cool slightly.

Mostly Veggies

*Mixed Vegetable
Coconut Curry*

Mixed Vegetable Coconut Curry

Tips

For the best flavor, toast the cumin and coriander seeds and grind them yourself. *To toast seeds:* Place in a dry skillet over medium heat and cook, stirring, until fragrant, about 3 minutes. Immediately transfer to a spice grinder or mortar and grind finely.

If you are halving this recipe, be sure to use a small (approx. 2 quart) slow cooker.

Make Ahead

Complete Step 1. Cover and refrigerate for up to 2 days. When you're ready to cook, complete the recipe.

Here's a great weeknight meal that can be made with ingredients you're likely to have on hand. Serve over hot steamed rice.

● **Medium to large (4 to 5 quart) slow cooker**

1 tbsp	vegetable or coconut oil	15 mL
3 cups	cubed (½ inch/1 cm) peeled carrots (about 4 medium)	750 mL
2	onions, finely chopped	2
2	stalks celery, diced	2
4	cloves garlic, minced	4
1 tbsp	minced gingerroot	15 mL
2 tsp	ground cumin (see Tips, left)	10 mL
2 tsp	ground coriander	10 mL
1 tsp	salt	5 mL
1 tsp	cracked black peppercorns	5 mL
½ tsp	ground turmeric	2 mL
1	bay leaf	1
1	can (28 oz/796 mL) diced tomatoes with juice	1
4 cups	cubed (1 inch/2.5 cm) peeled winter squash	1 L
1 cup	coconut milk	250 mL
1	red bell pepper, seeded and diced	1
1	long red or green chile pepper, seeded and minced	1

1. In a skillet, heat oil over medium heat. Add carrots, onions and celery and cook, stirring, until softened, about 7 minutes. Add garlic, ginger, cumin, coriander, salt, peppercorns, turmeric and bay leaf and cook, stirring, for 1 minute. Add tomatoes with juice and bring to a boil. Transfer to slow cooker stoneware.

2. Stir in squash. Cover and cook on Low for 6 hours or on High for 3 hours. Add coconut milk, bell pepper and chile pepper and stir well. Cover and cook on High for 15 minutes, until peppers are tender.

Vegan Friendly

Entertaining Worthy

Can Be Halved

Tips

I use Italian San Marzano tomatoes in this recipe. They are richer and thicker and have more tomato flavor than domestic varieties. If you are using a domestic variety, add 1 tbsp (15 mL) tomato paste along with the tomatoes.

Be sure to rinse the salted eggplant thoroughly after sweating. Otherwise it may retain salt and your ratatouille will be too salty.

If you are halving this recipe, be sure to use a small (approx. 1½ to 3½ quart) slow cooker.

Make Ahead

Complete Steps 1 through 3. Cover and refrigerate eggplant and zucchini mixtures separately for up to 2 days. When you're ready to cook, continue with Step 4.

Ratatouille

Ratatouille makes a great accompaniment to roast vegetables or served over polenta or baked tofu. I also think it's delicious on its own with some warm whole-grain bread.

- **Large (approx. 5 quart) slow cooker**
- **Preheat oven to 400°F (200°C)**
- **Rimmed baking sheet, ungreased**

2	medium eggplant (each about 12 oz/375 g), peeled, cubed (1 inch/2.5 cm), sweated and drained of excess moisture (see Tips, page 130)	2
3 tbsp	olive oil, divided	45 mL
4	medium zucchini (about 1½ lbs/750 g total), peeled and thinly sliced	4
2	cloves garlic, minced	2
2	onions, thinly sliced	2
1 tsp	herbes de Provence	5 mL
½ tsp	salt	2 mL
½ tsp	cracked black peppercorns	2 mL
8 oz	mushrooms, sliced	250 g
1	can (28 oz/796 mL) tomatoes with juice, coarsely chopped	1
2	green bell peppers, cut into ½-inch (1 cm) cubes	2
½ cup	chopped fresh parsley or basil	125 mL

1. On baking sheet, toss eggplant with 1 tbsp (15 mL) of the olive oil. Spread evenly on sheet. Cover with foil and bake in preheated oven until soft and fragrant, about 15 minutes. Remove from oven and transfer to slow cooker stoneware.

2. Meanwhile, heat 1 tbsp (15 mL) of the oil over medium-high heat. Add zucchini and cook, stirring, for 6 minutes. Add garlic and cook, stirring, until zucchini is soft and browned, about 1 minute. Transfer to a bowl. Cover and refrigerate.

3. Reduce heat to medium. Add remaining 1 tbsp (15 mL) oil. Add onions and cook, stirring, until softened, about 3 minutes. Add herbes de Provence, salt and peppercorns and cook, stirring, about 1 minute. Add mushrooms and toss until coated. Stir in tomatoes with juice and bring to a boil. Transfer to stoneware.

4. Cover and cook on Low for 6 hours or on High for 3 hours, until vegetables are tender. Add green peppers, reserved zucchini mixture and parsley and stir well. Cover and cook on High for 25 minutes, until peppers are tender and zucchini is heated through.

Louisiana Ratatouille

Tips

Okra, a tropical vegetable, has a great flavor but it becomes unpleasantly sticky when overcooked. Choose young okra pods, 2 to 4 inches (5 to 10 cm) long, that don't feel sticky to the touch (if sticky, they are too ripe). Gently scrub the pods and cut off the top and tail. Okra can also be found in the freezer section of the grocery store. Thaw before adding to slow cooker.

To sweat eggplant: Place cubed eggplant in a colander, sprinkle liberally with salt, toss well and set aside for 30 minutes to 1 hour. If time is short, blanch the pieces for a minute or two in heavily salted water. In either case, rinse thoroughly in fresh cold water and, using your hands, squeeze out excess moisture. Pat dry with paper towels and it's ready for cooking.

If you are halving this recipe, be sure to use a small (approx. $1\frac{1}{2}$ to $3\frac{1}{2}$ quart) slow cooker.

Make Ahead

Complete Steps 1 and 2. Cover and refrigerate for up to 2 days. When you're ready to cook, complete the recipe.

Eggplant, tomato and okra stew is a classic Southern dish that probably owes its origins to the famous Mediterranean mélange ratatouille. One secret to a successful result, even on top of the stove, is not overcooking the okra, which should be added after the flavors in the other ingredients have melded.

● **Medium (approx. 4 quart) slow cooker**

2	medium eggplants, peeled, cubed (2 inches/5 cm), sweated and drained of excess moisture (see Tips, left)	2
2 tbsp	oil	25 mL
2	onions, finely chopped	2
4	cloves garlic, minced	4
1 tsp	dried oregano	5 mL
1 tsp	salt	5 mL
$\frac{1}{2}$ tsp	cracked black peppercorns	2 mL
1	can (28 oz/796 mL) tomatoes with juice, coarsely chopped	1
2 tbsp	red wine vinegar	25 mL
1 lb	okra, trimmed and cut into 1-inch (2.5 cm) lengths, about 2 cups (500 mL) (see Tips, left)	500 g
1	green bell pepper, diced ($\frac{1}{4}$ inch/0.5 cm)	1

1. In a skillet, heat oil over medium-high heat. Add eggplant, in batches, and cook, stirring, until lightly browned. Transfer to slow cooker stoneware.

2. Reduce heat to medium. Add onions to pan and cook, stirring, until softened, about 3 minutes. Add garlic, oregano, salt and peppercorns and cook, stirring, for 1 minute. Stir in tomatoes with juice and red wine vinegar and bring to a boil. Transfer to slow cooker stoneware.

3. Cover and cook on Low for 6 hours or on High for 3 hours, until hot and bubbly. Add okra and bell pepper. Cover and cook on High for 30 minutes, until okra is tender.

Vegan Friendly

Can Be Halved

Tip

To sweat eggplant: Place cubed eggplant in a colander, sprinkle liberally with salt, toss well and set aside for 30 minutes to 1 hour. If time is short, blanch the pieces for a minute or two in heavily salted water. In either case, rinse thoroughly in fresh cold water and, using your hands, squeeze out excess moisture. Pat dry with paper towels and it's ready for cooking.

If you are halving this recipe, be sure to use a small (approx. $1\frac{1}{2}$ to $3\frac{1}{2}$ quart) slow cooker.

Make Ahead

Complete Steps 1 and 2. Cover and refrigerate for up to 2 days. When you're ready to cook, complete the recipe.

Eggplant Braised with Tomatoes and Mushrooms

This hearty combination makes a perfect dinner served over hot rice or a bowl of steaming orzo. If you feel the need, add a simple tossed green salad.

● **Medium (approx. 4 quart) slow cooker**

1	medium eggplant, peeled, cubed (2 inches/5 cm), sweated and drained of excess moisture (see Tips, left)	1
2 tbsp	olive oil	25 mL
2	onions, finely chopped	2
4	cloves garlic, minced	4
1 tsp	dried thyme	5 mL
1 tsp	salt	5 mL
1 tsp	cracked black peppercorns	5 mL
1	can (28 oz/796 mL) tomatoes with juice, coarsely chopped	1
2	potatoes, peeled and shredded	2
1 lb	cremini mushrooms, trimmed and sliced	500 g
$\frac{1}{2}$ cup	freshly grated Parmesan or vegan alternative	125 mL
$\frac{1}{4}$ cup	finely chopped fresh parsley	50 mL

1. In a skillet, heat oil over medium-high heat. Add eggplant, in batches, and cook, stirring, until lightly browned. Transfer to slow cooker stoneware as completed.

2. Reduce heat to medium. Add onions to pan and cook, stirring, until softened, about 3 minutes. Add garlic, thyme, salt and peppercorns and cook, stirring, for 1 minute. Stir in tomatoes with juice and bring to a boil. Transfer to slow cooker stoneware.

3. Add potatoes and mushrooms and stir well. Cover and cook on Low for 6 hours or on High for 3 hours, until hot and bubbly. Stir in Parmesan and garnish with parsley.

Vegan Friendly

Can Be Halved

Tips

Some curry pastes contain products such as shrimp paste or fish sauce, so if you're a vegetarian, check the label to ensure that yours is fish- and seafood-free.

If you're a heat seeker, you can increase the quantity of curry paste, but this quantity is quite enough for me.

If you are halving this recipe, be sure to use a small (approx. $1\frac{1}{2}$ to $3\frac{1}{2}$ quart) slow cooker.

Make Ahead

Complete Step 1. Cover and refrigerate for up to 2 days. When you're ready to cook, complete the recipe.

Variation

Crispy Onion Topping:
Cut 3 onions in half, then cut them vertically into paper-thin slices. In a large skillet, heat 1 tbsp (15 mL) oil or clarified butter over medium-high heat. Add the onion slices and cook, stirring constantly, until they are browned and crispy, about 15 minutes. Use instead of the cilantro garnish, if desired.

Potato and Pea Coconut Curry

Sweet and white potatoes cooked in an aromatic sauce make a simple but very tasty combination. If you have time, substituting Crispy Onion Topping (see Variation, left) or Crispy Shallot Topping (page 153) for the cilantro garnish will add delicious flavor and texture to the dish. Serve with warm naan or over hot rice.

● **Medium to large ($3\frac{1}{2}$ to 5 quart) slow cooker**

1 tbsp	oil	15 mL
2	onions, finely chopped	2
4	cloves garlic, minced	4
1 tbsp	minced gingerroot	15 mL
$\frac{1}{2}$ tsp	cracked black peppercorns	2 mL
1 cup	vegetable broth	250 mL
2	large sweet potatoes (each about 8 oz/ 250 g), peeled and cut into 1-inch (2.5 cm) cubes	2
2	potatoes, peeled and diced	2
2 tsp	Thai red curry paste (see Tips, left)	10 mL
1 cup	coconut milk, divided	250 mL
2 cups	sweet green peas, thawed if frozen	500 mL
	Finely chopped fresh cilantro	

1. In a skillet, heat oil over medium heat. Add onions and cook, stirring, until softened, about 3 minutes. Add garlic, ginger and peppercorns and cook, stirring, for 1 minute. Add broth and bring to a boil. Transfer to slow cooker stoneware.

2. Stir in sweet potatoes and potatoes. Cover and cook on Low for 6 to 8 hours or on High for 3 to 4 hours, until potatoes are tender.

3. In a small bowl, combine curry paste and $\frac{1}{4}$ cup (50 mL) of the coconut milk. Stir until blended. Add to stoneware, along with the remaining coconut milk, and stir well. Stir in peas. Cover and cook on High for 15 minutes, until peas are tender and flavors have melded. When serving, garnish with cilantro.

Potato and Eggplant Tian

Tips

Whether you peel the eggplant is simply a matter of taste.

To sweat eggplant: Place slices in a colander and sprinkle liberally with salt. Set aside for 30 minutes to 1 hour. Rinse thoroughly in fresh cold water and pat dry with paper towels.

If you are halving this recipe, be sure to use a small (1½ to 3½ quart) slow cooker.

I don't recommend making this dish ahead of time because the potatoes will become unpleasantly soggy.

In French cooking, a tian is a layered vegetable casserole. In this version, dried mushrooms combine with tomatoes, potatoes and eggplant to produce a dish that is rich in Provençal flavors. All you need to add is a simple green salad to complete the meal.

● **Medium to large (4 to 5 quart) slow cooker**

1	package (½ oz/14 g) dried mushrooms, such as porcini or portobello	1
1 cup	hot water	250 mL
2	large potatoes (each about 8 oz/250 g)	2
¼ cup	olive oil, divided	50 mL
2	medium eggplant (each about 1 lb/500 g) sliced (about ½ inch/1 cm) (see Tips, left)	2
2	onions, finely chopped	2
6	cloves garlic, minced	6
1 tsp	salt	5 mL
1 tsp	cracked black peppercorns	5 mL
1 tsp	dried thyme	5 mL
1	can (28 oz/796 mL) tomatoes with juice, coarsely chopped	1
1	red bell pepper, seeded and thinly sliced	1

1. In a bowl, combine dried mushrooms and hot water. Stir well and let stand for 30 minutes. Strain through a fine sieve and set ½ cup (125 mL) of the liquid aside, saving the remainder for another use. Chop mushrooms finely and set aside.

2. Meanwhile, peel potatoes and cut in half lengthwise. Cut each half into 4 wedges. Pat dry.

3. In a skillet, heat 2 tbsp (25 mL) of the oil over medium-high heat. Add potatoes, in batches, and cook until they are nicely browned on all sides, about 7 minutes per batch. Transfer to slow cooker stoneware as completed. Add remaining oil to pan. Add eggplant, in batches, and cook until lightly browned on both sides, about 2 minutes per side. Layer over potatoes in stoneware.

4. Reduce heat to medium. Add onions to pan and cook, stirring, until softened, about 3 minutes. Add garlic, salt, peppercorns, thyme and reserved chopped mushrooms and cook, stirring, for 1 minute. Add tomatoes with juice and ½ cup (125 mL) of the reserved mushroom liquid and bring to a boil. Pour over eggplant mixture. Cover and cook on Low for 6 hours or on High for 3 hours, until mixture is hot and bubbly and vegetables are tender. Lay bell pepper slices over top. Cover and cook on High for 15 minutes, until pepper is tender.

Tip

I prefer to use sun-dried tomatoes packed in olive oil, which are already reconstituted. If you are using the packaged dry variety, reconstitute them according to the package directions — they usually need to be blanched for about 5 minutes in boiling water.

Make Ahead

Complete Step 1. Cover and refrigerate for up to 2 days. When you're ready to cook, complete the recipe.

Leek and Tomato Cobbler

If you like tomatoes, you'll enjoy this cobbler. The addition of sun-dried tomatoes intensifies the tomato flavor. Combined with sweet mild leeks and a hint of Italian seasoning, this makes a very tasty main course. If you prefer a creamy finish, as I do, stir in the cheese before adding the topping.

• **Small to medium (2 to 4 quart) slow cooker**

2 tbsp	olive oil	25 mL
3	leeks, white part with just a bit of green, cleaned and sliced (see Tips, page 94)	3
4	cloves garlic, minced	4
1 tsp	salt	5 mL
1 tsp	dried Italian seasoning	5 mL
1/2 tsp	cracked black peppercorns	2 mL
2 tbsp	all-purpose flour	25 mL
1	can (28 oz/796 mL) diced tomatoes with juice	1
2 tbsp	finely chopped reconstituted sun-dried tomatoes (see Tip, left)	25 mL
1 cup	shredded Swiss cheese, optional	250 mL
Topping		
3/4 cup	all-purpose flour	175 mL
1/4 tsp	salt	1 mL
1 tsp	baking soda	5 mL
1/3 cup	buttermilk	75 mL
1 tbsp	olive oil	15 mL

1. In a skillet, heat oil over medium heat. Add leeks and cook, stirring, until softened, about 5 minutes. Add garlic, salt, Italian seasoning and peppercorns and cook, stirring, for 1 minute. Add flour and cook, stirring, for 1 minute. Add tomatoes with juice and sun-dried tomatoes and cook, stirring, until mixture comes to a boil and thickens, about 5 minutes. Transfer to slow cooker stoneware.

2. Cover and cook on Low for 4 hours or on High for $1\frac{1}{2}$ hours. Stir in cheese, if using, and turn heat to High, if necessary.

3. *Topping:* In a bowl, combine flour and salt. Make a well in the middle. In a cup or bowl with a pouring spout, combine baking soda, buttermilk and olive oil. Pour into well and mix until blended. Drop batter by spoonfuls over hot vegetable mixture. Cover and cook on High for 45 minutes, until a tester inserted in the center comes out clean.

Tips

If it better suits your schedule, instead of softening the leeks and onion in the slow cooker (Step 1) you can do it in on the stovetop in a skillet. Simply melt the butter over medium heat, add the leeks and onions and cook, stirring, until softened, about 5 minutes. Stir in the garlic, salt and peppercorns and cook for 1 minute. Transfer to the stoneware and continue with Step 2.

I like to use half whole wheat and half all-purpose flour in the biscuit topping because whole wheat flour is much more nutritious. If you prefer, substitute 1½ cups (375 mL) all-purpose flour for the combination.

If you are halving this recipe, be sure to use a small (1½ to 2 quart) slow cooker.

Make Ahead

Complete Step 1. Cover and refrigerate for up to 2 days. When you're ready to cook, complete the recipe.

Leek and Potato Cobbler with Stilton

This is great winter fare — rich, dense and flavorful, topped with a hearty biscuit. Serve smallish portions and balance the meal with something light, such as a simple green salad.

● **Medium (approx. 4 quart) slow cooker**

3	leeks, white part with just a bit of green, cleaned and sliced (see Tips, page 94)	3
1	onion, finely chopped	1
4	cloves garlic, minced	4
1 tsp	salt	5 mL
½ tsp	cracked black peppercorns	2 mL
2 tbsp	melted butter	25 mL
2 cups	vegetable broth or water	500 mL
3	potatoes, peeled and shredded	3
4 oz	Stilton cheese, crumbled	125 g

Topping

¾ cup	whole wheat flour	175 mL
¾ cup	all-purpose flour	175 mL
½ tsp	salt	2 mL
2 tsp	baking soda	10 mL
¾ cup	buttermilk	175 mL
2 tbsp	olive oil	25 mL

1. In slow cooker stoneware, combine leeks, onion, garlic, salt, peppercorns and melted butter. Stir to coat vegetables thoroughly. Cover and cook on High for 30 minutes to 1 hour, until vegetables are softened. Stir in vegetable broth.

2. Add potatoes and stir well. Cover and cook on Low for 4 hours or on High for 2 hours. Stir in Stilton and turn heat to High, if necessary.

3. *Topping:* In a bowl, combine whole wheat and all-purpose flours and salt. Make a well in the middle. In a cup or bowl with a pouring spout, combine baking soda, buttermilk and olive oil. Pour into well and mix until blended. Drop batter by spoonfuls over hot vegetable mixture. Cover and cook on High for 45 minutes, until a tester inserted in the center comes out clean.

Chard-Studded Stew with Cornmeal Dumplings

Tips

If you are halving this recipe, be sure to use a small (1½ to 2 quart) slow cooker.

Like spinach, Swiss chard can be very gritty, so swish it around in a basin of lukewarm water before rinsing under cold running water to ensure all grit is removed. Unless your chard is very young, you'll need to remove the thick vein running up the center of the leaf before chopping.

Make Ahead

Complete Step 1. Cover and refrigerate for up to 2 days. When you're ready to cook, complete the recipe.

In terms of old-fashioned goodness, it doesn't get much better than this. It's lusciously rich and flavorful comfort food, almost like grandma used to make.

- **Medium to large (3½ to 5 quart) slow cooker**

1 tbsp	oil	15 mL
2	onions, finely chopped	2
4	carrots, peeled and diced	4
4	stalks celery, diced	4
4	cloves garlic, minced	4
1 tsp	dried thyme	5 mL
1 tsp	salt	5 mL
½ tsp	cracked black peppercorns	2 mL
2 cups	vegetable broth	500 mL
¼ cup	white miso	50 mL
4 cups	packed chopped Swiss chard leaves (see Tips, left)	1 L

Cornmeal Dumplings

¾ cup	all-purpose flour	175 mL
¼ cup	fine cornmeal	50 mL
1½ tsp	baking powder	7 mL
¼ tsp	salt	1 mL
½ cup	warm milk	125 mL
2 tbsp	melted butter	25 mL

1. In a skillet, heat oil over medium heat. Add onions, carrots and celery and cook, stirring, until softened, about 7 minutes. Add garlic, thyme, salt and peppercorns and cook, stirring, for 1 minute. Stir in vegetable broth. Transfer to slow cooker stoneware.

2. Cover and cook on Low for 5 hours or on High for 2½ hours. Turn heat to High, if necessary. Add miso and stir until it dissolves. Add chard, in batches, stirring after each addition to submerge the leaves in the liquid. Cover and cook for 20 minutes, until mixture returns to a simmer.

3. *Cornmeal Dumplings:* Meanwhile, in a bowl, combine flour, cornmeal, baking powder and salt. Make a well in the center. Pour in milk and butter and mix with a fork, just until mixture comes together. Drop dough by spoonfuls onto vegetables. Cover and cook on High for 30 minutes, until dumplings are cooked through.

Tip

If you are halving this recipe, be sure to use a small (1½ to 2 quart) slow cooker.

Make Ahead

Complete Step 1. Cover and refrigerate for up to 2 days. When you're ready to cook, complete the recipe.

Variation

Greek Bean Sauce with Bulgur: If you're serving this sauce with pasta, you can boost the nutritional content by stirring in up to 2 cups (500 mL) soaked bulgur before adding the feta and dill. To soak 1 cup (250 mL) of bulgur, use 1½ cups (375 mL) of water. Stir well and set aside until liquid is absorbed, about 10 minutes. Use cold water for fine bulgur and hot or boiling water for coarser grinds.

Greek Bean Sauce with Feta

This lip-smacking sauce is particularly delicious as a topping for polenta, but it also works well with brown rice and pasta, especially orzo. If serving it with pasta, use a whole wheat version or boost the nutritional content by adding bulgur (see Variation, left).

● **Medium to large (3½ to 5 quart) slow cooker**

1 tbsp	olive oil	15 mL
2	onions, finely chopped	2
2	cloves garlic, minced	2
1	piece (1 inch/2.5 cm) cinnamon stick	1
1 tsp	dried oregano, crumbled	5 mL
1 tsp	salt	5 mL
½ tsp	cracked black peppercorns	2 mL
1	can (28 oz/796 mL) tomatoes with juice, coarsely crushed	1
3 cups	frozen sliced green beans	750 mL
½ cup	crumbled feta cheese	125 mL
¼ cup	finely chopped fresh dill	50 mL

1. In a large skillet, heat oil over medium heat. Add onions and cook, stirring, until softened, about 3 minutes. Add garlic, cinnamon stick, oregano, salt and peppercorns and cook, stirring, for 1 minute. Add tomatoes with juice, stirring and breaking up with a spoon. Transfer to slow cooker stoneware.

2. Stir in green beans. Cover and cook on Low for 6 hours or on High for 3 hours, until hot and bubbly. Discard cinnamon stick. When serving, sprinkle with feta and dill.

Tips

Crumbling the dried mushrooms with your fingers before soaking eliminates the need to chop them, and the powdery texture works well in this recipe.

I always use Italian flat-leaf parsley because it has much more flavor than the curly leaf variety.

Pot Pie with Biscuit Topping

This tasty dish has real robustness thanks to the dried portobello mushrooms. All you need to add is a tossed green salad.

● **Small to medium (2 to 4 quart) slow cooker**

1	package (½ oz/14 g) dried portobello mushrooms, crumbled (see Tips, left)	1
3 cups	hot water	750 mL
1 tbsp	oil	15 mL
1	onion, finely chopped	1
4	stalks celery, diced	4
2	carrots, peeled and diced	2
2	cloves garlic, minced	2
1 tsp	dried thyme	5 mL
1 tsp	salt	5 mL
1 tsp	cracked black peppercorns	5 mL
½ cup	all-purpose flour	125 mL
2 tbsp	dry sherry or vodka, optional	25 mL
¾ cup	green peas, thawed if frozen	175 mL
½ cup	heavy or whipping (35%) cream	125 mL
¼ cup	finely chopped Italian flat-leaf parsley (see Tips, left)	50 mL

Biscuit Topping

¾ cup	all-purpose flour	175 mL
1 tsp	baking powder	5 mL
½ tsp	salt	2 mL
¼ cup	cold butter, cut into 1-inch (2.5 cm) cubes	50 mL
¼ cup	milk	50 mL

1. In a bowl, combine dried mushrooms and hot water. Stir well and let stand for 30 minutes. Strain through a fine sieve, reserving mushrooms and liquid separately. Set aside.

2. In a skillet, heat oil over medium heat. Add onion, celery and carrots and cook, stirring, until softened, about 7 minutes. Add reserved mushrooms, garlic, thyme, salt and peppercorns and cook, stirring, for 1 minute. Sprinkle flour over top of mixture and stir well. Cook, stirring, for 1 minute. Add sherry, if using, and stir until it evaporates, about 30 seconds. Add reserved mushroom liquid and cook, stirring, until mixture begins to thicken, about 3 minutes. Transfer to slow cooker stoneware.

Make Ahead

Complete Steps 1 and 2. Cover and refrigerate for up to 2 days. When you're ready to cook, complete the recipe.

3. Cover and cook on Low for 4 hours or on High for 2 hours. Turn heat to High, if necessary. Stir in peas, cream and parsley.

4. *Biscuit Topping:* Meanwhile, in a bowl, combine flour, baking powder and salt. Using your fingers or a pastry blender, cut in butter until mixture resembles coarse crumbs. Drizzle with milk and stir with a fork until a batter forms. Using your hands, roll batter into small balls (about 2 inches/5 cm in diameter). Drop over hot vegetables. Cover and cook on High, for 1 hour until a toothpick inserted in the center of a biscuit comes out clean.

Onion-Braised Potatoes with Spinach

Tips

This dish cooks for longer than most vegetarian dishes because it contains potatoes, which, unless they are diced, take a long time to cook in the slow cooker. New potatoes cook more quickly than mature potatoes, but before adding the final ingredients in this recipe check to make sure the potatoes are tender. If not, continue cooking until the potatoes are cooked, increasing the temperature to High, if necessary.

If you don't have a 14-oz (398 mL) can of diced tomatoes, use 2 cups (500 mL) canned tomatoes with juice, coarsely chopped.

If you are using fresh spinach leaves in this recipe, take care to wash them thoroughly, as they can be quite gritty. *To wash spinach:* Fill a clean sink with lukewarm water. Remove the tough stems and submerge the tender leaves in the water, swishing to remove the grit. Rinse thoroughly in a colander under cold running water, checking carefully to ensure that no sand remains. If you are using frozen spinach in this recipe, thaw and squeeze the excess moisture out before adding to the slow cooker.

Make Ahead

Complete Step 1. Cover and refrigerate for up to 2 days. When you're ready to cook, complete the recipe.

Served with brown rice and a salad, this tasty braise makes a great weeknight dinner. It also works well as part of a multi-dish Indian meal.

● **Medium to large (3½ to 5 quart) slow cooker**

1 tbsp	oil	15 mL
4	onions, thinly sliced on the vertical	4
4	cloves garlic, minced	4
1 tbsp	minced gingerroot	15 mL
1 tbsp	ground cumin (see Tips, page 83)	15 mL
1 tsp	salt	5 mL
1 tsp	cracked black peppercorns	5 mL
2	black cardamom pods, crushed	2
1	can (14 oz/398 mL) diced tomatoes with juice (see Tips, left)	1
1 cup	vegetable broth	250 mL
2 lbs	new potatoes, quartered (about 24 potatoes)	1 kg
1 lb	fresh spinach, stems removed, or 1 package (10 oz/300 g) spinach leaves, thawed if frozen (see Tips, left)	500 g
¼ tsp	cayenne pepper, dissolved in 2 tbsp (25 mL) freshly squeezed lemon juice	1 mL

1. In a skillet, heat oil over medium heat. Add onions and cook, stirring, until softened, about 3 minutes. Add garlic, ginger, cumin, salt, peppercorns and cardamom and cook, stirring, for 1 minute. Add tomatoes with juice and vegetable broth and bring to a boil. Transfer to slow cooker stoneware.

2. Add potatoes and stir well. Cover and cook on Low for 8 hours or on High for 4 hours, until potatoes are tender. Discard cardamom pods. Add spinach, in batches, stirring after each addition until all the leaves are submerged in the liquid. Add cayenne pepper solution to slow cooker and stir well. Cover and cook on High for 10 minutes, until spinach is wilted and flavors have melded.

Vegan Friendly

Entertaining Worthy

Make Ahead

Complete Step 1. Cover and refrigerate for up to 2 days. When you're ready to cook, warm onion mixture in a saucepan on top of the stove or in a microwave oven. Complete the recipe.

Caramelized Onion Gratin

This luscious combination of caramelized onions, crunchy bread crumbs and melted cheese makes a deliciously different centerpiece for a meal. Serve this with a seasonal green vegetable or salad.

- **Small shallow ovenproof dish**
- **Small (approx. 2 quart) slow cooker**

6	onions, thinly sliced on the vertical	6
3 tbsp	melted butter or olive oil	45 mL
½ tsp	paprika	2 mL
½ tsp	salt	2 mL
½ tsp	freshly ground black pepper	2 mL
1 cup	fresh bread crumbs	250 mL
½ cup	shredded Swiss cheese or vegan alternative	125 mL

1. In slow cooker stoneware, combine onions and 2 tbsp (25 mL) of the butter. Stir well. Place a clean tea towel, folded in half (so you will have two layers), over top of stoneware to absorb moisture. Cover and cook on High for 5 hours, stirring two to three times to ensure the onions are browning evenly and replacing the towel each time, until onions are nicely caramelized. Add paprika, salt and pepper and stir well. Transfer to ovenproof dish.

2. Preheat broiler. In a bowl, combine bread crumbs and cheese. Stir well. Spread evenly over onions and drizzle with remaining 1 tbsp (15 mL) of melted butter. Broil until crumbs begin to brown and cheese melts. Serve immediately.

Tips

If you prefer, transfer beet mixture to an ovenproof serving dish before adding the bread crumb mixture.

If you are halving this recipe, be sure to use a small (1½ to 2 quart) slow cooker.

Make Ahead

Complete Steps 1 and 2. Cover and refrigerate for up to 2 days. When you're ready to cook, complete the recipe.

Braised Beets with Roquefort Gratin

I love the combination of sweet beets, robust mushrooms and in-your-face Roquefort cheese. If you prefer more timid cheeses, make this using soft goat cheese. I serve this with brown rice for a complete meal.

● **Medium (approx. 4 quart) slow cooker**

1	package (½ oz/14 g) dried mushrooms, such as porcini	1
2 cups	hot water	500 mL
2 tbsp	oil	25 mL
1 cup	chopped shallots	250 mL
4	cloves garlic, minced	4
2 tsp	dried tarragon	10 mL
1 tsp	salt	5 mL
½ tsp	cracked black peppercorns	2 mL
4	large beets, peeled and thinly sliced (about 2 lbs/1 kg)	4
1 cup	fresh bread crumbs	250 mL
½ cup	crumbled Roquefort or soft goat cheese	125 mL
1 tbsp	melted butter	15 mL

1. In a bowl, combine dried mushrooms and hot water. Let stand for 30 minutes. Strain through a fine sieve, reserving liquid. Remove stems. Pat mushrooms dry and chop finely. Set mushrooms and liquid aside separately.

2. In a skillet, heat oil over medium heat. Add shallots and cook, stirring, until softened, about 3 minutes. Add garlic, tarragon, salt, peppercorns and reserved mushrooms and cook, stirring, for 1 minute. Stir in reserved mushroom soaking liquid. Transfer to slow cooker stoneware.

3. Stir in beets. Cover and cook on Low for 6 hours or on High for 3 hours, until beets are tender.

4. Preheat broiler. In a bowl, combine bread crumbs and cheese. Stir well. Spread evenly over beets and drizzle with melted butter. Broil until crumbs begin to brown and cheese melts. Serve immediately.

Can Be Halved

Tips

To clean leeks: Fill sink full of lukewarm water. Split leeks in half lengthwise and submerge in water, swishing them around to remove all traces of dirt. Transfer to a colander and rinse under cold water.

If you don't have a 14-oz (398 mL) can of diced tomatoes, use 2 cups (500 mL) canned tomatoes with juice, coarsely chopped

Easy White Bean Purée: Heat 1 tbsp (15 mL) olive oil in a skillet over medium heat for 30 seconds. Add ½ cup (125 mL) finely chopped parsley and 2 cloves minced garlic and cook, stirring, for 1 minute. Add 2 cups (500 mL) cooked dried or canned white kidney beans, drained and rinsed. Cook, mashing with a fork, until beans are heated through. Season to taste with salt and freshly ground black pepper.

If you are halving this recipe, be sure to use a small (approx. 1½ to 3½ quart) slow cooker.

Make Ahead

Complete Step 1. Cover and refrigerate for up to 2 days. When you're ready to cook, complete the recipe.

Cheesy Fennel and Leek Bake

This Mediterranean-inspired dish is delightfully different and equally delicious over hot polenta, mashed potatoes or a white bean purée (see Tips, left).

- **Medium to large (3½ to 5 quart) slow cooker**

1 tbsp	oil (approx.)	15 mL
2	bulbs fennel, cored, leafy stems discarded, and sliced on the vertical	2
3	leeks, white part with a bit of green, cleaned and thinly sliced (see Tips, left)	3
4	cloves garlic, minced	4
2 tsp	dried Italian seasoning	10 mL
1 tsp	salt, or to taste	5 mL
½ tsp	cracked black peppercorns	2 mL
1	can (14 oz/398 mL) diced tomatoes with juice (see Tips, left)	1
1 cup	shredded Italian cheese, such as mozzarella or Fontina, or a prepared mix of shredded Italian cheeses	250 mL

1. In a skillet, heat oil over medium-high heat for 30 seconds. Add fennel, in batches, and cook, stirring, until lightly browned, about 5 minutes per batch. Transfer to slow cooker stoneware. Reduce heat to medium and add more oil to pan, if necessary. Add leeks and cook, stirring, until softened, about 5 minutes. Add garlic, Italian seasoning, salt and peppercorns and cook, stirring, for 1 minute. Add tomatoes with juice and bring to a boil. Transfer to slow cooker stoneware.

2. Cover and cook on Low for 6 hours or High for 3 hours, until fennel is tender. Stir in cheese. Cover and cook on High for 15 minutes, until cheese is melted and mixture is bubbly.

Tips

A grapefruit spoon does a great job of cleaning the pith and seeds from the chile pepper.

If you are halving this recipe, be sure to use a small ($1\frac{1}{2}$ to 2 quart) slow cooker.

Dum Phukt–Style Potatoes with Cauliflower

I first enjoyed dum phukt cooking, which involves sealing a clay pot with a paste, in Delhi, India. This style of cooking translates beautifully to the slow cooker. I like to serve this robust dish as a main course over steaming long-grain brown rice, but it also works as a side or as one dish in a multi-dish Indian meal.

- **Medium (approx. 4 quart) slow cooker**
- **Large sheet of parchment paper**

2	large potatoes (each about 8 oz/250 g)	2
2 tbsp	olive oil	25 mL
4 cups	sliced lengthwise cauliflower florets	1 L
2	onions, finely chopped	2
1 tbsp	minced gingerroot	15 mL
3	cloves garlic, minced	3
1 tsp	salt	5 mL
$\frac{1}{2}$ tsp	cracked black peppercorns	2 mL
1	piece (2 inches/5 cm) cinnamon stick	1
6	whole cloves	6
2	bay leaves	2
$\frac{1}{2}$ cup	water	125 mL
$\frac{1}{2}$ cup	full-fat yogurt	125 mL
1 tsp	curry powder, preferably Madras	5 mL
1 to 2	long red chile peppers, seeded and diced (see Tips, left)	1 to 2

1. Peel and cut potatoes in half lengthwise, then cut each half into 4 wedges. Pat dry.

2. In a large skillet, heat oil over medium-high heat. Add potatoes, in batches, and cook until they are nicely browned on all sides, about 7 minutes per batch. Using a slotted spoon transfer to slow cooker stoneware.

3. Add cauliflower to pan and cook, stirring constantly, until browned in spots, about 5 minutes. Using a slotted spoon, transfer to slow cooker stoneware. Add onions and cook, stirring, until softened, about 3 minutes. Add ginger, garlic, salt, peppercorns, cinnamon stick, cloves and bay leaves and cook, stirring, for 1 minute. Stir in water.

4. Transfer to slow cooker stoneware. Toss to combine ingredients as best you can. Place a large piece of parchment paper over the mixture, pressing it down to brush the food and extending up the sides of the stoneware so it overlaps the rim. Cover and cook on Low for 8 hours or on High for 4 hours, until potatoes are tender. Lift out parchment and remove, being careful not to spill the accumulated liquid into the dish. Discard cinnamon, cloves and bay leaves.

5. In a small bowl, combine yogurt, curry powder and chiles to taste, stirring until curry powder is well integrated into mixture. Add to stoneware and stir gently. Cover and cook on High for 10 minutes to blend flavors.

Vegan Friendly

Can Be Halved

Tips

If you prefer, substitute fresh green beans for the frozen. Blanch in boiling water for 4 minutes after the water returns to a boil and add to the slow cooker along with the cabbage.

Some curry pastes contain products such as shrimp paste or fish sauce, which vegetarians may wish to avoid. Check the label to ensure that yours is fish- and seafood-free.

If you are halving this recipe, be sure to use a small (approx. 2 quart) slow cooker.

Make Ahead

Complete Step 1. Cover and refrigerate for up to 2 days. When you're ready to cook, complete the recipe.

Variation

Add 2 cups (500 mL) cooked broccoli florets along with the cabbage.

Mixed Vegetables in Spicy Peanut Sauce

Here's one way to get kids to eat their vegetables, so long as they don't have peanut allergies — cook them in a spicy sauce made from peanut butter and add a garnish of chopped roasted peanuts. All you need to add is some steaming rice or brown rice noodles.

● **Medium to large (3$\frac{1}{2}$ to 5 quart) slow cooker**

1 tbsp	oil	15 mL
2	onions, finely chopped	2
6	medium carrots, peeled and thinly sliced (about 4 cups/1 L)	6
4	stalks celery, diced (about 2 cups/500 mL)	4
2 tbsp	minced gingerroot	25 mL
4	cloves garlic, minced	4
$\frac{1}{2}$ tsp	cracked black peppercorns	2 mL
1 cup	vegetable broth	250 mL
3 cups	frozen sliced green beans (see Tips, left)	750 mL
$\frac{1}{2}$ cup	smooth natural peanut butter	125 mL
2 tbsp	soy sauce	25 mL
2 tbsp	freshly squeezed lemon juice	25 mL
1 tbsp	pure maple syrup	15 mL
2 tsp	Thai red curry paste (see Tips, left)	10 mL
4 cups	shredded Napa cabbage	1 L
2 cups	bean sprouts	500 mL
$\frac{1}{2}$ cup	finely chopped green onions, white part only	125 mL
$\frac{1}{2}$ cup	chopped dry roasted peanuts	125 mL

1. In a large skillet, heat oil over medium heat. Add onions, carrots and celery and cook, stirring, until softened, about 7 minutes. Add ginger, garlic and peppercorns and cook, stirring, for 1 minute. Transfer to slow cooker stoneware. Add vegetable broth and stir well.

2. Add green beans and stir well. Cover and cook on Low for 6 hours or on High for 3 hours, until vegetables are tender.

3. In a bowl, beat together peanut butter, soy sauce, lemon juice, maple syrup and red curry paste until blended. Add to slow cooker stoneware and stir well. Add Napa cabbage, in batches, stirring until each addition is submerged in liquid. Cover and cook for 10 minutes, until heated through. Stir in bean sprouts. Garnish each serving with a sprinkle of green onions, then peanuts.

African-Style Peanut Stew

Tips

Try substituting coconut oil for the olive oil. It adds a hint of coconut flavor to this stew that is quite appealing.

If you are halving this recipe, be sure to use a small (approx. 2 quart) slow cooker.

Make Ahead

Complete Step 1. Cover and refrigerate for up to 2 days. When you're ready to cook, complete the recipe.

Groundnuts, as peanuts are known in Africa, play an important role in that continent's cuisine. This tasty mélange provides just one example of the versatility offered by this nutritious food. I like to serve this over brown rice for a nutrient-dense meal.

● **Medium to large (3 $\frac{1}{2}$ to 5 quart) slow cooker**

2 tbsp	olive, coconut or peanut oil (see Tips, left)	25 mL
2	onions, finely chopped	2
2	stalks celery, diced	2
2	carrots, peeled and diced	2
4	cloves garlic, minced	4
1 tbsp	minced gingerroot	15 mL
1 tsp	salt	5 mL
1 tsp	cracked black peppercorns	5 mL
1	can (28 oz/796 mL) tomatoes with juice	1
2 cups	vegetable broth	500 mL
2 cups	cubed sweet potato (1 inch/2.5 cm) (about 1)	500 mL
2	dried mild chile peppers, such as passilla, guajillo or ancho	2
$\frac{1}{2}$ to 1	jalapeño pepper, seeded and coarsely chopped	$\frac{1}{2}$ to 1
$\frac{1}{2}$ cup	smooth natural peanut butter	125 mL
$\frac{1}{4}$ cup	fresh cilantro	50 mL
1	green bell pepper, seeded and diced	1
$\frac{1}{4}$ cup	chopped roasted peanuts	50 mL

1. In a skillet, heat oil over medium heat. Add onions, celery and carrots and cook, stirring, until softened, about 7 minutes. Add garlic, ginger, salt and peppercorns and cook, stirring, for 1 minute. Add tomatoes with juice and stir well. Transfer to slow cooker stoneware.

2. Add vegetable broth and sweet potato. Cover and cook on Low for 5 hours or on High for 2 $\frac{1}{2}$ hours, until hot and bubbly.

3. About an hour before the stew has finished cooking, in a heatproof bowl, soak dried chile peppers in boiling water for 30 minutes, weighing down with a cup to ensure they remain submerged. Drain, discarding soaking liquid and stems. Transfer to a blender. Add jalapeño pepper to taste, peanut butter and cilantro. Scoop out about $\frac{1}{2}$ cup (125 mL) of the cooking liquid from slow cooker and add to blender. Purée. Add to stoneware along with bell pepper. Cover and cook on High for 15 minutes, until pepper is tender and flavors meld. Serve garnished with roasted peanuts.

Tips

For best results, toast and grind the cumin yourself. *To toast seeds:* Place in a dry skillet and cook, stirring, until fragrant, about 3 minutes. Immediately transfer to a mortar or a spice grinder and grind.

If you are halving this recipe, be sure to use a small (approx. 1½ to 3½ quart) slow cooker.

Make Ahead

Complete Step 1. Cover and refrigerate for up to 2 days. When you're ready to cook, complete the recipe.

Parsnip and Coconut Curry with Crispy Shallots

The combination of sweet parsnips, spicy curry, mellow coconut milk and crispy shallots is absolutely delicious. I like to serve this over hot rice or with a warm Indian bread such as naan, alongside a small platter of stir-fried bok choy drizzled with toasted sesame oil and sprinkled with toasted sesame seeds.

● **Small to medium (2 to 4 quart) slow cooker**

1 tbsp	oil	15 mL
1	large onion, fined chopped	1
4	stalks celery, thinly sliced	4
6	parsnips, peeled and diced	6
1 tbsp	minced gingerroot	15 mL
2 tsp	curry powder	10 mL
2 tsp	ground cumin (see Tip, left)	10 mL
1 cup	vegetable broth	250 mL
1 cup	coconut milk	250 mL
1 cup	green peas, thawed if frozen	250 mL

Crispy Shallot Topping

2 tbsp	oil or clarified butter	25 mL
½ cup	thinly sliced shallots	125 mL
1	red chile pepper, seeded and minced, optional	

1. In a skillet, heat oil over medium heat. Add onion, celery and parsnips and cook, stirring, until softened, about 7 minutes. Add ginger, curry powder and cumin and cook, stirring for 1 minute. Stir in vegetable broth. Transfer to slow cooker stoneware.

2. Cover and cook on Low for 6 hours or High for 3 hours, until vegetables are tender. Stir in coconut milk and green peas. Cover and cook on High for 20 to 30 minutes, until peas are cooked and mixture is bubbly.

3. *Crispy Shallot Topping:* In a skillet, heat oil over medium-high heat. Add shallots and cook, stirring, until browned and crispy, about 5 minutes. Add chile pepper, if using, and cook, stirring, for 1 minute. Ladle curry into individual serving bowls and top with shallots.

Pasta and Grains

*Mushroom and
Artichoke Lasagna*

Tips

If you are looking for a gluten-free alternative, substitute 12 brown rice lasagna noodles for the oven-ready ones. Cook them in a pot of boiling salted water until slightly undercooked, or according to package instructions, undercooking by 2 minutes. Drain, toss with 1 tbsp (15 mL) olive oil and set aside until ready to use.

Unlike many recipes for lasagna, this one is not terribly saucy. As a result, the noodles on the top layer tend to dry out. Leave a small amount of the cooking liquid from the mushroom mixture behind in the pan, after adding to the slow cooker. Pour that over the top layer of noodles, particularly around the edges, where they are most likely to dry out.

Use white or cremini mushrooms or a combination of the two in this recipe.

Make Ahead

Complete Steps 1 and 2. Cover and refrigerate overnight. The next morning, complete the recipe.

Mushroom and Artichoke Lasagna

I love the unusual combination of flavors in this lasagna, which reminds me of a Provençal gratin. In addition to adding flavor and color, the baby spinach is a great time saver because it doesn't require pre-cooking.

- **Large (approx. 5 quart) oval slow cooker**
- **Greased slow cooker stoneware**

2 tbsp	butter	25 mL
1	onion, finely chopped	1
1 lb	mushrooms, stemmed and sliced	500 g
4	cloves garlic, minced	4
3½ cups	quartered artichoke hearts, packed in water, drained, or thawed if frozen	875 mL
¾ cup	dry white wine or vegetable broth	175 mL
12	oven-ready lasagna noodles (see Tips, left)	12
2½ cups	ricotta cheese	625 mL
2 cups	baby spinach	500 mL
2½ cups	shredded mozzarella cheese	625 mL
½ cup	freshly grated Parmesan	125 mL

1. In a skillet, melt butter over medium heat. Add onion and cook, stirring, until softened, about 3 minutes. Add mushrooms and garlic and cook, stirring, just until mushrooms begin to lose their liquid, about 7 minutes. Stir in artichokes and wine and bring to a boil. Cook, stirring, for 1 or 2 minutes, until liquid reduces slightly. Set aside.

2. Cover bottom of slow cooker stoneware with 4 noodles, breaking to fit where necessary. Spread with half of the ricotta, half of the mushroom mixture, half of the spinach and one-third each of the mozzarella and Parmesan. Repeat. Arrange final layer of noodles over cheeses. Pour any liquid remaining from mushroom mixture over noodles (see Tips, left) and sprinkle with remaining mozzarella and Parmesan.

3. Cover and cook on Low for 6 hours or on High for 3 hours, until hot and bubbly.

Sweet Potato Lasagna

Tip

I've used brown rice noodles in this pasta because they are a gluten-free alternative. If you prefer, substitute whole wheat lasagna noodles, which are higher in fiber, or oven-ready noodles for convenience. If using oven-ready noodles, skip Step 1.

Make Ahead

Complete Steps 1 and 2. Cover and refrigerate overnight. The next morning, complete the recipe.

This delicious lasagna is very easy to make. I like to serve it with steamed spinach sprinkled with toasted sesame seeds or a tossed green salad topped with sliced avocado.

- **Large (minimum 5 quart) oval slow cooker**
- **Greased slow cooker stoneware**

12	brown rice lasagna noodles (see Tip, left)	12
1 tbsp	olive oil	15 mL
4 cups	tomato sauce	1 L
2 cups	ricotta cheese	500 mL
3	medium sweet potatoes (about 2 lbs/1 kg), peeled and thinly sliced	3
1 tbsp	dried Italian seasoning	15 mL
2 cups	shredded mozzarella cheese	500 mL
1/4 cup	freshly grated Parmesan	50 mL

1. Cook lasagna noodles in a pot of boiling salted water, until slightly undercooked, or according to package instructions, undercooking by 2 minutes. Drain, toss with oil and set aside.

2. Spread 1 cup (250 mL) of the tomato sauce over bottom of prepared slow cooker stoneware. Cover with 3 noodles. Spread with one-third each of the ricotta, sweet potatoes and dried Italian seasoning and one-quarter of the tomato sauce and mozzarella. Repeat twice. Cover with final layer of noodles. Pour remaining sauce over top. Sprinkle with remaining mozzarella and Parmesan.

3. Cover and cook on Low for 6 hours or on High for 3 hours, until sweet potatoes are tender and mixture is hot and bubbly.

Tips

Be sure to use oven-ready cannelloni or manicotti in this recipe. It is a great time saver and it cooks to perfection in the slow cooker.

To sweat eggplant: Place cubed eggplant in a colander, sprinkle liberally with salt, toss well and set aside for 30 minutes to 1 hour. If time is short, blanch the pieces for a minute or two in heavily salted water. In either case, rinse thoroughly in fresh cold water and, using your hands, squeeze out excess moisture. Pat dry with paper towels and it's ready for cooking.

If you are halving this recipe, be sure to use a small ($1\frac{1}{2}$ to $3\frac{1}{2}$ quart) slow cooker.

Make Ahead

Complete Steps 1 and 2. Cover and refrigerate overnight. The next morning, complete the recipe. Be sure not to turn the slow cooker on until you've inserted the stoneware to prevent cracking.

Cannelloni with Tomato Eggplant Sauce

Here's a great recipe for cannelloni that is remarkably easy to make. Oven-ready pasta is filled with ricotta and baby spinach and bathed in a tomato eggplant sauce. Add some crusty bread and a salad of roasted peppers or crisp greens for a terrific meal.

● **Medium to large (4 to 5 quart) slow cooker**

Sauce

1	medium eggplant, peeled, cubed (2 inches/5 cm) sweated and drained of excess moisture (see Tips, left)	1
2 tbsp	olive oil (approx.)	25 mL
2	cloves garlic, minced	2
$\frac{1}{4}$ tsp	freshly ground black pepper	1 mL
3 cups	tomato sauce	750 mL

Filling

2 cups	ricotta cheese	500 mL
$\frac{1}{2}$ cup	freshly grated Parmesan	125 mL
$1\frac{1}{2}$ cups	chopped baby spinach	375 mL
1 tsp	freshly grated nutmeg	5 mL
1	egg, beaten	1
$\frac{1}{4}$ tsp	salt	1 mL
$\frac{1}{4}$ tsp	freshly ground black pepper	1 mL
24	oven-ready cannelloni shells	24

1. *Sauce:* In a skillet, heat oil over medium-high heat. Add eggplant, in batches, and cook until it begins to brown. Return all eggplant to pan. Add garlic and black pepper and cook, stirring, for 1 minute. Add tomato sauce, stir well and bring to a boil. Remove from heat and set aside.

2. *Filling:* In a bowl, combine ricotta, Parmesan, spinach, nutmeg, egg, salt and pepper. Using your fingers, fill pasta shells with mixture and place filled shells side by side in slow cooker stoneware, then on top of each other when bottom layer is complete. Pour sauce over shells.

3. Cover and cook on Low for 6 hours or on High for 3 hours, until hot and bubbly.

Tip

If you are halving this recipe, be sure to use a small ($1\frac{1}{2}$ to $3\frac{1}{2}$ quart) slow cooker.

Make Ahead

Complete Step 1. Cover and refrigerate caramelized onions for up to 2 days. When you're ready to cook, complete the recipe.

Variation

Polenta with Caramelized Onions: Skip Steps 2 and 3. Substitute 1 recipe (see page 182) Slow-Cooked Polenta for the pasta.

Penne with Caramelized Onions

With the help of your slow cooker, this luscious sauce is very easy to make. Use whole-grain pasta to maximize nutrition and add a tossed green salad to complete the meal.

- **Medium to large ($3\frac{1}{2}$ to 5 quart) slow cooker**

6	onions, thinly sliced on the vertical	6
2 tbsp	extra virgin olive oil	25 mL
4	cloves garlic, minced, optional	4
2	sprigs fresh thyme, optional	2
	Salt and freshly ground black pepper	
12 oz	penne	375 g
$\frac{1}{2}$ cup	freshly grated Parmesan or vegan alternative	125 mL
2 tbsp	drained tiny capers, optional	25 mL

1. In slow cooker stoneware, combine onions, olive oil, garlic, if using, and thyme, if using. Stir well. Place a clean tea towel, folded in half (so you will have two layers), over top of stoneware to absorb moisture. Cover and cook on High for 5 hours, stirring two or three times to ensure onions are browning evenly, and replacing towel each time, until onions are nicely caramelized. Season to taste with salt and pepper.

2. In a large pot of boiling salted water over high heat, cook penne, uncovered, until pasta is al dente. Scoop out 1 cup (250 mL) of pasta cooking water and set aside. Drain pasta.

3. In a skillet over medium heat, bring $\frac{1}{2}$ cup (125 mL) of reserved pasta water to a boil. Stir in Parmesan, capers, if using, and caramelized onions. Add pasta and cook, stirring, with a wooden spoon, until evenly coated with sauce, adding more pasta water, if necessary. Serve immediately.

Tips

If you prefer, use frozen diced squash in this recipe. You can add it to the slow cooker, without defrosting.

One chile pepper produces a mildly spiced result. If you like heat, add the second.

If you are halving this recipe, be sure to use a small (1½ to 3½ quart) slow cooker.

Variation

If you prefer, substitute an equal quantity of penne for the rigatoni.

Rigatoni with Caramelized Onions and Spicy Squash

This tasty mélange was inspired by a recipe from Mario Batali. The combination of caramelized onions and sweet squash accented with spicy chiles is quite lovely.

● **Medium to large (3½ to 5 quart) slow cooker**

2	onions, thinly sliced on the vertical	2
4	cloves garlic, minced	4
1 tsp	dried thyme	5 mL
2 tbsp	olive oil	25 mL
3 cups	diced (½ inch/1 cm) winter squash, such as butternut or acorn (see Tips, left)	750 mL
1 to 2	dried red chile peppers, crumbled (see Tips, left)	1 to 2
	Salt and freshly ground black pepper	
12 oz	rigatoni	375 g
½ cup	freshly grated Parmesan or vegan alternative	125 mL

1. In slow cooker stoneware, combine onions, garlic, thyme and olive oil. Stir well. Place a clean tea towel, folded in half (so you will have two layers), over top of stoneware to absorb moisture. Cover and cook on High for 5 hours, stirring two or three times to ensure onions are browning evenly, and replacing towel each time, until onions are nicely caramelized. Add squash and chile peppers to taste and season to taste with salt and pepper. Stir well. Cover and cook on High until squash is tender, about 45 minutes.

2. Meanwhile, in a large pot of boiling salted water over high heat, cook rigatoni, uncovered, until pasta is al dente. Scoop out 1 cup (250 mL) of pasta cooking water and set aside. Drain pasta.

3. In a skillet over medium heat, bring ½ cup (125 mL) of reserved pasta water to a boil. Stir in onion-squash mixture. Add pasta and cook, stirring, with a wooden spoon, until evenly coated with sauce, adding more pasta water, if necessary. Sprinkle with Parmesan and serve immediately.

Tips

If you're pressed for time you can soften the onions on the stovetop. Heat the oil over medium heat for 30 seconds in a large skillet. Add the onions and cook, stirring, until they soften, about 5 minutes. Transfer to the stoneware and continue with Step 2.

If you prefer a smoother sauce, combine the arugula with 1 cup (250 mL) of the tomato sauce in a food processor and pulse several times until the arugula is finely chopped and integrated into the sauce. Add to the onion mixture along with the remaining sauce.

If you are halving this recipe, be sure to use a small (1½ to 3½ quart) slow cooker.

Make Ahead

Complete Steps 1 and 2. Cover and refrigerate onions for up to 2 days. When you're ready to complete the recipe, in a saucepan, bring tomato sauce, miso and caramelized onions to a simmer over medium heat. Add arugula, return to a simmer and cook until nicely wilted and flavors meld.

Arugula-Laced Caramelized Onion Sauce

I love the bittersweet flavor of caramelized onions but on the stovetop caramelizing onions is a laborious process of slow, constant stirring. Made in the slow cooker, caramelized onions require almost no attention. In this recipe, I have added sugar to the onions to ensure deeper flavor. Serve this luscious sauce over whole wheat pasta, Slow-Cooked Polenta (page 182) or Basic Grits (page 183). Complete the meal with a tossed green salad topped with shredded carrots for a splash of healthy color.

● **Medium to large (3½ to 5 quart) slow cooker**

2 tbsp	olive oil	25 mL
6	onions, thinly sliced on the vertical (about 3 lbs/1.5 kg)	6
1 tsp	granulated sugar	5 mL
1 tsp	cracked black peppercorns	5 mL
1 tbsp	white or red miso	15 mL
3 cups	tomato sauce	750 mL
2	bunches arugula, stems removed and chopped (see Tips, left)	2
	Cooked pasta, preferably whole-grain, polenta or grits	

1. In slow cooker stoneware, combine olive oil and onions. Stir well to coat onions thoroughly. Cover and cook on High for 1 hour, until onions are softened (see Tips, left).

2. Add sugar and peppercorns and stir well. Place a clean tea towel, folded in half (so you will have two layers), over top of stoneware to absorb moisture. Cover and cook on High for 4 hours, stirring two or three times to ensure that the onions are browning evenly and replacing towel each time.

3. Remove towels, add miso and stir well to ensure it is well integrated into the onions. Add tomato sauce and arugula and stir well to blend. Cover and cook on High for 30 minutes, until mixture is hot and flavors have blended. Serve over hot whole-grain pasta, polenta or grits.

Basic Tomato Sauce

Not only is this sauce tasty and easy to make, it is also much lower in sodium than prepared sauces. It keeps covered for up to 1 week in the refrigerator and can be frozen for up to 6 months.

Vegan Friendly

Can Be Halved

Tips

If you are in a hurry, you can soften the vegetables on the stovetop. Heat oil in a skillet for 30 seconds. Add onions and carrots and cook, stirring, until carrots are softened, about 7 minutes. Add garlic, thyme and peppercorns and cook, stirring, for 1 minute. Transfer to slow cooker stoneware. Add tomatoes with juice and continue with Step 2.

If you are halving this recipe, be sure to use a small ($1\frac{1}{2}$ to $3\frac{1}{2}$ quart) slow cooker.

- **Medium to large ($3\frac{1}{2}$ to 5 quart) slow cooker**

1 tbsp	olive oil	15 mL
2	onions, finely chopped	2
2	carrots, peeled and diced	2
4	cloves garlic, minced	4
1 tsp	dried thyme, crumbled	5 mL
$\frac{1}{2}$ tsp	cracked black peppercorns	2 mL
2	cans (each 28 oz/796 mL) tomatoes with juice, coarsely chopped	2
	Salt, optional	

1. In slow cooker stoneware, combine olive oil, onions and carrots. Stir well to ensure vegetables are coated with oil. Cover and cook on High for 1 hour, until vegetables are softened. Add garlic, thyme and peppercorns. Stir well. Stir in tomatoes with juice.

2. Place a clean tea towel, folded in half (so you will have two layers), over top of stoneware to absorb moisture. Cover and cook on Low for 6 hours or on High for 3 hours, until sauce is thickened and flavors are melded. Season to taste with salt, if using.

Mushroom Tomato Sauce

Tips

For an easy and delicious meal, make this sauce ahead of time and refrigerate for up to 2 days. Prepare 1 batch of Slow-Cooked or Creamy Polenta (page 182), and just before it is ready to serve, reheat Mushroom Tomato Sauce. To serve, spoon polenta onto a warm plate and top with the sauce. Sprinkle with grated Parmesan, if desired.

If you are halving this recipe, be sure to use a small ($1\frac{1}{2}$ to $3\frac{1}{2}$ quart) slow cooker.

Make Ahead

Complete Step 1. Cover and refrigerate for up 2 days. When you're ready to cook, complete the recipe.

Variations

Whole Grain Bolognese: In a bowl, combine 1 cup (250 mL) coarse bulgur and $1\frac{1}{2}$ cups (375 mL) boiling water. Set aside for 20 minutes until water is absorbed. Add to sauce after it has finished cooking. Stir well, cover and cook on High for 10 minutes to meld flavors.

Double Mushroom Tomato Sauce: Soak 1 package ($\frac{1}{2}$ oz/14 g) dried porcini mushrooms in 1 cup (250 mL) hot water for 20 minutes. Drain, pat dry and chop finely. Save soaking liquid for another use. Add mushrooms to pan along with peppercorns.

One way of adding variety to your diet is by expanding the kinds of grains you use with sauces traditionally served with pasta. I like to serve this classic sauce over polenta or grits, as well as whole wheat pasta. Accompanied by a tossed green salad, it makes a great weeknight meal.

- **Medium to large ($3\frac{1}{2}$ to 5 quart) slow cooker**

1 tbsp	olive oil	15 mL
1	onion, finely chopped	1
2	stalks celery, diced	2
4	cloves garlic, minced	4
1 tbsp	finely chopped fresh rosemary or 2 tsp (10 mL) dried rosemary, crumbled	15 mL
1 tsp	salt	5 mL
$\frac{1}{2}$ tsp	cracked black peppercorns	2 mL
8 oz	cremini mushrooms, sliced	250 g
$\frac{1}{2}$ cup	dry white wine or vegetable broth	125 mL
1 tbsp	tomato paste	15 mL
1	can (28 oz/796 mL) tomatoes with juice, coarsely chopped	1
	Hot pepper flakes, optional	
	Cooked whole-grain pasta, polenta or grits	
	Freshly grated Parmesan or vegan alternative, optional	

1. In a skillet, heat oil over medium heat. Add onion and celery and cook, stirring, until softened, about 5 minutes. Add garlic, rosemary, salt and peppercorns and cook, stirring, for 1 minute. Add mushrooms and toss to coat. Add wine and cook for 1 minute. Stir in tomato paste and tomatoes with juice and bring to a boil. Transfer to slow cooker stoneware.

2. Place a clean tea towel, folded in half (so you will have two layers), over top of stoneware to absorb moisture. Cover and cook on Low for 6 hours or on High for 3 hours, until hot and bubbly. Stir in pepper flakes, if using. Serve over hot cooked pasta, polenta or grits. Garnish with Parmesan to taste, if using.

Tips

To sweat eggplant: Place cubed eggplant in a colander, sprinkle liberally with salt, toss well and set aside for 30 minutes to 1 hour. If time is short, blanch the pieces for a minute or two in heavily salted water. In either case, rinse thoroughly in fresh cold water and, using your hands, squeeze out excess moisture. Pat dry with paper towels and it's ready for cooking.

If you are halving this recipe, be sure to use a small (1½ to 3½ quart) slow cooker.

Make Ahead

Complete Steps 1 and 2. Cover and refrigerate for up to 2 days. When you're ready to cook, continue with Step 3.

Syracuse Sauce

Serve this rich and delicious sauce over hot whole-grain pasta or polenta for a great Italian-themed meal. Add a simple green salad and crusty whole-grain rolls to complete the meal.

● **Medium to large (3½ to 5 quart) slow cooker**

1	large eggplant, peeled, cubed (2 inches/5 cm), sweated and drained of excess moisture (see Tips, left)	1
2 tbsp	olive oil, divided (approx.)	25 mL
2	onions, finely chopped	2
4	cloves garlic, minced	4
1	can (28 oz/796 mL) tomatoes with juice, coarsely chopped	1
1 tbsp	tomato paste	15 mL
2	roasted red bell peppers, diced	2
½ cup	black olives, pitted and chopped (about 20 olives)	125 mL
½ cup	finely chopped fresh parsley	125 mL
2 tbsp	capers, drained and minced	25 mL
1 tbsp	white or red miso	15 mL
	Cooked pasta, preferably whole-grain, or polenta	

1. In a skillet, heat 1 tbsp (15 mL) of the oil over medium-high heat. Add sweated eggplant, in batches, and cook until lightly browned, adding more oil as necessary. Transfer to slow cooker stoneware.

2. Add onions to pan, adding oil, if necessary, and cook, stirring, until softened, about 3 minutes. Add garlic and cook, stirring, for 1 minute. Add tomatoes with juice and tomato paste and bring to a boil. Transfer to slow cooker stoneware.

3. Place a clean tea towel, folded in half (so you will have two layers), over top of stoneware to absorb moisture. Cover and cook on Low for 6 hours or on High for 3 hours, until hot and bubbly. Add roasted red peppers, olives, parsley, capers and miso. Stir well. Cover and cook on High for 20 minutes, until heated through. To serve, ladle over hot cooked pasta or polenta.

Tips

I like to make this using cremini mushrooms because they have a more intense flavor, but white mushrooms work well, too.

Add the mushroom soaking liquid to vegetable broth to enhance the flavor.

Variation

Substitute an equal quantity of penne for the fusilli.

Fusilli and Mushroom Timbale

Fragrant mushrooms and creamy cheese wrapped around hot succulent pasta — what's not to love about this delicious dish? If you want to impress, unmold it onto a platter; it makes a very elegant presentation. No one needs to know how easy it was to make.

- **8-cup (2 L) baking dish, lightly greased**
- **Large (minimum 5 quart) oval slow cooker**

8 oz	fusilli (about 2 cups/500 mL)	250 g
2 tbsp	extra virgin olive oil, divided	25 mL
1	small package (1/2 oz/14 g) dried porcini mushrooms	1
1 cup	hot water	250 mL
8 oz	sliced mushrooms (see Tips, left)	250 g
2	cloves garlic, minced	2
1 tsp	dried tarragon	5 mL
1 tsp	salt	5 mL
1/2 tsp	cracked black peppercorns	2 mL
1	can (14 oz/398 mL) diced tomatoes with juice	1
1/4 cup	finely chopped fresh parsley	50 mL
2	eggs, beaten	2
8	thin slices Fontina cheese (about 6 oz/175 g)	8
1/2 cup	freshly grated Parmesan	125 mL

1. In a large pot of boiling salted water over high heat, cook fusilli until pasta is al dente. Drain and transfer to a large bowl. Add 1 tbsp (15 mL) of the olive oil and toss well. Set aside and let cool.

2. Meanwhile, in a bowl, soak dried mushrooms in hot water for 30 minutes. Strain through a fine sieve. Chop mushrooms finely and set aside. Save liquid for another use (see Tips, left).

3. In a skillet, heat remaining olive oil over medium-high heat. Add sliced mushrooms and cook, stirring, until they begin to brown and lose their liquid, about 5 minutes. Add garlic, tarragon, salt, peppercorns and reserved reconstituted mushrooms and cook, stirring, for 1 minute. Add tomatoes with juice and bring to a simmer. Remove from heat and stir in parsley.

4. Add eggs to cooled pasta and stir well. Arrange half of pasta mixture in bottom of prepared dish. Add one-third of mushroom mixture and cover with 4 slices of Fontina. Repeat. Spread remaining mushroom mixture over top layer of Fontina and sprinkle with Parmesan. Cover with foil and secure tightly. Place dish in slow cooker stoneware and add boiling water to reach 1 inch (2.5 cm) up the sides of dish. Cover and cook on High for 3 hours until set. Remove from stoneware and let cool slightly. If desired, unmold to serve.

Tip

To sweat eggplant: Place cubed eggplant in a colander, sprinkle liberally with salt, toss well and set aside for 30 minutes to 1 hour. If time is short, blanch the pieces for a minute or two in heavily salted water. In either case, rinse thoroughly in fresh cold water and, using your hands, squeeze out excess moisture. Pat dry with paper towels and it's ready for cooking.

Variation

Substitute an equal quantity of fusilli for the penne.

Eggplant and Penne Timbale

If you like luscious baked pasta dishes like lasagna, here's a simplified version that I think is every bit as delicious and much easier to make. It can be unmolded onto a serving dish for a more impressive presentation. Add a tossed green salad or some sliced tomatoes for a simply delicious meal.

- **8-cup (2 L) baking dish, lightly greased**
- **Large (minimum 5 quart) slow cooker**

1	eggplant, peeled, cubed (1 inch/2.5 cm), sweated and drained of excess moisture (see Tip, left)	1
8 oz	penne (about 2 cups/500 mL)	250 g
1 tbsp	butter or extra virgin olive oil	15 mL
2 tbsp	extra virgin olive oil (approx.)	25 mL
4	cloves garlic, minced	4
1 tsp	dried oregano	5 mL
1 tsp	salt	5 mL
$\frac{1}{2}$ tsp	cracked black peppercorns	2 mL
1	can (14 oz/398 mL) diced tomatoes with juice	1
1 cup	freshly grated Parmesan or vegan alternative, divided	250 mL
2	eggs, beaten	2

1. In a large pot of boiling salted water over high heat, cook penne until pasta is al dente. Drain and transfer to a large bowl. Add butter and toss well. Set aside and let cool.

2. In a skillet, heat 2 tbsp (25 mL) oil over medium-high heat. Add sweated eggplant, in batches, if necessary, and cook, stirring, until nicely browned. Add garlic, oregano, salt and peppercorns and cook, stirring, for 1 minute. Add tomatoes with juice and bring to a simmer. Remove from heat and stir in half of the Parmesan.

3. Add eggs to cooled pasta and stir well. Arrange half of the pasta mixture in bottom of prepared dish. Add half of the eggplant mixture. Repeat. Sprinkle remaining Parmesan evenly over top. Cover dish tightly with foil and secure with a string. Place dish in slow cooker stoneware and add boiling water to reach 1 inch (2.5 cm) up the sides of dish. Cover and cook on High for 3 hours until set. Remove from stoneware and let cool slightly. If desired, unmold to serve.

Cauliflower Rice Timbale

Tips

I like to use brown rice because it is more nutritious than the refined variety, but white Arborio rice works well in this recipe, too. The important thing is to use rice that is glutinous, which helps to hold the dish together.

When being combined with the other ingredients, the rice should have cooled enough that you don't have to worry about the eggs curdling but be warm enough to make the butter blend smoothly. If you are using cold rice, melt the butter before adding.

I always use unsalted butter, not only because I prefer the taste, but also because it allows me more control over the quantity of salt I consume.

I'm a great fan of timbales because they are so easy to make yet give the impression they must be complicated. Your family or guests will be impressed with your culinary acumen if you take the time to unmold the timbale. Add a green salad or, in season, sliced tomatoes in a vinaigrette for a very tasty meal.

- **7-inch (18 cm) 6-cup (1.5 L) soufflé dish**
- **Large (minimum 5 quart) oval slow cooker**

2 cups	cooled cooked short-grain brown rice (see Tips, left)	500 mL
1/4 cup	butter, softened (see Tips, left)	50 mL
1 cup	freshly grated Parmesan, divided	250 mL
2	egg yolks	2
2 tbsp	oil	25 mL
3 cups	vertically sliced (about 1/4 inch/0.5 cm) cauliflower florets	750 mL
1 tsp	salt	5 mL
1 tsp	paprika	5 mL
	Freshly ground black pepper	
1/2 cup	heavy or whipping (35%) cream	125 mL

1. In a bowl, combine rice, butter, 1/2 cup (125 mL) of the Parmesan and egg yolks. Mix well and set aside.

2. In a skillet, heat oil over medium heat. Add cauliflower and cook, stirring, until it is nicely browned in many spots (it will look splotchy), about 5 minutes. Add salt, paprika, and pepper, to taste and stir well. Stir in cream and remaining Parmesan. Bring to a simmer and remove from heat.

3. In prepared dish, spread one-third of the rice mixture. Add half of the cauliflower mixture. Repeat. Finish with a layer of rice. Cover dish tightly with foil and secure with a string. Place dish in slow cooker stoneware and pour in enough boiling water to reach 1 inch (2.5 cm) up the sides of the dish. Cover and cook on High for 3 to 4 hours, until set. Serve warm, unmolded, or directly from the dish.

Squash-Laced Wild Rice and Barley Casserole

This hearty casserole is great winter fare. It's simple and very tasty. A tossed green salad is all you need to add.

- **Medium to large ($3\frac{1}{2}$ to 5 quart) slow cooker**

1 tbsp	oil	15 mL
2	leeks, white part with just a bit of green, cleaned and thinly sliced (see Tips, left)	2
2	carrots, peeled and diced	2
2	stalks celery, diced	2
4	cloves garlic, minced	4
1 tsp	salt	5 mL
1 tsp	cracked black peppercorns	5 mL
$\frac{1}{2}$ tsp	dried thyme or 2 sprigs fresh thyme	2 mL
1	bay leaf	1
$\frac{1}{2}$ cup	barley, rinsed (see Tips, left)	125 mL
$\frac{1}{2}$ cup	wild rice, rinsed	125 mL
4 cups	vegetable broth, divided	1 L
4 cups	diced ($\frac{1}{2}$ inch /1 cm) butternut squash (about 1)	1 L

1. In a skillet, heat oil over medium heat. Add leeks, carrots and celery and cook, stirring, until softened, about 7 minutes. Add garlic, salt, peppercorns, thyme and bay leaf and cook, stirring, for 1 minute. Add barley and wild rice and toss until well coated. Add 2 cups (500 mL) of the vegetable broth, stir well and bring to a boil. Boil for 2 minutes. Transfer to slow cooker stoneware.

2. Stir in squash and remaining 2 cups (500 mL) of broth. Cover and cook on Low for 8 hours or on High for 4 hours, until barley is tender. Discard bay leaf.

Can Be Halved

Tips

For the best flavor, toast cumin and coriander seeds and grind them yourself. *To toast seeds:* Place in a dry skillet over medium heat and cook, stirring, until fragrant, about 3 minutes. Immediately transfer to a spice grinder or mortar and grind finely.

A grapefruit spoon does a great job of cleaning the pith and seeds from the chile pepper.

If you are halving this recipe, be sure to use a small ($1^1/_2$ to $3^1/_2$ quart) slow cooker.

Variations

Vegetable Biriyani with Crispy Shallot or Onion Topping: Make Crispy Shallot Topping (page 153) or Crispy Onion Topping (Variation, page 132). When serving, ladle biriyani onto plates and garnish liberally with topping.

Vegetable Biriyani

Here's a tasty and nutritious main course that is very easy to make. If you have time, make the Crispy Shallot or Onion Topping (see Variations, left). It adds delicious flavor and texture to the end result.

- **Medium to large ($3^1/_2$ to 5 quart) slow cooker**
- **Lightly greased slow cooker stoneware**

3 tbsp	oil, divided	45 mL
1 tsp	cumin seeds	5 mL
$^1/_2$ tsp	ground turmeric	2 mL
2 cups	cubed ($^1/_2$ inch/1 cm) peeled potatoes	500 mL
1	red or sweet onion, thinly sliced on the vertical	1
2	carrots, peeled and diced	2
2 cups	diced fennel bulb	500 mL
$1^1/_2$ cups	long-grain brown rice, rinsed and drained	375 mL
2 tsp	ground cumin	10 mL
1 tsp	ground coriander	5 mL
1 tsp	salt	5 mL
1 tsp	cracked black peppercorns	5 mL
2	green cardamom pods, crushed	2
4 cups	vegetable broth	1 L

1. In a skillet, heat 2 tbsp (25 mL) of the oil over medium-high heat. Add cumin seeds and cook until they sizzle, about 10 seconds. Stir in turmeric. Add potatoes and cook, stirring, until they begin to brown, about 3 minutes. Add red onion and cook, stirring, for 1 minute. Add carrots and fennel and cook, stirring, until well coated with mixture. Transfer to a bowl and set aside.

2. Add remaining tbsp (15 mL) of oil, rice, ground cumin and coriander, salt, peppercorns and cardamom pods to pan and cook, stirring, until well coated. Add vegetable broth and bring to a boil. Boil for 2 minutes. Using a slotted spoon, layer half the rice mixture over bottom of prepared slow cooker. Spread vegetables over it. Add remaining rice mixture plus all of the liquid. Place a clean tea towel, folded in half (so you will have two layers), over top of stoneware to absorb moisture. Cover and cook on Low for 6 hours or on High for 3 hours, until rice is tender and liquid has been absorbed. Serve hot.

Tips

Soaking the beans and removing their skins produces a lovely melt-in-your-mouth texture. *To soak the beans for this recipe:* Bring beans to a boil in 4 cups (1 L) water over medium heat. Boil rapidly for 3 minutes. Cover, turn off element and let stand for 1 hour. Drain in a colander placed over a sink and rinse thoroughly under cold running water. Using your hands, pop the beans out of their skins. Discard skins.

Use the type of barley you prefer — whole, pot or pearled. I prefer whole barley because it is the most nutritious form of the grain.

If you like your risotto to be on the dry side, use 2 cups (500 mL) of broth. For a moist result, use the larger quantity, or something in between.

If you are halving this recipe, be sure to use a small (1$\frac{1}{2}$ to 3$\frac{1}{2}$ quart) slow cooker.

Make Ahead

Complete Steps 1 and 2, using 3 cups (750 mL) broth because the barley soaks up liquid on sitting. Cover and refrigerate for up to 2 days. When you're ready to cook, add 1 cup (250 mL) extra broth and complete the recipe.

Mushroom-Spiked Butterbean and Barley Risotto

Containing ample servings of both a whole grain and a legume, and therefore qualifying as a complete protein, this delicious "risotto" makes a great main course or a perfect dish for a buffet.

- **Medium (approx. 4 quart) slow cooker**

1 cup	dried butterbeans, lima beans or gigantes, soaked, drained and popped out of their skins (see Tips, left)	250 mL
1	package ($\frac{1}{2}$ oz/14 g) dried porcini mushrooms	1
1 cup	hot water	250 mL
1 tbsp	oil	15 mL
2	onions, finely chopped	2
4	cloves garlic, minced	4
1 tsp	dried thyme	5 mL
1 tsp	salt	5 mL
$\frac{1}{2}$ tsp	cracked black peppercorns	2 mL
1 cup	barley, rinsed (see Tips, left)	250 mL
2 to 3 cups	vegetable broth (see Tips, left)	500 to 750 mL
	Freshly grated Parmesan or vegan alternative	

1. In a bowl, combine dried mushrooms with hot water. Let stand for 30 minutes. Strain through a fine sieve, reserving liquid. Pat mushrooms dry and chop finely. Set mushrooms and soaking liquid aside, separately.

2. In a skillet, heat oil over medium heat. Add onions and cook, stirring, until softened, about 3 minutes. Add garlic, thyme, salt, peppercorns and reserved mushrooms and cook, stirring, for 1 minute. Add barley and toss until well coated with mixture. Add broth and reserved mushroom liquid and bring to a boil. If using whole barley, boil for 2 minutes. Transfer to slow cooker stoneware. Stir in butterbeans.

3. Cover and cook on Low for 8 hours or on High for 4 hours, until barley is tender. Pass the Parmesan at the table.

Tips

If possible use golden or yellow zucchini, which has more flavor than the green version. If you're not peeling it, scrub the skin thoroughly with a vegetable brush.

If you prefer, complete Step 3 while the zucchini sweats. When finished, wipe skillet clean and complete Step 2.

If you are halving this recipe, be sure to use a small ($1\frac{1}{2}$ to $3\frac{1}{2}$ quart) slow cooker.

Make Ahead

Complete Steps 1 through 3. Cover and refrigerate zucchini and tomato mixtures separately for up to 2 days. When you're ready to cook, continue with Step 4. Because the barley soaks up liquid on sitting, add an extra 1 cup (250 mL) of broth or water before cooking.

Variation

Greek-Style Bean and Potato Stew: Omit vegetable broth and tomato paste. Substitute 2 medium potatoes, peeled and diced, for the barley. Serve over orzo, whole wheat couscous, rice or another grain.

Greek-Style Beans and Barley

Here's a tasty casserole the whole family can enjoy. Add a simple green or shredded carrot salad for a great weekday meal.

● **Medium to large ($3\frac{1}{2}$ to 5 quart) slow cooker**

2	zucchini, thinly sliced into $\frac{1}{2}$-inch (1 cm) slices (see Tips, left)	2
$\frac{1}{2}$ tsp	salt	2 mL
2 tbsp	olive oil, divided	25 mL
4	cloves garlic, minced	4
	Freshly ground black pepper	
2	onions, finely chopped	2
2 tsp	dried oregano, crumbled	10 mL
$\frac{1}{2}$ tsp	cracked black peppercorns	2 mL
1 cup	barley, rinsed (see Tips, page 174)	250 mL
1	can (28 oz/796 mL) tomatoes with juice, coarsely chopped	1
2 tbsp	tomato paste	25 mL
2 cups	vegetable broth	500 mL
3 cups	frozen sliced green beans	750 mL
	Crumbled feta cheese, optional	

1. In a colander over a sink, combine zucchini and salt. Toss well and set aside for 30 minutes to allow zucchini to sweat. Rinse thoroughly. Pat dry with paper towel.

2. In a skillet, heat 1 tbsp (15 mL) of the oil over medium heat. Add zucchini and cook, stirring, for 3 minutes. Add garlic and cook, stirring, until zucchini softens and just begins to brown, about 4 minutes. Season to taste with freshly ground black pepper. Transfer to a bowl, cover and refrigerate.

3. In same skillet, heat remaining oil over medium heat. Add onions and cook, stirring, until softened, about 3 minutes. Add oregano and peppercorns and cook, stirring, for 1 minute. Add barley and toss until coated. Add tomatoes with juice, tomato paste and vegetable broth and bring to a boil. Transfer to slow cooker stoneware.

4. Add green beans and stir well. Cover and cook on Low for 6 hours or on High for 3 hours, until barley is tender. Add reserved zucchini and stir well. Cover and cook on High for 15 minutes, until zucchini is heated through. Sprinkle with crumbled feta to taste, if using.

Tips

Celery root oxidizes quickly on contact with air. Tossing it with lemon juice keeps it from discoloring.

I always use Italian flat-leaf parsley because it has much more flavor than the curly leaf variety.

Use the type of barley you prefer — whole, pot or pearled. I prefer whole barley because it is the most nutritious form of the grain.

If your supermarket carries 19-oz (540 mL) cans of diced tomatoes, by all means substitute for the 14-oz (398 mL) can called for in the recipe.

If you are halving this recipe, be sure to use a small (1$\frac{1}{2}$ to 3$\frac{1}{2}$ quart) slow cooker.

Make Ahead

Complete Step 2. Cover and refrigerate for up to 2 days. When you're ready to cook, continue with Steps 1 and 3. Because the barley soaks up liquid on sitting, add an extra $\frac{1}{2}$ cup (125 mL) of broth or water before cooking.

Barley-Spiked Winter Vegetable Casserole

Here's a great dish to make during the dark days of winter. The combination of root vegetables, seasoned with caraway seeds, produces a great-tasting dish that is seasonally appropriate — I like to imagine my pioneer ancestors sitting down to a similar meal. I serve this with rye bread and steamed broccoli, but creamed spinach works well, too.

• **Large (approx. 5 quart) slow cooker**

1	large celery root, peeled and shredded	1
1 tbsp	freshly squeezed lemon juice (see Tips, left)	15 mL
1 tbsp	oil	15 mL
2	leeks, white and light green parts only, cleaned and thinly sliced (see Tips, page 179)	2
4	carrots, peeled and sliced	4
4	parsnips, peeled and sliced	4
2	cloves garlic, minced	2
1 tsp	caraway seeds	5 mL
1 tsp	salt	5 mL
$\frac{1}{2}$ tsp	cracked black peppercorns	2 mL
$\frac{1}{2}$ cup	barley, rinsed	125 mL
1	can (14 oz/398 mL) diced tomatoes with juice (see Tips, left)	1
2 cups	vegetable broth	500 mL
$\frac{1}{2}$ cup	finely chopped Italian flat-leaf parsley	125 mL

1. In a bowl, toss celery root and lemon juice. Set aside.

2. In a large skillet, heat oil over medium heat. Add leeks, carrots and parsnips and cook, stirring, until softened, about 7 minutes. Add garlic, caraway seeds, salt and peppercorns and cook, stirring for 1 minute. Add barley and toss until coated. Add tomatoes with juice and vegetable broth and bring to a boil.

3. Transfer vegetable mixture to stoneware. Add celery root and stir well. Cover and cook on Low for 6 hours or on High for 3 hours, until vegetables and barley are tender. Sprinkle with parsley and serve.

Vegan Friendly

Can Be Halved

Tips

You can use either hard or soft wheat berries in this recipe. You can also substitute spelt or Kamut berries if you prefer.

If you are halving this recipe, be sure to use a small ($1\frac{1}{2}$ to $3\frac{1}{2}$ quart) slow cooker.

Make Ahead

Complete Step 1. Cover and refrigerate for up to 2 days. When you're ready to cook, complete the recipe. Because the wheat berries soak up liquid on sitting, add an extra 1 cup (250 mL) of broth or water before cooking.

Wheat Berry Gratin

This very simple dish is easy to make, yet surprisingly delicious. Serve it with a tossed green salad or sliced tomatoes for a great weeknight meal.

- **Medium (approx. $3\frac{1}{2}$ quart) slow cooker**
- **Long, shallow baking dish**

1 tbsp	oil	15 mL
2	onions, finely chopped	2
4	stalks celery	4
4	cloves garlic, minced	4
1 tsp	dried thyme	5 mL
1 tsp	salt	5 mL
$\frac{1}{2}$ tsp	cracked black peppercorns	2 mL
1 cup	wheat berries, rinsed	250 mL
2 cups	vegetable broth	500 mL
$\frac{1}{3}$ cup	heavy or whipping (35%) cream or soy milk, optional	75 mL
$\frac{1}{2}$ cup	freshly grated Parmesan or vegan alternative	125 mL
4	tomatoes, thinly sliced	4
	Extra virgin olive oil	

1. In a skillet, heat oil over medium heat. Add onions and celery and cook, stirring, until softened, about 5 minutes. Add garlic, thyme, salt and peppercorns and cook, stirring, for 1 minute. Add wheat berries and toss to coat. Add vegetable broth and bring to a boil. Boil for 2 minutes. Transfer to slow cooker stoneware.

2. Cover and cook on Low for 8 hours or on High for 4 hours, until wheat berries are tender. Add cream, if using, and Parmesan and stir well.

3. Preheat broiler. Transfer mixture to a baking dish. Lay tomatoes evenly over top of wheat berry mixture. Drizzle with olive oil. Broil until edges begin to brown. Serve immediately.

Wheat Berry Ragoût

Tips

To clean leeks: Fill sink full of lukewarm water. Split leeks in half lengthwise and submerge in water, swishing them around to remove all traces of dirt. Transfer to a colander and rinse under cold water.

Celery root oxidizes quickly on contact with air. To prevent browning, immediately after shredding place in a large bowl of acidulated water (6 cups/1.5 L water combined with 2 tbsp/25 mL lemon juice.) Drain well before adding to recipe.

I like my wheat berries a tad crunchy, the texture produced by cooking them for 6 hours on Low. If you prefer a softer texture, cook them longer.

If you are halving this recipe, be sure to use a small (1½ to 3½ quart) slow cooker.

Make Ahead

Complete Step 1. Cover and refrigerate for up to 2 days. When you're ready to cook, complete the recipe. Because the wheat berries soak up liquid on sitting, add an extra 1 cup (250 mL) of broth or water before cooking.

The dish has great flavor, some of which comes from the herbes de Provence. This pungent blend of dried herbs — such as thyme, savory, sage, lavender and fennel — really boosts the flavor of a dish with virtually no effort on your part. I love the way the celery root dissolves into the liquid and acts as a thickener. I like the hint of creaminess the Parmesan adds, but the choice is yours.

● **Medium to large (4 to 5 quart) slow cooker**

1 tbsp	oil	15 mL
3	leeks, white and light green parts only, cleaned and sliced (see Tips, left)	3
2	carrots, peeled and diced	2
4	cloves garlic, minced	4
1½ tsp	herbes de Provence or dried thyme	7 mL
1 tsp	salt	5 mL
1 tsp	cracked black peppercorns	5 mL
2 cups	shredded peeled celery root (about 1 small) (see Tips, left)	500 mL
1 cup	wheat berries, rinsed (see Tips, page 178)	250 mL
1	can (28 oz/796 mL) diced tomatoes with juice	1
3 cups	vegetable broth, divided	750 mL
	Freshly grated Parmesan or vegan alternative, optional	

1. In a large skillet, heat oil over medium heat. Add leeks and carrots and cook, stirring, until softened, about 7 minutes. Add garlic, herbes de Provence, salt and peppercorns and cook, stirring, for 1 minute. Add celery root and wheat berries and toss to coat. Add tomatoes with juice and 1 cup (250 mL) of the broth and bring to a boil. Boil for 2 minutes. Transfer to slow cooker stoneware.

2. Add remaining 2 cups (500 mL) of broth. Cover and cook on Low for 6 to 8 hours or on High for 3 to 4 hours (see Tips, left), until wheat berries reach the degree of crunchiness you prefer. Serve immediately in soup plates, topped with Parmesan, if using.

Tips

I always use stone-ground cornmeal because it has not been hulled or degermed. It is the most nutritious version of cornmeal and has more texture and flavor than the refined version.

If you are halving this recipe, be sure to use a small ($1\frac{1}{2}$ to 2 quart) slow cooker.

Creamy Polenta with Corn and Chiles

In my opinion, polenta is a quintessential comfort food. I love it as side dish, where it is particularly apt at complementing robust stews, or as a main course topped with a traditional pasta sauce. This version, which contains the luscious combination of corn and chiles, also works as a main course on its own. I like to serve it with a tossed salad, sliced tomatoes with vinaigrette or some marinated roasted peppers.

- **Small to medium (2 to $3\frac{1}{2}$ quart) slow cooker**
- **Greased slow cooker stoneware**

3 cups	milk	750 mL
2	cloves garlic, minced	2
1 tsp	finely chopped fresh rosemary or $\frac{1}{2}$ tsp (2 mL) dried rosemary, crumbled	5 mL
$\frac{1}{2}$ tsp	salt	2 mL
	Freshly ground black pepper	
$\frac{3}{4}$ cup	coarse yellow cornmeal, preferably stone-ground (see Tips, left)	175 mL
1 cup	corn kernels	250 mL
1 cup	shredded Monterey Jack cheese	250 mL
$\frac{1}{2}$ cup	freshly grated Parmesan	125 mL
1	can ($4\frac{1}{2}$ oz/127 mL) diced mild green chiles	1

1. In a large saucepan over medium heat, bring milk, garlic, rosemary, salt, and black pepper, to taste, to a boil. Gradually add cornmeal, in a steady stream, whisking to remove all lumps. Continue whisking until mixture begins to thicken and bubbles like lava, about 5 minutes. Add corn, Jack and Parmesan cheeses and chiles and mix well. Transfer to prepared slow cooker stoneware.

2. Cover and cook on Low for 2 hours, until mixture is firm and just beginning to brown around the edges.

Slow-Cooked Polenta

Tips

You can cook polenta directly in the slow cooker stoneware or in a 6-cup (1.5 L) baking dish, lightly greased, depending upon your preference. If you are cooking directly in the stoneware, I recommend using a small (maximum 3½ quart) slow cooker, lightly greased. If you are using a baking dish, you will need a large (minimum 5 quart) oval slow cooker.

If you are halving this recipe and cooking directly in the stoneware, be sure to use a small (1½ to 2 quart) slow cooker.

Variation

Creamy Polenta: Substitute 2 cups (500 mL) milk or cream and 1¼ cups (300 mL) vegetable broth for the quantity of liquid above. If desired, stir in ¼ cup (50 mL) finely chopped fresh parsley and/or 2 tbsp (25 mL) freshly grated Parmesan, after the cornmeal has been added to the liquid.

Polenta, an extremely versatile dish from northern Italy, is basically cornmeal cooked in seasoned liquid. It is one of my favorite grains. Depending upon the method used, making polenta can be a laborious process. These slow-cooked versions produce excellent results with a minimum of effort.

- **Small or large oval (2 or minimum 5 quart) slow cooker, depending upon method**

4 cups	vegetable broth or water	1 L
1 tsp	salt	5 mL
¼ tsp	freshly ground black pepper	1 mL
1 cup	coarse yellow cornmeal, preferably stone-ground	250 mL

1. In a saucepan over medium heat, bring broth, salt and pepper to a boil. Add cornmeal in a thin stream, stirring constantly.

2. *Direct method:* Transfer mixture to prepared slow cooker stoneware (see Tips, left). Cover and cook on Low for 1½ hours.

3. *Baking dish method:* Transfer mixture to prepared baking dish (see Tips, left). Cover dish tightly with foil and secure with a string. Place dish in slow cooker stoneware and pour in enough boiling water to come 1 inch (2.5 cm) up the sides of the dish. Cover and cook on Low for 1½ hours.

Tips

Whole-grain stone-ground grits (the tastiest and most nutritious kind) take a long time to cook. Preparing them on the stovetop requires about 2 hours of attention and frequent stirring. If, like me, you're a grits lover, having a slow cooker is very advantageous. Once you put them in the stoneware and turn the appliance on, you can forget about them until they are done.

If you are halving this recipe, be sure to use a small (1½ to 2 quart) slow cooker.

Basic Grits

Add variety to your diet by serving grits, instead of pasta, topped with a tasty sauce for a light lunch or dinner. Grits are dried broken grains of corn with a pleasant nutty taste that adapts well to many flavors. In fact, they are one of my favorite grains.

- **Small to medium (2 to 3½ quart) slow cooker**
- **Lightly greased slow cooker stoneware**

4 cups	water	1 L
1 tbsp	olive oil	15 mL
½ tsp	salt	2 mL
½ tsp	freshly ground black pepper	2 mL
1 cup	grits (not instant, preferably stone-ground)	250 mL

1. In a saucepan over medium heat, bring water, olive oil, salt and pepper to a boil. Gradually add grits, stirring constantly, until smooth and blended. Continue cooking and stirring, until grits are slightly thickened, about 4 minutes. Transfer to prepared stoneware. Cover and cook on Low for 6 hours or on High for 3 hours, until set. Serve immediately.

Tips

I always use unsalted butter, not only because I prefer the taste, but also because it allows me more control over the quantity of salt I consume.

If you are halving this recipe, be sure to use a small ($1\frac{1}{2}$ to 2 quart) slow cooker.

Grits 'n' Cheddar Cheese

I think I must have lived in the American South in a previous life because I'm absolutely crazy about grits. I could eat them for breakfast, lunch and dinner, which is unfortunate, because they can be difficult to find north of the Mason-Dixon Line. They make a great accompaniment to many dishes, embellished with cheese or on their own.

- **Small to medium (2 to $3\frac{1}{2}$ quart) slow cooker**
- **Lightly greased slow cooker stoneware**

2 cups	water	500 mL
1 tbsp	butter (see Tips, left)	15 mL
1 tsp	salt	5 mL
$\frac{1}{2}$ tsp	freshly ground black pepper	2 mL
$\frac{1}{2}$ cup	grits (not instant), preferably stone-ground	125 mL
1 cup	milk	250 mL
2	eggs, beaten	2
1 cup	shredded Cheddar cheese	250 mL

1. In a saucepan over medium heat, bring water, butter, salt and pepper to a boil. Gradually add grits, stirring until smooth.

2. Remove from heat. Add milk, eggs and cheese and stir to blend. Transfer to prepared stoneware. Cover and cook on High for 3 to 4 hours, until set. Serve immediately.

Tips
If you prefer, use frozen chopped butternut squash in this recipe. Reduce the quantity to 2 cups (500 mL).

Be sure to rinse the quinoa thoroughly before using because some quinoa has a resinous coating called saponin, which needs to be rinsed off. To ensure your quinoa is saponin-free, before cooking fill a bowl with warm water and swish the kernels around, then transfer to a sieve and rinse thoroughly under cold running water.

You'll know if your quinoa is cooked when a white line forms around the seeds.

If you are halving this recipe, be sure to use a small ($1\frac{1}{2}$ to 2 quart) slow cooker.

Make Ahead
Complete Step 1. Cover and refrigerate overnight or for up to 2 days. When you're ready to cook, continue with Steps 2 and 3.

Squash with Quinoa and Apricots

Banish the blahs with this robust combination of fruits, vegetables and a nutritious whole grain seasoned with ginger, orange and a hint of cinnamon. In season, accompany with a serving of watercress tossed in a simple vinaigrette.

- **Medium to large ($3\frac{1}{2}$ to 5 quart) slow cooker**

1 tbsp	oil	15 mL
2	onions, finely chopped	2
2	cloves garlic, minced	2
1 tbsp	minced gingerroot	15 mL
1 tbsp	ground cumin (see Tip, page 153)	15 mL
2 tsp	finely grated orange zest	10 mL
1	piece (2 inches/5 cm) cinnamon stick	1
1 tsp	ground turmeric	5 mL
1 tsp	salt	5 mL
$\frac{1}{2}$ tsp	cracked black peppercorns	2 mL
1 cup	vegetable broth	250 mL
$\frac{1}{2}$ cup	orange juice	125 mL
4 cups	cubed (1 inch/2.5 cm) peeled winter squash (see Tips, left)	1 L
2	apples, peeled, cored and sliced	2
$\frac{1}{2}$ cup	chopped dried apricots	125 mL
$1\frac{1}{2}$ cups	quinoa, rinsed	375 mL

1. In a skillet, heat oil over medium heat. Add onions and cook, stirring, until softened, about 3 minutes. Add garlic, ginger, cumin, orange zest, cinnamon stick, turmeric, salt and peppercorns and cook, stirring, for 1 minute. Add vegetable broth and orange juice and bring to a boil. Transfer to slow cooker stoneware.

2. Add squash, apples and apricots to stoneware and stir well. Cover and cook on Low for 6 hours or on High for 3 hours, until vegetables are tender. Discard cinnamon stick.

3. In a pot, bring 3 cups (750 mL) of water to a boil. Add quinoa in a steady stream, stirring to prevent lumps, and return to a boil. Cover, reduce heat to low and simmer for 15 minutes, until tender and liquid is absorbed. Add to slow cooker and stir well. Serve immediately.

Beans, Lentils, Tempeh and Tofu

Flageolet Gratin with Fennel

continued next page…

Tips

Some prepared vegetable broths are so concentrated they resemble vegetable juice. That's why I recommend diluting them with an equal amount of water. If you are using homemade vegetable broth, substitute 4 cups (1 L) for the vegetable broth and the water.

Aleppo pepper is a mild chile pepper from Syria. It is available in specialty stores or supermarkets with a well-stocked spice section.

If you're serving guests, rather than serving in the stoneware you may want to transfer the cooked dish to a heatproof serving dish or individual tureens, then add the topping and place under broiler.

If you are halving this recipe, be sure to use a small (1½ to 3½ quart) slow cooker.

Make Ahead

Complete Steps 1 and 2. Cover and refrigerate for up to 2 days. When you're ready to cook, complete the recipe.

Flageolet Gratin with Fennel

Flageolets, small dried French beans, which many consider to be the Rolls Royce of legumes, seem to have a particular affinity for fennel. Here, I've complemented the mild licorice flavor of that vegetable with herbes de Provence, a classic blend, which includes fennel seeds. The crisp gratin adds a pleasant finishing touch.

● **Medium to large (4 to 5 quart) slow cooker**

1½ cups	dried flageolets (see Tips, page 190)	375 mL
2 cups	vegetable broth (see Tips, left)	500 mL
2 cups	water	500 mL
2 tbsp	olive oil	25 mL
2	leeks, white part with just a hint of green, cleaned and sliced (see Tips, page 146)	2
1	bulb fennel, trimmed, cored and diced	1
4	cloves garlic, minced	4
1½ tsp	herbes de Provence or dried thyme	7 mL
2	bay leaves	2
1 tsp	salt	5 mL
½ tsp	cracked black peppercorns	2 mL

Topping

2 cups	dry bread crumbs	500 mL
½ cup	finely chopped fresh parsley	125 mL
1 tsp	ground Aleppo pepper or ¼ tsp (1 mL) cayenne (see Tips, left)	5 mL
¼ tsp	salt	1 mL
¼ cup	melted butter or olive oil	50 mL

1. In a saucepan, combine flageolets, broth and water. Bring to a boil and boil rapidly for 2 minutes. Set aside for 20 minutes.

2. In a skillet, heat oil over medium heat. Add leeks and fennel and cook, stirring, until softened, about 5 minutes. Add garlic, herbes de Provence, bay leaves, salt and peppercorns and cook, stirring, for 1 minute. Transfer to slow cooker stoneware. Add flageolets with liquid and stir well.

3. Cover and cook on Low for 6 to 8 hours or on High for 3 to 4 hours, until flageolets are tender. Discard bay leaves.

4. *Topping:* Preheat broiler. In a bowl, combine bread crumbs, parsley, Aleppo pepper and salt. Stir well. Add butter and mix until combined. Sprinkle evenly over bean mixture and broil until topping is lightly browned and flageolets are bubbly.

Tips

Flageolets are available in well-stocked supermarkets or specialty stores. Although they usually do not need to be soaked before using, I find they cook better in the slow cooker if they receive a quick soak as directed.

If you're serving guests, rather than serving in the stoneware you may want to transfer the cooked dish to a heatproof serving dish or individual tureens, then add the topping and place under broiler.

Kale-Laced Flageolet and Mushroom Gratin

It's hard to believe that such a delicious mélange is also incredibly good for you. The combination of flageolets (in France, the ne plus ultra of dried beans), an excellent source of many B vitamins, calcium and fiber, and kale, a dark leafy green that some believe to be a super-food, make this dish a nutritional powerhouse.

● **Medium to large (4 to 5 quart) slow cooker**

1	package (½ oz/14 g) dried porcini mushrooms	1
1 cup	hot water	250 mL
1 cup	dried flageolets (see Tips, left)	250 mL
2 cups	vegetable broth	500 mL
1 tbsp	olive oil	15 mL
2	onions, finely chopped	2
4	stalks celery, diced	4
4	gloves garlic, minced	4
1 tsp	dried rosemary	5 mL
1 tsp	salt	5 mL
½ tsp	cracked black peppercorns	2 mL
4 cups	finely chopped stemmed kale	1 L

Topping

2 cups	dry bread crumbs	500 mL
½ cup	finely chopped fresh parsley	125 mL
¼ cup	melted butter or margarine, or olive oil	50 mL

1. In a bowl, combine dried mushrooms and hot water. Stir well and let stand for 30 minutes. Strain through a fine sieve, reserving mushrooms and liquid separately. Chop mushrooms finely. Set aside.

2. Meanwhile, in a saucepan, combine flageolets and vegetable broth. Bring to a boil and boil rapidly for 2 minutes. Set aside for 20 minutes.

3. In a skillet, heat oil over medium heat. Add onions and celery and cook, stirring, until softened, about 5 minutes. Add garlic, rosemary, salt, peppercorns and reserved chopped mushrooms and cook, stirring, for 1 minute. Add flageolets with broth. Transfer to slow cooker stoneware. Stir in reserved mushroom soaking liquid.

4. Cover and cook on Low for 6 to 8 hours or on High for 3 to 4 hours, until flageolets are tender. Add kale, in batches, stirring until each is submerged. Cover and cook on High for 15 minutes, until kale is tender.

5. *Topping:* Preheat broiler. In a bowl, combine bread crumbs and parsley. Stir well. Add butter and mix until combined. Sprinkle evenly over bean mixture and broil, until topping is lightly browned and mixture is bubbly.

Traditional Succotash

Tips

If you prefer, substitute 4 cups (1 L) frozen lima beans for the dried ones and skip Step 1.

Use the type of paprika you prefer, sweet, hot or even smoked. The results will be different, but all will be good.

This dish works best made with a robust vegetable broth such as Enhanced Vegetable Broth (Variation, page 103). If you don't have time to make Enhanced Vegetable Broth and you think your broth may be lacking in flavor, add a bit of vegetable bouillon powder, but be aware that you may have to reduce the quantity of salt in the recipe.

If you are halving this recipe, be sure to use a small (1½ to 3½ quart) slow cooker.

Make Ahead

Complete Steps 1 and 2. Cover and refrigerate for up to 2 days. When you're ready to cook, complete the recipe.

Made with freshly picked corn, succotash has become a late summer and autumn tradition. This makes a large batch, but it keeps well.

- **Large (approx. 5 quart) slow cooker**

2 cups	dried lima beans (see Tips, left)	500 mL
1 tbsp	oil	15 mL
2	onions, finely chopped	2
4	stalks celery, peeled and thinly sliced	4
2	large carrots, peeled, cut in quarters lengthwise, then thinly sliced	2
4	cloves garlic, minced	4
2	sprigs fresh rosemary or 1 tbsp (15 mL) dried rosemary	2
1 tsp	salt	5 mL
1 tsp	cracked black peppercorns	5 mL
1	can (28 oz/796 mL) tomatoes with juice, coarsely chopped	1
3 cups	vegetable broth (see Tips, left)	750 mL
2 tsp	paprika	10 mL
2 cups	corn kernels	500 mL
½ cup	heavy or whipping (35%) cream, optional	125 mL
	Freshly grated Parmesan or vegan alternative, optional	
	Freshly grated nutmeg	

1. In a large saucepan, bring beans to a boil with 6 cups (1.5 L) water. Boil rapidly for 3 minutes. Turn off heat and let stand for 1 hour. Drain and rinse under cold water. Using your fingers, pop beans out of their skins and transfer to a bowl. Cover with cold water and set aside. Discard skins. Drain beans before using.

2. In a skillet, heat oil over medium heat. Add onions, celery and carrots and cook, stirring, until softened, about 7 minutes. Add garlic, rosemary, salt and peppercorns and cook, stirring, for 1 minute. Stir in tomatoes with juice and vegetable broth and bring to a boil. Transfer to slow cooker stoneware. Stir in lima beans.

3. Cover and cook on Low for 8 hours or on High for 4 hours, until beans are tender.

4. Scoop out ¼ cup (50 mL) of cooking liquid. Place paprika in a small bowl. Gradually add hot liquid, stirring until smooth. Add to stoneware and stir well. Stir in corn. Cover and cook on High for 15 minutes until corn is tender and flavors meld. Stir in cream and Parmesan, if using, and season to taste with nutmeg.

New Age Succotash

Tips

I always use Italian flat-leaf parsley because it has much more flavor than the curly leaf variety.

If you are halving this recipe, be sure to use a small (1½ to 3½ quart) slow cooker.

Make Ahead

Complete Step 1. Cover and refrigerate for up to 2 days. When you're ready to cook, complete the recipe.

Variations

Barley Succotash: For a more substantial dish, add ½ cup (125 mL) barley along with the edamame. Add 1 cup (250 mL) of vegetable broth to the mixture. Use the type of barley you prefer: whole (hulled), pot or pearled, being aware that whole barley is the most nutritious form of the grain.

Spicy Succotash: For a livelier dish, stir in 1 can (4½ oz/127 mL) mild green chiles along with the red peppers.

I call this dish "new age" because it uses edamame, or soybeans, instead of traditional lima beans. I've also finished it with a smattering of mouth-watering roasted red peppers, usually not included in the dish. I like to serve this with steamed asparagus, in season.

● **Medium to large (3½ to 5 quart) slow cooker**

1 tbsp	oil	15 mL
2	onions, finely chopped	2
4	stalks celery, diced	4
2	carrots, peeled and diced	2
4	cloves garlic, minced	4
1	sprig fresh rosemary or 2 tsp (10 mL) dried rosemary, crumbled	1
1 tsp	salt	5 mL
½ tsp	cracked black peppercorns	2 mL
1	can (28 oz/796 mL) tomatoes with juice, coarsely chopped	1
1½ cups	vegetable broth	375 mL
4 cups	frozen shelled edamame	1 L
4 cups	corn kernels	1 L
2	roasted red bell peppers, seeded and diced	2
½ cup	finely chopped Italian flat-leaf parsley	125 mL
2 tsp	paprika, dissolved in 2 tbsp (25 mL) water	10 mL

1. In a skillet, heat oil over medium heat. Add onions, celery and carrots and cook, stirring, until softened, about 7 minutes. Add garlic, rosemary, salt and peppercorns and cook, stirring, for 1 minute. Stir in tomatoes with juices and vegetable broth and bring to a boil. Transfer to slow cooker stoneware.

2. Add edamame and stir well. Cover and cook on Low for 6 to 8 hours or on High for 3 to 4 hours, until mixture is hot and bubbly. Stir in corn, roasted red peppers, parsley and paprika solution. Cover and cook on High for 20 minutes, until corn is tender and mixture is heated through.

Mushroom Cholent

Cholent, which is prepared on Friday and left to cook overnight, is the traditional midday meal for the Jewish Sabbath. In this version, portobello mushrooms provide the heartiness usually derived from meat and a mirepoix containing parsnips, as well as the traditional vegetables, adds sweetness and flavor. The mushrooms contribute to a surprisingly rich gravy and the results are very good indeed.

● **Large (approx. 5 quart) slow cooker**

1 cup	dried white navy beans	250 mL
1 tbsp	oil	15 mL
2	onions, finely chopped	2
4	stalks celery, diced	4
2	carrots, peeled and diced	2
2	parsnips, peeled and diced	2
6	cloves garlic, minced	6
1 tbsp	minced gingerroot	15 mL
2 tsp	paprika	10 mL
1 tsp	salt	5 mL
1 tsp	cracked black peppercorns	5 mL
4 cups	vegetable broth	1 L
2	potatoes, peeled and cut into $\frac{1}{2}$-inch (1 cm) cubes	2
12 oz	portobello mushroom caps (about 4 large)	375 g
1 cup	barley, rinsed (see Tips, left)	250 mL

1. Soak beans according to either method in Basic Beans (see page 239). Drain and rinse and set aside.

2. In a large skillet, heat oil over medium heat. Add onions, celery, carrots and parsnips and cook, stirring, until softened, about 7 minutes. Add garlic, ginger, paprika, salt and peppercorns and cook, stirring, for 1 minute. Stir in vegetable broth and remove from heat.

3. Pour half the contents of pan into slow cooker stoneware. Set remainder aside. Spread potatoes evenly over mixture. Arrange mushrooms evenly over potatoes, cutting one to fit, if necessary. Spread barley and reserved beans evenly over mushrooms. Add remaining onion mixture to stoneware.

4. Cover and cook on Low for 10 to 12 hours or on High for 5 to 6 hours, until potatoes and beans are tender.

Cider-Baked Beans

Tip

If you are halving this recipe, be sure to use a small ($1\frac{1}{2}$ to $3\frac{1}{2}$ quart) slow cooker.

Make Ahead

To manage your time most effectively when making this dish, soak the dried beans overnight. Chop and peel the onions, celery, carrots, parsnips and garlic the night before you plan to cook. Cover and refrigerate overnight. Measure the dried spices and cover. Combine apple cider, water and maple syrup in a 4-cup (1 L) measure. Cover and refrigerate overnight. The next morning, drain and rinse the beans and proceed with the recipe.

Variation

Cider-Baked Beans with Caramelized Apples: Thanks to Cinda Chavich for this idea. When beans are almost cooked, peel and core 4 apples, then slice them vertically into thin slices. In a skillet, over medium heat, melt 3 tbsp (45 mL) butter. Add $\frac{1}{4}$ cup (50 mL) brown sugar and cook, stirring, for about 2 minutes. Add apple slices and stir to coat with sugar mixture. Add $\frac{1}{4}$ cup (50 mL) rum. Increase heat to medium-high and cook, turning, until the liquid evaporates and the apples are tender. Arrange apple slices on top of beans, cover and cook on High for 1 hour.

If, like me, you often have small quantities of several varieties of dried beans in your pantry, here is a great way to use them up. For a festive presentation, add the bread crumb or caramelized apple topping, both of which are Entertaining Worthy. I like to serve this with a salad of shredded carrots and steamed brown bread.

• **Large (approx. 5 quart) slow cooker**

2 cups	assorted dried beans	500 mL
2	onions, finely chopped	2
3	stalks celery, peeled and thinly sliced	3
2	carrots, peeled and thinly sliced	2
2	large parsnips, peeled and thinly sliced	2
2	cloves garlic, minced	2
2 tsp	chili powder	10 mL
1 tsp	salt	5 mL
1 tsp	cracked black peppercorns	5 mL
4	whole cloves	4
1	piece (2 inches/5 cm) cinnamon stick	1
1 cup	apple cider or juice	250 mL
1 cup	water	250 mL
$\frac{1}{2}$ cup	pure maple syrup	125 mL
2 tbsp	cornstarch, dissolved in 2 tbsp (25 mL) cold water	25 mL

Bread Crumb Topping, optional

1 cup	dry bread crumbs	250 mL
$\frac{1}{4}$ cup	melted butter or olive oil	50 mL
$\frac{1}{4}$ cup	finely chopped Italian flat-leaf parsley	50 mL

1. Soak beans according to either method in Basic Beans (see page 239). Drain and rinse and set aside.

2. In slow cooker stoneware, combine beans, onions, celery, carrots, parsnips, garlic, chili powder, salt, peppercorns, cloves and cinnamon stick and stir well. Add apple cider, water and maple syrup. Cover and cook on Low for 10 to 12 hours or on High for 5 to 6 hours, until beans are tender. Discard cinnamon.

3. In a bowl, combine dissolved cornstarch with 2 tbsp (25 mL) hot cooking liquid from beans and stir until smooth. Gradually add up to $\frac{1}{4}$ cup (50 mL) hot bean liquid, stirring until mixture is smooth. Return mixture to stoneware and stir well until sauce thickens.

4. *Bread Crumb Topping, if using:* Preheat broiler. Ladle beans into individual heatproof tureens or baking dish. In a bowl, combine bread crumbs, butter and parsley. Sprinkle over beans and place under broiler until topping is lightly browned and beans are bubbly.

Vegan Friendly

Can Be Halved

Tips

For this quantity of beans, use 2 cans (14 to 19 oz/398 to 540 mL) drained and rinsed, or cook 2 cups (500 mL) dried beans (see Basic Beans, page 239).

If you are halving this recipe, be sure to use a small (approx. 2 quart) slow cooker.

Make Ahead

Complete Steps 1 and 2. Cover and refrigerate for up to 2 days. When you're ready to cook, complete the recipe.

Barbecue Baked Beans

This dish is evidence that vegetarians can also enjoy the robust pleasures of down-home baked beans. The addition of dried mushrooms, miso and smoked paprika provide the robust flavors associated with Southern barbecue. Make this a main course served with multi-grain bread and, if you're not a vegan, Cheddar cheese, or serve it as part of a multi-dish meal. It is also great on a buffet.

● **Medium (approx. 4 quart) slow cooker**

1	package ($1/2$ oz/14 g) dried porcini mushrooms	1
1 cup	hot water	250 mL
1 tbsp	oil	15 mL
2	onions, finely chopped	2
4	stalks celery, diced	4
2	carrots, peeled and diced	2
2	cloves garlic, minced	2
1 tsp	minced gingerroot	5 mL
1 tsp	salt	5 mL
1 tsp	cracked black peppercorns	5 mL
1	bay leaf	1
1	piece (2 inches/5 cm) cinnamon stick	1
1	can (14 oz/398 mL) crushed tomatoes	1
4 cups	drained cooked white beans, such as navy	1 L
$1/4$ cup	pure maple syrup	50 mL
1 tbsp	dark miso	15 mL
1 to 2 tsp	smoked paprika	5 to 10 mL

1. In a bowl, combine dried mushrooms and hot water. Stir well and let stand for 30 minutes. Strain through a fine sieve, reserving mushrooms and liquid separately. Chop mushrooms finely. Set aside.

2. In a skillet, heat oil over medium heat. Add onions, celery and carrots and cook, stirring, until softened, about 7 minutes. Add garlic, ginger, salt, peppercorns, bay leaf, cinnamon stick and reserved mushrooms and cook, stirring, for 1 minute. Stir in crushed tomatoes and reserved mushroom soaking liquid. Transfer to slow cooker stoneware.

3. Add beans and stir well. Cover and cook on Low for 6 hours or on High for 3 hours, until beans are tender. Discard bay leaf and cinnamon.

4. In a small bowl, combine maple syrup, miso and paprika. Add to stoneware and stir well. Cover and cook on High for 20 minutes to meld flavors. Serve hot.

Tips

Try substituting coconut oil for the olive oil. It adds a hint of coconut flavor to this chili that is quite appealing.

For the best flavor, toast cumin seeds and grind them yourself. *To toast seeds:* Place in a dry skillet over medium heat and cook, stirring, until fragrant about 3 minutes. Immediately transfer to a spice grinder or mortar and grind finely

For this quantity of beans, use 1 can (14 to 19 oz/398 to 540 mL) drained and rinsed, or cook 1 cup (250 mL) dried beans (see Basic Beans, page 239).

If you are halving this recipe, be sure to use a small (1½ to 3½ quart) slow cooker.

Make Ahead

Complete Step 1. Cover and refrigerate for up to 2 days. When you're ready to cook, complete the recipe.

Squash and Black Bean Chili

Nicely flavored with hot smoky chipotle pepper and a hint of cinnamon, this luscious chili makes a fabulous weeknight meal. Add a tossed green salad and some whole-grain rolls, relax and enjoy.

- **Medium to large (3½ to 5 quart) slow cooker**

1 tbsp	oil	15 mL
2	onions, finely chopped	2
4	cloves garlic, minced	4
2 tsp	chili powder	10 mL
1 tsp	dried oregano	5 mL
1 tsp	ground cumin (see Tips, left)	5 mL
1 tsp	salt	5 mL
1	piece (3 inches/7.5 cm) cinnamon stick	1
1	can (28 oz/796 mL) tomatoes with juice, coarsely chopped	1
2 cups	drained cooked black beans (see Tips, left)	500 mL
4 cups	cubed (1 inch/2.5 cm) peeled butternut squash	1 L
2	green bell peppers, diced	2
1	can (4½ oz/127 mL) chopped mild green chiles	1
1	finely chopped canned chipotle pepper in adobo sauce, optional	1
	Finely chopped fresh cilantro	

1. In a skillet, heat oil over medium heat. Add onions and cook, stirring, until softened, about 3 minutes. Add garlic, chili powder, oregano, cumin, salt and cinnamon stick and cook, stirring, for 1 minute. Add tomatoes with juice and bring to a boil. Transfer to slow cooker stoneware.

2. Add beans and squash and stir well. Cover and cook on Low for 6 hours or on High for 3 hours, until squash is tender. Add bell peppers, chiles, and chipotle pepper, if using. Cover and cook on High for 20 minutes, until bell pepper is tender. Discard cinnamon stick. When ready to serve, ladle into bowls and garnish with cilantro.

Vegan Friendly

Entertaining Worthy

Can Be Halved

Tips

For the best flavor, toast cumin seeds and grind them yourself. *To toast seeds:* Place in a dry skillet over medium heat and cook, stirring, until fragrant about 3 minutes. Immediately transfer to a spice grinder or mortar and grind finely.

For this quantity of beans, use 1 can (14 to 19 oz/398 to 540 mL) drained and rinsed, or cook 1 cup (250 mL) dried beans (see Basic Beans, page 239).

If you are halving this recipe, be sure to use a small (1½ to 3½ quart) slow cooker.

Make Ahead

Complete Steps 1 and 3. Cover and refrigerate tomato and chile mixtures separately for up to 2 days, being aware that the chile mixture will lose some of its vibrancy if held for this long. (For best results, rehydrate the chiles while the dish is cooking or no sooner than the night before you plan to cook.) When you're ready to cook, complete the recipe.

Easy Vegetable Chili

Not only is this chili easy to make, it is also delicious. The mild dried chiles add interesting flavor, along with a nice bit of heat. Only add the jalapeño if you're a heat seeker.

● **Medium to large (3½ to 5 quart) slow cooker**

1 tbsp	oil	15 mL
2	onions, chopped	2
4	stalks celery, thinly sliced	4
4	cloves garlic, minced	4
2 tsp	ground cumin (see Tips, page 199)	10 mL
2 tsp	dried oregano, crumbled	10 mL
1 tsp	salt	5 mL
1	can (14 oz/398 mL) diced tomatoes with juice	1
2 cups	cooked dried or canned red kidney beans, drained and rinsed (see Basic Beans, page 239)	500 mL
2	dried New Mexico, ancho or guajillo chile peppers	2
2 cups	boiling water	500 mL
1 cup	coarsely chopped cilantro, leaves and stems	250 mL
1 cup	vegetable broth, tomato juice or water	250 mL
1	jalapeño pepper, coarsely chopped, optional	1
2 cups	corn kernels	500 mL
1	green bell pepper, chopped	1

1. In a skillet, heat oil over medium heat. Add onions and celery and cook, stirring, until softened, about 5 minutes. Add garlic, cumin, oregano and salt and cook, stirring, for 1 minute. Add tomatoes with juice and bring to a boil. Transfer to slow cooker stoneware.

2. Add beans and stir well. Cover and cook on Low for 6 hours or on High for 3 hours, until hot and bubbly.

3. About an hour before the recipe is finished cooking, in a heatproof bowl, soak dried chiles in boiling water for 30 minutes, weighing down with a cup to ensure they remain submerged. Drain and discard soaking liquid. Discard stems and chop peppers coarsely. Transfer to a blender. Add cilantro, broth, and jalapeño, if using. Purée.

4. Add chile mixture to stoneware and stir well. Add corn and bell pepper and stir well. Cover and cook on High for 20 minutes, until pepper is tender and mixture is hot and bubbly.

Tips

For the best flavor, toast cumin seeds and grind them yourself. *To toast seeds:* Place in a dry skillet over medium heat and cook, stirring, until fragrant about 3 minutes. Immediately transfer to a spice grinder or mortar and grind finely.

For this quantity of beans, use 1 can (14 to 19 oz/398 to 540 mL) drained and rinsed, or cook 1 cup (250 mL) dried beans (see Basic Beans, page 239).

If you are halving this recipe, be sure to use a small (1½ to 3½ quart) slow cooker.

Make Ahead

Chop jalapeño and bell peppers and shred cheese. Cover and refrigerate. Complete Step 1. Cover and refrigerate for up to 2 days. When you're ready to cook, complete the recipe.

Light Chili

I love the rich, creamy sauce and the flavors of the spices in this luscious chili. Serve this with a good dollop of sour cream or a non-dairy alternative, your favorite salsa and a sprinkling of chopped cilantro.

● **Medium to large (3½ to 5 quart) slow cooker**

1 tbsp	oil	15 mL
2	onions, finely chopped	2
6	cloves garlic, minced	6
1 tbsp	ground cumin (see Tips, left)	15 mL
1 tbsp	dried oregano	15 mL
1 tsp	salt	5 mL
1 tsp	cracked black peppercorns	5 mL
1	can (28 oz/796 mL) tomatoes with juice, chopped	1
2 cups	vegetable broth	500 mL
8 oz	portobello mushrooms, stems removed, cut into 1-inch (2.5 cm) cubes	250 g
2 cups	drained cooked white kidney beans, (see Tips, left)	500 mL
1 to 2	jalapeño peppers, finely chopped	1 to 2
2	green bell peppers, diced	2
1½ cups	shredded Monterey Jack cheese or vegan alternative	375 mL
1	can (4½ oz/127 mL) diced mild green chiles, drained	1
	Sour cream or vegan alternative	
	Salsa	
	Finely chopped cilantro	

1. In a skillet, heat oil over medium heat. Add onions and cook, stirring, until softened, about 3 minutes. Add garlic, cumin, oregano, salt and peppercorns and cook, stirring, for 1 minute. Add tomatoes with juice and broth and bring to a boil. Cook, stirring, until liquid is reduced by one-third, about 5 minutes. Transfer to slow cooker stoneware.

2. Add mushrooms and beans and stir to combine. Cover and cook on Low for 6 hours or on High for 3 hours, until mixture is hot and bubbly. Stir in jalapeño peppers, bell peppers, cheese and mild green chiles. Cover and cook on High for 20 minutes, until peppers are tender and cheese is melted. Ladle into bowls and top with sour cream, salsa and chopped cilantro.

Hominy-Spiked Light Chili

Combining a whole grain (hominy) with a legume (white beans), this tasty chili provides a complete protein. It's also delicious and a meal in itself.

Tips

To sweat eggplant: Place cubed eggplant in a colander, sprinkle liberally with salt, toss well and set aside for 30 minutes to 1 hour. If time is short, blanch the pieces for a minute or two in heavily salted water. In either case, rinse thoroughly in fresh cold water and, using your hands, squeeze out excess moisture. Pat dry with paper towels and it's ready for cooking.

For the best flavor, toast cumin seeds and grind them yourself. *To toast seeds:* Place in a dry skillet over medium heat and cook, stirring, until fragrant about 3 minutes. Immediately transfer to a spice grinder or mortar and grind finely.

For this quantity of beans, use 1 can (14 to 19 oz/398 to 540 mL) drained and rinsed, or cook 1 cup (250 mL) dried beans (see Basic Beans, page 239).

If you are halving this recipe, be sure to use a small (1½ to 3½ quart) slow cooker.

Make Ahead

Complete Steps 1 and 2. Cover and refrigerate for up to 2 days. When you're ready to cook, complete the recipe.

● **Medium to large (3½ to 5 quart) slow cooker**

1	large eggplant, peeled, cubed (2 inches/5 cm), sweated and drained of excess moisture (see Tips, left)	1
2 tbsp	oil (approx.)	25 mL
2	onions, finely chopped	2
4	cloves garlic, minced	4
1 tbsp	ground cumin (see Tips, left)	15 mL
2 tsp	dried oregano	10 mL
1	can (14 oz/398 mL) crushed tomatoes	1
2 cups	vegetable broth	500 mL
2 cups	drained cooked white beans, such as navy or cannellini (see Tips, left)	500 mL
1	can (15 oz/425 mL) hominy, drained and rinsed	1
1	green bell pepper, seeded and diced	1
1	jalapeño pepper, seeded and minced	1
1½ cups	shredded Monterey Jack cheese or vegan alternative	375 mL
	Shredded lettuce, optional	
	Sliced avocado, optional	

1. In a skillet, heat oil over medium-high heat. Add eggplant, in batches, and cook, stirring, until lightly browned. Transfer to slow cooker stoneware as completed.

2. Reduce heat to medium. Add onions to pan, adding more oil if necessary, and cook, stirring, until softened, about 3 minutes. Add garlic, cumin and oregano and cook, stirring, for 1 minute. Add tomatoes and bring to a boil. Transfer to slow cooker stoneware.

3. Add vegetable broth, beans and hominy and stir well. Cover and cook on Low for 6 hours or on High for 3 hours, until hot and bubbly. Add bell pepper and jalapeño. Cover and cook on High for 20 minutes, until peppers are tender. Stir in cheese. Serve garnished with lettuce and/or avocado, if using.

Vegan Friendly

Can Be Halved

Tips

Use the type of barley you prefer — pearled, pot or whole. Whole (also known as hulled) barley is the most nutritious form of the grain.

For this quantity of beans, use 1 can (14 to 19 oz/398 to 540 mL) drained and rinsed, or cook 1 cup (250 mL) dried beans (see Basic Beans, page 239).

Use your favorite chili powder blend in this recipe or, if you prefer, ground ancho, New Mexico or guajillo peppers.

I prefer the slightly smoky flavor that a chipotle pepper in adobo sauce lends to this recipe, but it's not to everyone's taste. If you're unfamiliar with the flavor, add just half a pepper and a bit of the sauce. If you're a heat seeker, use a whole one and increase the quantity of adobo sauce.

If you are halving this recipe, be sure to use a small ($1\frac{1}{2}$ to $3\frac{1}{2}$ quart) slow cooker.

Make Ahead

Complete Step 1. Cover and refrigerate overnight for up to 2 days. When you're ready to cook, complete the recipe. Because the barley soaks up liquid on sitting, add an extra $\frac{1}{2}$ cup (125 mL) of broth or water before cooking.

Barley and Sweet Potato Chili

This unusual chili has great flavor and with the addition of optional toppings, such as sliced roasted pepper strips (either bottled or freshly roasted) and cilantro, it can be enhanced and varied to suit many tastes. I like to serve this with a simple green salad topped with sliced avocado.

● **Medium to large ($3\frac{1}{2}$ to 5 quart) slow cooker**

1 tbsp	oil	15 mL
2	onions, finely chopped	2
2	cloves garlic, minced	2
1 tbsp	ground cumin (see Tips, opposite)	15 mL
1 tsp	dried oregano, crumbled	5 mL
1 tsp	salt	5 mL
$\frac{1}{2}$ tsp	cracked black peppercorns	2 mL
$\frac{1}{2}$ cup	barley (see Tips, left)	125 mL
1	can (28 oz/796 mL) tomatoes with juice, coarsely crushed	1
1 cup	vegetable broth	250 mL
2	medium sweet potatoes, peeled and cut into 1-inch (2.5 cm) cubes	2
2 cups	drained cooked red kidney or black beans (see Tips, left)	500 mL
1 tbsp	chili powder, dissolved in 2 tbsp (25 mL) lime juice (see Tips, left)	15 mL
1	jalapeño pepper, minced, or $\frac{1}{2}$ to 1 canned chipotle pepper in adobo sauce, minced (see Tips, left)	1
1	green bell pepper, diced, optional	1
	Sliced roasted bell peppers, optional	
	Finely chopped cilantro	

1. In a large skillet, heat oil over medium heat. Add onions and cook, stirring, until softened, about 3 minutes. Add garlic, cumin, oregano, salt and peppercorns and cook, stirring, for 1 minute. Add barley and toss to coat. Add tomatoes with juice and bring to a boil. Transfer to slow cooker stoneware.

2. Add vegetable broth, sweet potatoes and beans. Cover and cook on Low for 6 to 8 hours or on High for 3 to 4 hours, until barley and sweet potatoes are tender. Stir in chili powder solution, jalapeño pepper, and bell pepper, if using. Cover and cook on High for 20 to 30 minutes, until flavors have melded and bell pepper is tender. To serve, ladle into soup plates and garnish with roasted pepper strips, if using, and cilantro.

Vegan Friendly

Can Be Halved

Tips

For the best flavor, toast cumin seeds and grind them yourself. *To toast seeds:* Place in a dry skillet over medium heat and cook, stirring, until fragrant, about 3 minutes. Immediately transfer to a spice grinder or mortar and grind finely.

For this quantity of beans, use 2 cans (14 to 19 oz/398 to 540 mL) drained and rinsed and save excess for another use, or cook 1½ cups (375 mL) dried beans (see Basic Beans, page 239).

If you are halving this recipe, be sure to use a small (1½ to 3½ quart) slow cooker.

Make Ahead

Complete Steps 1 and 3. Cover and refrigerate vegetable and chile mixtures separately for up to 2 days. (The chile mixture will lose some of its vibrancy.) For best results, complete Step 3 while the recipe is cooking. When you're ready to cook, complete the recipe.

Orange-Spiked Black Bean Chili

If you're looking for a light and easy chili that is a bit different from the norm, try this. The hint of orange combines beautifully with the chiles. If you're a heat seeker, add an extra jalapeño.

● **Medium to large (3½ to 5 quart) slow cooker**

1 tbsp	oil	15 mL
2	onions, finely chopped	2
4	carrots, peeled and diced	4
2	stalks celery, diced	2
4	cloves garlic, minced	4
1 tbsp	ground cumin (see Tips, left)	15 mL
2 tsp	dried oregano	10 mL
1 tsp	salt	5 mL
1 tsp	cracked black peppercorns	5 mL
1 tbsp	finely grated orange zest	15 mL
2 cups	vegetable broth	500 mL
3 cups	drained cooked black beans (see Tips, left)	750 mL
1	sweet potato, peeled and cut into ½-inch (1 cm) cubes	1
2	dried ancho, New Mexico or guajillo chile peppers	2
½ cup	freshly squeezed orange juice (about 1 orange)	125 mL
1	jalapeño pepper, seeded and coarsely chopped, optional	1
¼ cup	chopped cilantro	50 mL
1	green bell pepper, seeded and diced	1

1. In a skillet, heat oil over medium heat. Add onions, carrots and celery and cook, stirring, until softened, about 7 minutes. Add garlic, cumin, oregano, salt, peppercorns and orange zest and cook, stirring, for 1 minute. Stir in vegetable broth. Transfer to slow cooker stoneware.

2. Add beans and sweet potato and stir well. Cover and cook on Low for 6 hours or on High for 3 hours, until mixture is hot and bubbly.

3. About an hour before the chili has finished cooking, in a heatproof bowl, soak dried chile peppers in boiling water for 30 minutes, weighing down with a cup to ensure they remain submerged. Drain and discard soaking water. Discard stems and chop peppers coarsely. Transfer to a blender. Add orange juice, jalapeño, if using and cilantro. Purée.

4. Add chile mixture to stoneware and stir well. Stir in bell pepper. Cover and cook on High for 20 minutes, until pepper is tender and flavors meld.

Tips

For the best flavor, toast cumin seeds and grind them yourself. *To toast seeds:* Place in a dry skillet over medium heat and cook, stirring, until fragrant, about 3 minutes. Immediately transfer to a spice grinder or mortar and grind finely.

For this quantity of beans, use 1 can (14 to 19 oz/398 to 540 mL) drained and rinsed, or cook 1 cup (250 mL) dried beans (see Basic Beans, page 239).

Substitute cranberry, Romano or red kidney beans for the pinto beans, if desired.

If you are halving this recipe, be sure to use a small (1½ to 3½ quart) slow cooker.

Two-Bean Chili with Zucchini

This delicious version of vegetarian chili combines fresh green beans with dried beans and adds corn kernels and sautéed zucchini for a tasty finish.

● **Medium to large (4 to 5 quart) slow cooker**

2	small zucchini, cut into ½-inch (1 cm) lengths and sweated	2
1 tbsp	oil	15 mL
2	onions, finely chopped	2
2	cloves garlic, minced	2
1 tbsp	ground cumin (see Tips, left)	15 mL
1 tbsp	dried oregano	15 mL
1 tsp	salt	5 mL
½ tsp	cracked black peppercorns	2 mL
1	can (28 oz/796 mL) tomatoes with juice, coarsely chopped	1
2 cups	vegetable broth	500 mL
2 cups	green beans, cut into 2-inch (5 cm) lengths	500 mL
2 cups	drained cooked pinto beans (see Tips, left)	500 mL
2	dried ancho chile peppers	2
2 cups	boiling water	500 mL
1	jalapeño pepper, seeded and coarsely chopped, optional	1
½ cup	coarsely chopped cilantro	125 mL
1½ cups	corn kernels	375 mL
1 cup	shredded Monterey Jack cheese or vegan alternative, optional	250 mL
	Sour cream or vegan alternative, optional	

1. In a skillet, heat oil over medium heat. Add zucchini and cook, stirring, until it begins to brown. Transfer to a bowl using a slotted spoon, cover and refrigerate.

2. In same skillet, add onions and cook, stirring, until softened, about 3 minutes. Add garlic, cumin, oregano, salt and peppercorns and cook, stirring, for 1 minute. Add tomatoes with juice and bring to a boil. Transfer to slow cooker stoneware.

3. Add vegetable broth, green beans and pinto beans and stir to combine. Cover and cook on Low for 6 hours or on High for 3 hours, until mixture is hot and bubbly.

Make Ahead

Complete Steps 1, 2 and 4. Cover and refrigerate zucchini, tomato mixture and chile mixture separately for up to 2 days. (The chile mixture will lose some of its vibrancy. For best results, complete Step 4 while the recipe is cooking.) When you're ready to cook, complete the recipe.

4. About an hour before the chili has finished cooking, in a heatproof bowl, soak ancho chiles in boiling water for 30 minutes, weighing down with a cup to ensure they remain submerged. Drain and set soaking water aside. Discard stems and chop peppers coarsely. Transfer to a blender. Add jalapeño, if using, cilantro and $1/2$ cup (125 mL) of the chile soaking liquid (discard remainder). Purée.

5. Add chile mixture to stoneware and stir well. Stir in corn and reserved zucchini. Cover and cook on High for 30 minutes, until corn is tender and flavors meld. Ladle into bowls and garnish with cheese or sour cream, if using.

Vegan Friendly

Can Be Halved

Tips

I like to make this with collard greens but other dark leafy greens such as kale work well, too.

The smoked paprika makes the dish more robust and adds a pleasant hint of smokiness.

If halving this recipe, be sure to use a small to medium (2 to 3½ quart) slow cooker.

Make Ahead

Complete Steps 1 and 2. Cover and refrigerate for up to 2 days. When you're ready to cook, complete the recipe.

Red Beans and Greens

Few meals could be more healthful than this delicious combination of hot leafy greens over flavorful beans. If you're cooking for a smaller group, make the full quantity of beans, spoon off what is needed, and serve with the appropriate quantity of cooked greens. Refrigerate or freeze the leftover beans for another meal.

● **Large (approx. 5 quart) slow cooker**

2 cups	dried kidney beans	500 mL
1 tbsp	oil	15 mL
2	onions, finely chopped	2
2	stalks celery, finely chopped	2
4	cloves garlic, minced	4
1 tsp	dried oregano	5 mL
1 tsp	salt	5 mL
½ tsp	cracked black peppercorns	2 mL
½ tsp	dried thyme	2 mL
2	bay leaves	2
¼ tsp	ground allspice, or 6 whole allspice, tied in a piece of cheesecloth	1 mL
4 cups	vegetable broth	1 L
1 tsp	smoked paprika, dissolved in 1 tbsp (15 mL) boiling water, optional	5 mL

Greens

8 cups	greens, thoroughly washed, stems removed and chopped	2 L
	Butter or olive oil	
1 tbsp	balsamic vinegar	15 mL
	Salt and freshly ground black pepper	

1. Soak beans according to either method in Basic Beans (see page 239). Drain and rinse and set aside.

2. In a skillet, heat oil over medium heat. Add onions and celery and cook, stirring, until softened, about 5 minutes. Add garlic, oregano, salt, peppercorns, thyme, allspice and bay leaves and cook, stirring, for 1 minute. Add 2 cups (500 mL) of the broth and stir well. Transfer to slow cooker stoneware.

3. Add remaining 2 cups (500 mL) of broth and soaked beans to stoneware. Cover and cook on Low for 8 to 10 hours or on High for 4 to 5 hours, until beans are tender. Discard bay leaves, and allspice in cheesecloth, if using. Stir in smoked paprika solution, if using.

4. *Greens:* Steam greens until tender, about 10 minutes for collards. Toss with butter and balsamic vinegar. Season to taste with salt and pepper. Add to beans and stir to combine. Serve immediately.

Vegan Friendly

Can Be Halved

Tips

If you prefer, use coconut oil for softening the vegetables. It will add a pleasant nutty flavor to the dish.

For the best flavor, toast cumin and coriander seeds and grind them yourself. *To toast seeds:* Place in a dry skillet over medium heat and cook, stirring, until fragrant, about 3 minutes. Immediately transfer to a spice grinder or mortar and grind finely.

Can sizes vary from location to location. If your supermarket carries 19-oz (540 mL) cans of diced tomatoes, by all means substitute for the 14-oz (398 mL) called for in the recipe.

If you are halving this recipe, be sure to use a small (1¹⁄₂ to 3¹⁄₂ quart) slow cooker.

Make Ahead

Complete Steps 1 and 2. Cover and refrigerate for up to 2 days. When you're ready to cook, complete the recipe.

Indian Peas and Beans

Simple yet delicious served with Indian bread and a cucumber salad, this Indian-inspired dish makes a great weeknight dinner. It also makes a nice addition to a multi-dish Indian meal.

● **Medium to large (3¹⁄₂ to 5 quart) slow cooker**

1 cup	yellow split peas, rinsed	250 mL
1 tbsp	oil (see Tips, left)	15 mL
2	onions, finely chopped	2
4	cloves garlic, minced	4
1 tbsp	minced gingerroot	15 mL
1 tbsp	ground cumin (see Tips, left)	15 mL
2 tsp	ground coriander	10 mL
1 tsp	ground turmeric	5 mL
1 tsp	cracked black peppercorns	5 mL
2	bay leaves	2
1	can (14 oz/398 mL) diced tomatoes with juice (see Tips, left)	1
2 cups	vegetable broth	500 mL
2 cups	frozen sliced green beans	500 mL
¹⁄₄ tsp	cayenne pepper, dissolved in 1 tbsp (15 mL) freshly squeezed lemon juice	1 mL
1 cup	coconut milk, optional	250 mL
¹⁄₂ cup	finely chopped cilantro	125 mL

1. In a large saucepan, combine peas with 6 cups (1.5 L) cold water. Bring to a boil and boil rapidly for 3 minutes. Remove from heat and set aside for 1 hour. Rinse thoroughly under cold water, drain and set aside.

2. In a large skillet, heat oil over medium heat. Add onions and cook, stirring, until softened, about 3 minutes. Add garlic, ginger, cumin, coriander, turmeric, peppercorns and bay leaves and cook, stirring, for 1 minute. Add tomatoes with juice and reserved split peas and bring to a boil. Transfer to slow cooker stoneware.

3. Add vegetable broth and green beans and stir well. Cover and cook on Low for 8 to 10 hours or on High for 4 to 5 hours, until peas are tender. Stir in cayenne solution, and coconut milk, if using. Add cilantro and stir well. Cover and cook on High for 20 minutes, until heated through. Discard bay leaves.

Tomato Dal with Spinach

Tips

For the best flavor, toast cumin and coriander seeds and grind them yourself. *To toast seeds:* Place in a dry skillet over medium heat and cook, stirring, until fragrant, about 3 minutes. Immediately transfer to a spice grinder or mortar and grind finely.

If halving this recipe, be sure to use a small (approx. 3 quart) slow cooker.

Make Ahead

Complete Steps 1 and 2. Cover and refrigerate for up to 2 days. When you're ready to cook, complete the recipe.

Variation

If you prefer, substitute 2 parsnips for 2 of the carrots.

This mildly spiced but tasty dal is delicious over hot cooked rice or as a substantial side dish. Add the yogurt, if you prefer a creamy finish.

● **Large (approx. 5 quart) slow cooker**

2 cups	yellow split peas, rinsed	500 mL
1 tbsp	oil	15 mL
1	onion, finely chopped	1
6	carrots, peeled and diced	6
6	cloves garlic, finely chopped	6
1 tbsp	minced gingerroot	15 mL
1 tbsp	ground cumin (see Tips, left)	15 mL
1 tbsp	ground coriander	15 mL
1 tsp	salt	5 mL
1 tsp	cracked black peppercorns	5 mL
1	can (28 oz/796 mL) tomatoes with juice, coarsely chopped	1
4 cups	vegetable broth	1 L
1 tsp	curry powder, dissolved in 1 tbsp (15 mL) freshly squeezed lemon juice	5 mL
8 oz	trimmed fresh spinach leaves (about 8 cups/2 L) or 1 package (10 oz/300 g) frozen spinach, thawed	250 g
	Plain yogurt or vegan alternative, optional	

1. In a large saucepan, combine peas with 8 cups (2 L) cold water. Bring to a boil. Reduce heat and boil for 25 minutes or until peas are just tender. Drain.

2. Meanwhile, in a skillet, heat oil over medium heat. Add onion and carrots and cook, stirring, until softened, about 7 minutes. Add garlic, ginger, cumin, coriander, salt and peppercorns and cook, stirring, for 1 minute. Add tomatoes with juice and bring to a boil, breaking up with a spoon. Transfer to slow cooker stoneware. Add vegetable broth and reserved split peas and stir to combine.

3. Cover and cook on Low for 8 hours or on High for 4 hours, until peas are soft. Stir in curry powder solution. Add spinach, in batches, stirring to submerge each before adding the next. Cover and cook on High for 20 minutes, until spinach is cooked and mixture is bubbly. Ladle into bowls and drizzle with yogurt, if using.

Vegan Friendly

Can Be Halved

Tips

To prepare fennel: Before removing the core, chop off the top shoots (which resemble celery) and discard. If desired, save the feathery green fronds to use as a garnish. If the outer sections of the bulb seem old and dry, peel them with a vegetable peeler before using.

Toasting fennel seeds intensifies their flavor. *To toast fennel seeds*: Place in a dry skillet over medium heat and stir until fragrant, about 3 minutes. Immediately transfer to a mortar or spice grinder and grind.

For this quantity of peas, use 1 can (14 to 19 oz/398 to 540 mL) drained and rinsed black-eyed peas, or cook 1 cup (250 mL) dried peas (see Basic Beans, page 239).

You can use any kind of paprika in this recipe: Regular; hot, which produces a nicely peppery version; or smoked, which adds a delicious note of smokiness. If you have regular paprika and would like a bit a heat, dissolve ¼ tsp (1 mL) cayenne pepper in the lemon juice along with the paprika.

If you are halving this recipe, see Tips, page 210.

Make Ahead

Complete Step 1. Cover and refrigerate for up to 2 days. When you're ready to cook, complete the recipe.

Peas and Greens

This delicious combination of black-eyed peas and greens is a great dish for busy weeknights. Just add some whole-grain bread.

● **Medium to large (3½ to 5 quart) slow cooker**

1 tbsp	oil	15 mL
2	onions, finely chopped	2
1	bulb fennel, trimmed, cored and thinly sliced on the vertical (see Tips, left)	1
4	cloves garlic, minced	4
½ tsp	salt, or to taste	2 mL
½ tsp	cracked black peppercorns	2 mL
¼ tsp	fennel seeds, toasted and ground (see Tips, left)	1 mL
1	can (14 oz/398 mL) diced tomatoes with juice	1
2 cups	drained cooked black-eyed peas (see Tips, left)	500 mL
1 tsp	paprika, dissolved in 2 tbsp (25 mL) freshly squeezed lemon juice (see Tips, left)	5 mL
4 cups	chopped spinach or Swiss chard (about 1 bunch), stems removed	1 L

1. In a skillet, heat oil over medium heat. Add onions and fennel and cook, stirring, until fennel is softened, about 5 minutes. Add garlic, salt, peppercorns and fennel seeds and cook, stirring, for 1 minute. Add tomatoes with juice and bring to a boil. Transfer to slow cooker stoneware.

2. Stir in peas. Cover and cook on Low for 8 hours or on High for 4 hours, until peas are tender. Stir in paprika solution. Add spinach, in batches, stirring after each to submerge the leaves in the liquid. Cover and cook on High for 20 minutes, until spinach is tender.

Vegan Friendly

Can Be Halved

Tips

For the best flavor, toast coriander and cumin seeds and grind them yourself. *To toast seeds:* Place in a dry skillet over medium heat and cook, stirring, until fragrant, about 3 minutes. Immediately transfer to a spice grinder or mortar and grind finely.

You can use fresh or canned tomatoes in this recipe. If using canned tomatoes, drain them thoroughly before chopping.

For this quantity of chickpeas, use 2 cans (14 to 19 oz/398 to 540 mL) drained and rinsed, or cook 2 cups (500 mL) dried chickpeas (see Basic Beans, page 239).

If you are halving this recipe, be sure to use a small (1½ to 3½ quart) slow cooker.

Make Ahead

Complete Step 1 and refrigerate for up to 2 days. When you're ready to cook, complete the recipe.

Gingery Chickpeas in Spicy Tomato Gravy

This zesty stew can be served as a main course or as a rich side dish. At our house, we like to eat it with hot naan or pita bread and a cool cucumber salad.

● **Medium to large (3½ to 5 quart) slow cooker**

1 tbsp	oil	15 mL
2	onions, finely chopped	2
4	cloves garlic, finely chopped	4
2 tbsp	minced gingerroot	25 mL
2 tsp	ground coriander (see Tips, left)	10 mL
1 tsp	ground cumin	5 mL
1 tsp	salt	5 mL
½ tsp	cracked black peppercorns	2 mL
2 tsp	balsamic vinegar	10 mL
2 cups	coarsely chopped canned or fresh tomatoes (see Tips, left)	500 mL
4 cups	drained cooked chickpeas (see Tips, left)	1 L
	Chopped green onion, optional	

1. In a skillet, heat oil over medium heat. Add onions and cook, stirring, until they begin to brown, about 10 minutes. Add garlic, ginger, coriander, cumin, salt and peppercorns and cook, stirring, for 1 minute. Add balsamic vinegar and tomatoes and bring to a boil. Transfer to slow cooker stoneware.

2. Add chickpeas. Cover and cook on Low for 6 to 8 hours or on High for 3 to 4 hours, until hot and bubbly. Garnish with chopped green onion, if using.

Tips

For this quantity of chickpeas, use 2 cans (14 to 19 oz/398 to 540 mL) drained and rinsed, reserve the excess, or cook 1½ cups (375 mL) dried beans (see Basic Beans, page 239).

Harissa is a North African condiment made from hot peppers and various seasonings. It is available in specialty food stores. *To make your own harissa:* In a mini food processor, combine 3 dried red chile peppers (reconstituted in boiling water for 30 minutes), 2 tsp (10 mL) each toasted caraway, coriander and cumin seeds, 2 reconstituted sun-dried tomatoes, 4 cloves garlic, 2 tbsp (25 mL) freshly squeezed lemon juice, 1 tbsp (15 mL) sweet paprika and ½ tsp (2 mL) salt and process until combined. Add 3 tbsp (45 mL) extra virgin olive oil and process until smooth. Store, covered, in the refrigerator for up to 1 month, covering the paste with a bit of olive oil every time you use it. Makes about ⅓ cup (75 mL).

If you are halving this recipe, be sure to use a small (1½ to 3½ quart) slow cooker.

Make Ahead

Complete Step 1. Cover and refrigerate for up to 2 days. When you're ready to cook, complete the recipe.

Spicy Chickpeas with Okra

This tasty combination, which is Moroccan inspired, makes a nice main course accompanied by salad or a side. It is also a great dish for a buffet. The flavors are deep and deliciously different: hints of cumin and ginger and a sparkle of harissa-induced heat.

● **Medium to large (3½ to 5 quart) slow cooker**

1 tbsp	olive oil	15 mL
2	onions, finely chopped	2
4	cloves garlic, minced	4
1 tbsp	minced gingerroot	15 mL
1 tbsp	ground cumin (see Tips, page 214)	15 mL
1 tsp	salt	5 mL
1 tsp	crushed black peppercorns	5 mL
1 cup	vegetable broth	250 mL
3 cups	drained cooked chickpeas (see Tips, left)	750 mL
2 cups	trimmed sliced (½ inch/1 cm) okra	500 mL
1 tsp	harissa (see Tips, left)	5 mL

1. In a skillet, heat oil over medium heat. Add onions and cook, stirring, until softened, about 3 minutes. Add garlic, ginger, cumin, salt and peppercorns and cook, stirring, for 1 minute. Add vegetable broth and bring to a boil. Transfer to slow cooker stoneware.

2. Stir in chickpeas. Cover and cook on Low for 6 hours or on High for 3 hours. Stir in okra and harissa. Cover and cook on High for 20 minutes, until okra is tender.

Vegan Friendly

Can Be Halved

Tips

I use Italian San Marzano tomatoes when making this dish. They are particularly luscious and rich. If you're using domestic tomatoes, you may want to add 1 tbsp (15 mL) of tomato paste along with the tomatoes to ensure that the tomato flavor has enough intensity to stand up to the smoked paprika.

For this quantity of chickpeas, use 2 cans (14 to 19 oz/398 to 540 mL) drained and rinsed and reserve the excess, or cook 1½ cups (375 mL) dried chickpeas (see Basic Beans, page 239).

Use hot or sweet smoked paprika to suit your taste. Although I love its flavor, I find smoked paprika can easily overwhelm a dish, so I advise starting with 1 tsp (5 mL) and increasing the quantity, if necessary, to suit your taste.

If you are halving this recipe, be sure to use a small (1½ to 3½ quart) slow cooker.

Make Ahead

Complete Step 1. Cover and refrigerate for up to 2 days. When you're ready to cook, complete the recipe.

Smoky Chickpeas

Although this dish is very easy to make, the results are quite delicious. Serve it as a centerpiece of a meal with a vegetable side or over a whole grain such as polenta or wheat berries.

● **Medium (approx. 4 quart) slow cooker**

1 tbsp	oil	15 mL
2	onions, chopped	2
4	cloves garlic, minced	4
1 tsp	dried thyme	5 mL
1 tsp	salt	5 mL
1 tsp	cracked black peppercorns	5 mL
1	can (14 oz/398 mL) tomatoes with juice (see Tips, left)	1
3 cups	drained cooked chickpeas (see Tips, left)	750 mL
1 to 2 tsp	smoked paprika (see Tips, left)	5 to 10 mL

1. In a skillet, heat oil over medium heat. Add onions and cook, stirring, until softened, about 3 minutes. Add garlic, thyme, salt and peppercorns and cook, stirring, for 1 minute. Add tomatoes with juice and bring a boil. Transfer to slow cooker stoneware.

2. Stir in chickpeas. Cover and cook on Low for 6 hours or on High for 3 hours, until hot and bubbly. Stir in paprika to taste. Cover and cook on High for 15 minutes to meld flavors.

Tips

For the best flavor, toast cumin seeds and grind them yourself. *To toast seeds:* Place seeds in a dry skillet over medium heat and cook, stirring, until fragrant, about 3 minutes. Immediately transfer to a spice grinder or mortar and grind finely.

For this quantity of chickpeas, use 1 can (14 to 19 oz/398 to 540 mL) drained and rinsed, or cook 1 cup (250 mL) dried chickpeas (see Basic Beans, page 239).

If you are halving this recipe, be sure to use a small ($1\frac{1}{2}$ to $3\frac{1}{2}$ quart) slow cooker.

Make Ahead

Complete Step 1 but do not add the potato. Cover and refrigerate for up to 2 days. When you're ready to cook, shred the potato, add to stoneware and complete the recipe.

Spanish-Style Chickpeas with Spinach

Served with salad, this tasty mixture makes a great main course. It is also a nice addition to a buffet.

- **Small to medium (2 to 4 quart) slow cooker**

1 tbsp	olive oil	15 mL
2	onions, finely chopped	2
6	cloves garlic, minced	6
1 tbsp	ground cumin (see Tips, left)	15 mL
1 tsp	salt	5 mL
$\frac{1}{2}$ tsp	cracked black peppercorns	2 mL
Pinch	saffron threads, crumbled	Pinch
1	potato, peeled and shredded	1
2 cups	drained cooked chickpeas (see Tips, left)	500 mL
1 tbsp	sweet paprika	15 mL
1 tbsp	sherry vinegar	15 mL
1 tbsp	water	15 mL
6 cups	loosely packed spinach leaves (about 6 oz/175 g)	1.5 L

1. In a skillet, heat oil over medium heat. Add onions and cook, stirring, until softened, about 3 minutes. Add garlic, cumin, salt, peppercorns and saffron and cook, stirring, for 1 minute. Add potato and toss until coated. Transfer to slow cooker stoneware.

2. Stir in chickpeas. Cover and cook on Low for 6 hours or on High for 3 hours, until hot and bubbly.

3. In a small bowl, combine paprika, vinegar and water. Stir to blend. Add to stoneware and stir well. Add spinach, in batches, stirring after each to submerge the leaves in the liquid. Cover and cook on High for 10 minutes, until spinach is heated through.

Tips

I prefer a strong gingery flavor in this dish. If you're ginger-averse, reduce the amount.

For this quantity of chickpeas, use 1 can (14 to 19 oz/398 to 540 mL) drained and rinsed, or cook 1 cup (250 mL) dried chickpeas (see Basic Beans, page 239).

If halving this recipe, be sure to use a small (approx. 2 quart) slow cooker.

Make Ahead

Complete Step 1. Cover and refrigerate for up to 2 days. When you're ready to cook, complete the recipe.

Tagine of Squash and Chickpeas with Mushrooms

I love the unusual combination of flavorings in this dish. The tastes of the cinnamon and ginger really come through, and the bittersweet mixture of lemon and honey, with a sprinkling of currants, adds a perfect finish. Serve this over whole-grain couscous to complement the Middle Eastern flavors. Add spinach or Swiss chard to complete the meal.

● **Medium to large (3½ to 5 quart) slow cooker**

1 tbsp	oil	15 mL
1	onion, finely chopped	1
2	carrots, peeled and diced (about 1 cup/250 mL)	2
4	cloves garlic, minced	4
1	piece (2 inches/5 cm) cinnamon stick	1
2 tbsp	minced gingerroot (see Tips, left)	25 mL
1 tsp	ground turmeric	5 mL
½ tsp	salt	2 mL
½ tsp	cracked black peppercorns	2 mL
1	can (28 oz/796 mL) tomatoes with juice, coarsely chopped	1
3 cups	cubed peeled butternut squash or pumpkin (1 inch/2.5 cm cubes)	750 mL
2 cups	drained cooked chickpeas (see Tips, left)	500 mL
8 oz	cremini mushrooms, stemmed and halved	250 g
1 tbsp	liquid honey	15 mL
1 tbsp	freshly squeezed lemon juice	15 mL
¼ cup	currants, optional	50 mL

1. In a large skillet, heat oil over medium heat. Add onion and carrots and cook, stirring, until carrots are softened, about 7 minutes. Add garlic, cinnamon stick, ginger, turmeric, salt and peppercorns and cook, stirring, for 1 minute. Add tomatoes with juice and bring to a boil. Transfer to slow cooker stoneware.

2. Stir in squash, chickpeas and mushrooms. Cover and cook on Low for 8 hours or on High for 4 hours, until vegetables are tender. Discard cinnamon stick.

3. In a small bowl, combine honey and lemon juice. Add to slow cooker and stir well. When serving, sprinkle with currants, if using.

Eggplant Lentil Ragoût

This is a delicious combination of flavors and textures. Just add a green salad for a satisfying meal.

Tips

To sweat eggplant: Place cubed eggplant in a colander, sprinkle liberally with salt, toss well and set aside for 30 minutes to 1 hour. If time is short, blanch the pieces for a minute or two in heavily salted water. In either case, rinse thoroughly in fresh cold water and, using your hands, squeeze out excess moisture. Pat dry with paper towels and it's ready for cooking.

For the best flavor, toast cumin seeds and grind them yourself. *To toast seeds:* Place seeds in a dry skillet over medium heat and cook, stirring, until fragrant, about 3 minutes. Immediately transfer to a spice grinder or mortar and grind finely.

If you are halving this recipe, be sure to use a small (1½ to 3½ quart) slow cooker.

Make Ahead

Complete Step 1. Cover and refrigerate for up to 2 days. When you're ready to cook, complete the recipe.

• **Medium (approx. 4 quart) slow cooker**

1	medium eggplant (about 1 lb/500 g) peeled, cubed (2 inch/5 cm) and sweated (see Tips, left)	1
2 tbsp	olive oil (approx.)	25 mL
2	onions, finely chopped	2
4	cloves garlic, minced	4
1 tbsp	ground cumin (see Tips, left)	15 mL
1 tsp	finely grated lemon zest	5 mL
1 tsp	salt	5 mL
½ tsp	cracked black peppercorns	2 mL
1 cup	brown or green lentils, rinsed	250 mL
3 cups	vegetable broth	750 mL
1 tbsp	freshly squeezed lemon juice	15 mL
½ cup	finely chopped dill	125 mL

1. In a skillet, heat oil over medium-high heat. Add eggplant, in batches, and cook until browned, adding more oil as necessary. Transfer to slow cooker stoneware.

2. Add onions to pan, adding more oil, if necessary, and cook, stirring, until softened, about 3 minutes. Add garlic, cumin, lemon zest, salt and peppercorns and cook, stirring, for 1 minute. Add lentils and toss until coated. Transfer to slow cooker stoneware. Stir in broth.

3. Cover and cook on Low for 6 to 8 hours or on High for 3 to 4 hours, until lentils are tender. Stir in lemon juice and dill.

Fennel-Spiked Lentil Cobbler with Red Pepper and Goat Cheese

I love the flavors in this delicious casserole: the mild licorice flavor of the fennel combines beautifully with the hint of heat from the black peppercorns and the nicely acidic balsamic vinegar. The crisp crumbs provide texture and the goat cheese adds a pleasant bit of tang. Add a simple green salad to complete the meal.

- **Medium to large (4 to 5 quart) slow cooker (see Tips, left)**

1 tbsp	olive oil	15 mL
2	onions, diced	2
1	large fennel bulb, trimmed, cored and diced	1
4	cloves garlic, minced	4
1 tsp	dried thyme	5 mL
1 tsp	cracked black peppercorns (see Tips, left)	5 mL
½ tsp	salt (see Tips, left)	2 mL
1 cup	brown or green lentils, rinsed	250 mL
1 tbsp	balsamic vinegar	15 mL
3 cups	vegetable broth	750 mL
1	red bell pepper, seeded and diced	1
2 cups	fresh bread crumbs	500 mL
4 oz	soft goat cheese, crumbled	125 g

1. In a skillet, heat oil over medium heat. Add onions and fennel and cook, stirring, until softened, about 5 minutes. Add garlic, thyme, peppercorns and salt and cook, stirring, for 1 minute. Add lentils and toss until well coated. Stir in vinegar and vegetable broth and bring to a boil. Transfer to slow cooker stoneware.

2. Cover and cook on Low for 6 hours or on High for 3 hours, until lentils are tender. Stir in bell pepper. Cover and cook on High for 15 minutes, until pepper is tender.

3. Meanwhile, preheat broiler. In a bowl, combine bread crumbs and goat cheese. Stir until combined. Spread as best you can over lentil mixture and broil until crumbs and cheese begin to brown. Serve immediately.

Tips

For best results, toast and grind the cumin and coriander seeds yourself. *To toast seeds:* Place in a dry skillet over medium heat and cook, stirring, until fragrant, about 3 minutes. Immediately transfer to a spice grinder or mortar and grind finely.

If halving this recipe, be sure to use a small (approx. 2 quart) slow cooker.

Make Ahead

Complete Step 1. Cover and refrigerate for up to 2 days. When you're ready to cook, complete the recipe.

Indian-Spiced Lentils with Peppery Apricots

Although the flavors are exotic, this delicious mélange qualifies as comfort food. Savory lentils seasoned with spices that are traditionally associated with the East are punctuated by sweet chewy apricots sprinkled with piquant cayenne. It's a marriage made in heaven.

● **Medium (approx. 4 quarts) slow cooker**

1 tbsp	oil	15 mL
2	onions, finely chopped	2
4	stalks celery, diced	4
4	cloves garlic, minced	4
1 tbsp	minced gingerroot	15 mL
2 tsp	ground cumin (see Tips, left)	10 mL
2 tsp	ground coriander	10 mL
1 tsp	ground turmeric	5 mL
1	piece (2 inches/5 cm) cinnamon stick	1
1½ cups	brown or green lentils, rinsed	375 mL
4 cups	vegetable broth	1 L
1	sweet potato, peeled and diced	1
½ tsp	cayenne pepper	2 mL
1 cup	chopped dried apricots	250 mL
	Finely chopped fresh parsley	

1. In a skillet, heat oil over medium heat. Add onions and celery and cook, stirring, until softened, about 5 minutes. Add garlic, ginger, cumin, coriander, turmeric and cinnamon stick and cook, stirring, for 1 minute. Transfer to slow cooker stoneware. Stir in lentils and vegetable broth.

2. Add sweet potato and stir well. Cover and cook on Low for 6 to 8 hours or on High for 3 to 4 hours, until lentils are tender.

3. In a small bowl, sprinkle cayenne evenly over apricots. Add to stoneware and stir well. Cover and cook on High for 15 minutes to meld flavors. Discard cinnamon stick. Garnish with parsley.

Tips

I like to use some red lentils in this recipe because they dissolve into the liquid, producing a lusciously creamy result, but if you don't have any, use brown or green lentils for the total quantity.

If you don't have sun-dried tomatoes, substitute 1 tbsp (15 mL) tomato paste.

If you don't have harissa, make your own (page 215), or dissolve $\frac{1}{2}$ tsp (2 mL) cayenne pepper in 1 tbsp (15 mL) freshly squeezed lemon juice and stir in along with the red peppers.

If you are halving this recipe, be sure to use a small ($1\frac{1}{2}$ to $3\frac{1}{2}$ quart) slow cooker.

Make Ahead

Complete Step 1. Cover and refrigerate for up to 2 days. When you're ready to cook, complete the recipe.

Cumin-Laced Lentils with Sun-Dried Tomatoes and Roasted Peppers

I love the slightly Middle Eastern flavors that underscore this luscious dish. It is very forgiving. If you don't have sun-dried tomatoes, substitute tomato paste. As for harissa, substitute cayenne or make your own (see Tips, left).

● **Medium (approx. 4 quart) slow cooker**

1 tbsp	olive oil	15 mL
1	onion, finely chopped	1
2	stalks celery, diced	2
4	cloves garlic, minced	4
1 tbsp	ground cumin (see Tips, page 222)	15 mL
1 tbsp	ground coriander	15 mL
1 tsp	salt	5 mL
1 tsp	cracked black peppercorns	5 mL
1 cup	brown or green lentils, rinsed	250 mL
$\frac{1}{2}$ cup	red lentils, rinsed (see Tips, left)	125 mL
1	can (14 oz/398 mL) diced tomatoes with juice	1
2	finely chopped sun-dried tomatoes (see Tips, left)	2
2 cups	vegetable broth	500 mL
2	roasted red peppers, thinly sliced	2
1 to 2 tsp	harissa (see Tips, left)	5 to 10 mL
	Finely chopped cilantro	

1. In a skillet, heat oil over medium heat. Add onion and celery and cook, stirring, until softened, about 5 minutes. Add garlic, cumin, coriander, salt and peppercorns and cook, stirring, for 1 minute. Add brown and red lentils and toss until well coated with mixture. Add tomatoes with juice and sun-dried tomatoes. Transfer to slow cooker stoneware.

2. Stir in vegetable broth. Cover and cook on Low for 6 hours or on High for 3 hours, until lentils are tender. Add roasted peppers and harissa and stir well. Cover and cook on High for 15 minutes to meld flavors. Garnish with cilantro.

Tips

To poach eggs: In a deep skillet, bring about 2 inches (5 cm) lightly salted water to a boil over medium heat. Reduce heat to low. Break eggs into a measuring cup and, holding the cup close to the surface of the water, slip the eggs into the pan. Cook until whites are set and centers are still soft, 3 to 4 minutes. Remove with a slotted spoon.

If you are halving this recipe, be sure to use a small ($1\frac{1}{2}$ to $3\frac{1}{2}$ quart) slow cooker.

Make Ahead

Complete Step 1. Cover and refrigerate for up to 2 days. When you're ready to cook, complete the recipe.

Variation

Egg and Lentil Curry: Substitute 4 to 6 hard-cooked eggs for the poached. Peel them and cut into halves. Ladle the curry into a serving dish, arrange the eggs on top and garnish.

Poached Eggs on Spicy Lentils

This delicious combination is a great cold-weather dish. Add the chiles if you prefer a little spice and accompany with warm Indian bread, such as naan, and hot rice. The Egg and Lentil Curry (see Variation, left) is a great dish for a buffet table or as part of an Indian-themed meal.

● **Medium (approx. 4 quart) slow cooker**

1 tbsp	oil	15 mL
2	onions, finely chopped	2
1 tbsp	minced garlic	15 mL
1 tbsp	minced gingerroot	15 mL
1 tsp	ground coriander	5 mL
1 tsp	ground cumin	5 mL
1 tsp	cracked black peppercorns	5 mL
1 cup	red lentils, rinsed	250 mL
1	can (28 oz/796 mL) tomatoes with juice, coarsely chopped	1
2 cups	vegetable broth	500 mL
1 cup	coconut milk	250 mL
	Salt	
1	long green chile pepper or 2 Thai birds-eye chiles, finely chopped, optional	1
4	eggs	4
	Finely chopped fresh parsley, optional	

1. In a large skillet, heat oil over medium heat. Add onions and cook, stirring, until softened, about 3 minutes. Add garlic, ginger, coriander, cumin and peppercorns and cook, stirring, for 1 minute. Add lentils, tomatoes with juice and vegetable broth and bring to a boil. Transfer to slow cooker stoneware.

2. Cover and cook on Low for 6 hours or on High for 3 hours, until lentils are tender and mixture is bubbly. Stir in coconut milk, salt, to taste, and chile pepper, if using. Cover and cook for 20 to 30 minutes until heated through.

3. When ready to serve, ladle into soup bowls and top each serving with a poached egg (see Tip, left). Garnish with parsley, if using.

Lentil Sloppy Joes

Tip

Use 1 can (14 to 19 oz/398 to 540 mL) green or brown lentils, drained and rinsed, or cook 1 cup (250 mL) dried lentils (see Basic Beans, page 239).

Make Ahead

Complete Step 1. Cover and refrigerate for up to 2 days. When you're ready to cook, complete the recipe.

Here's a kids' favorite that grown-ups enjoy, too. It makes a great dinner for those busy nights when everyone is coming and going at different times. Leave the slow cooker on Low or Warm, the buns on the counter, the fixins' of salad in the fridge and let everyone help themselves.

● **Small to medium (1½ to 4 quart) slow cooker**

1 tbsp	oil	15 mL
1	onion, finely chopped	1
4	stalks celery, diced	4
4	cloves garlic, minced	4
½ tsp	dried oregano	2 mL
½ tsp	salt	2 mL
	Freshly ground black pepper	
½ cup	tomato ketchup	125 mL
¼ cup	water	50 mL
1 tbsp	balsamic vinegar	15 mL
1 tbsp	brown sugar	15 mL
1 tbsp	Dijon mustard	15 mL
2 cups	cooked brown or green lentils, drained and rinsed (see Tip, left)	500 mL
	Hot pepper sauce, optional	
	Toasted hamburger buns	

1. In a skillet, heat oil over medium heat. Add onion and celery and cook, stirring, until softened, about 5 minutes. Add garlic, oregano, salt, and pepper, to taste, and cook, stirring, for 1 minute. Stir in ketchup, water, balsamic vinegar, brown sugar and mustard. Transfer to slow cooker stoneware. Add lentils and stir well.

2. Cover and cook on Low for 6 hours or on High for 3 hours, until hot and bubbly. Add hot pepper sauce, to taste, if using. Ladle over hot toasted buns and serve immediately.

Tips

You can use leftover mashed potatoes in this recipe. If they have solidified after refrigeration, remove them from the container, place on a cutting board and cut into thin slices. Lay the slices as evenly as you can over top of the lentil mixture. They will soften as they heat in the hot liquid.

If you are halving this recipe, be sure to use a small ($1\frac{1}{2}$ to $3\frac{1}{2}$ quart) slow cooker.

Make Ahead

Complete Step 1 and make the mashed potatoes. Cover and refrigerate lentil mixture and potatoes separately for up to 2 days. When you're ready to cook, complete the recipe.

Variation

After the topping has been added, sprinkle 1 cup (250 mL) shredded Cheddar cheese evenly over the top.

Lentil Shepherd's Pie

This flavorful combination is the ultimate comfort food dish. Don't worry if you're serving fewer people — the leftovers taste great reheated.

● **Large (approx. 5 quart) oval slow cooker**

Filling

1 tbsp	oil	15 mL
2	onions, finely chopped	2
4	stalks celery, thinly sliced	4
2	large carrots, peeled and thinly sliced	2
1 tbsp	finely chopped garlic	15 mL
1 tsp	salt	5 mL
$\frac{1}{2}$ tsp	dried thyme	2 mL
$\frac{1}{2}$ tsp	cracked black peppercorns	2 mL
$1\frac{1}{2}$ cups	brown or green lentils, rinsed	375 mL
1	can (28 oz/796 mL) tomatoes with juice, coarsely chopped	1
2 cups	vegetable broth	500 mL

Topping

4 cups	mashed potatoes (see Tip, left)	1 L
1 cup	dry bread crumbs	250 mL

1. In a large skillet, heat oil over medium heat. Add onions, celery and carrots and cook, stirring, for 7 minutes, until vegetables are softened. Add garlic, salt, thyme and peppercorns and cook, stirring, for 1 minute. Add lentils and tomatoes with juice and bring to boil. Transfer to slow cooker stoneware and stir in vegetable broth.

2. Cover and cook on Low for 6 hours or on High for 3 to hours, until lentils are tender.

3. *Topping:* In a bowl, combine mashed potatoes and bread crumbs. Mix well. Spread evenly over lentil mixture. Cover and cook on High for 1 hour, until mixture is hot and bubbly.

Vegan Friendly

Entertaining Worthy

Can Be Halved

Tips

You can vary the kind of paprika to suit your taste. Hot, sweet and smoked will all work well in this recipe and provide different flavors. If you're using smoked paprika, I recommend using just 1 tsp (5 mL) and mixing it with 2 tsp (10 mL) of an unsmoked variety (hot or sweet).

If you are halving this recipe, be sure to use a small (1 1/2 to 3 1/2 quart) slow cooker.

Make Ahead

Complete Steps 1 and 2. Cover and refrigerate tempeh and vegetable mixture separately for up to 2 days. When you're ready to cook, complete the recipe.

Tempeh Paprikash

If you're feeling the need for some cold weather comfort food, look no further. This hearty stew is enhanced with the robust flavors of caraway and cremini mushrooms and finished with a good hit of paprika and a garnish of dill. Serve it over broad noodles such as pappardelle for a traditional presentation. Steaming brown rice or garlic mashed potatoes are delicious options as well.

- **Medium (approx. 3 quart) slow cooker**

2 tbsp	oil	25 mL
8 oz	tempeh, sliced (1/4 inch/0.5 cm)	250 g
2	onions, finely chopped	2
2	stalks celery, diced	2
4	cloves garlic, minced	4
1 tbsp	caraway seeds, crushed	15 mL
1 tsp	dried thyme	5 mL
	Finely grated zest of 1 lemon	
1/2 tsp	salt	2 mL
1/2 tsp	cracked black peppercorns	2 mL
1/4 cup	all-purpose flour	50 mL
2 tbsp	tomato paste	25 mL
2 cups	Enhanced Vegetable Broth (see Variation, page 103)	500 mL
12 oz	cremini mushrooms, trimmed and quartered	375 g
1 tbsp	paprika (see Tip, left), dissolved in 2 tbsp (25 mL) freshly squeezed lemon juice	15 mL
1	green or red bell pepper, seeded and diced	1
1/2 cup	sour cream or vegan alternative	125 mL
	Finely chopped dill	

1. In a skillet, heat oil over medium-high heat. Add tempeh and cook, turning once, until browned on both sides, about 4 minutes. Transfer to a bowl, cover and refrigerate until ready to use.

2. Reduce heat to medium. Add onions and celery and cook, stirring, until softened, about 3 minutes. Add garlic, caraway seeds, thyme, lemon zest, salt and peppercorns and cook, stirring, for 1 minute. Add flour and cook, stirring, for 1 minute. Add tomato paste and stir well. Add broth and cook, stirring and scraping up brown bits from bottom of pan, until mixture thickens, about 5 minutes. Transfer to stoneware.

3. Stir in mushrooms. Cover and cook on Low for 6 hours or on High for 3 hours.

4. Add paprika solution to stoneware along with bell pepper and reserved tempeh. Cover and cook on High for 20 minutes, until pepper is tender and tempeh is heated through. To serve, ladle into bowls and top with a dollop of sour cream. Garnish with dill.

Tips

Dried and frozen lime leaves are available in Asian markets or specialty stores.

If halving this recipe, be sure to use a small (approx. 2 quart) slow cooker.

Make Ahead

Complete Steps 1 and 2. Cover and refrigerate tempeh and vegetable mixtures separately for up to 2 days. When you're ready to cook, complete the recipe.

Thai-Style Coconut Tempeh Curry

Here's a version of a typical Thai green curry made with tempeh. I like to serve this over steamed brown rice.

● **Medium (approx. 4 quart) slow cooker**

1 tsp	mild curry powder	5 mL
8 oz	tempeh, sliced (¼ inch/0.5 cm)	250 g
2 tbsp	olive or coconut oil	25 mL
2	onions, finely chopped	2
2	carrots, peeled and sliced	2
4	cloves garlic, minced	4
1 tbsp	minced gingerroot	15 mL
1 tsp	cracked black peppercorns	5 mL
½ tsp	salt	2 mL
2	dried or frozen wild lime leaves (see Tips, left)	2
2 cups	vegetable broth	500 mL
2 tsp	Thai-style green curry paste	10 mL
1	can (14 oz/400 mL) coconut milk, divided	1
1 tbsp	white miso	15 mL
1 cup	green peas, thawed if frozen	250 mL

1. Sprinkle curry powder evenly over tempeh slices. In a skillet, heat oil over medium-high heat. Add tempeh and cook, turning once, until browned, about 4 minutes. Transfer to a bowl. Cover and refrigerate until ready to use.

2. Reduce heat to medium. Add onions and carrots to pan and cook, stirring, until softened, about 5 minutes. Add garlic, ginger, peppercorns, salt and lime leaves and cook, stirring, for 1 minute. Stir in vegetable broth. Transfer to slow cooker stoneware.

3. Cover and cook on Low for 6 hours or on High for 3 hours. In a small bowl, combine curry paste and ¼ cup (50 mL) of the coconut milk. Stir until blended. Add miso and stir well. Add to stoneware along with peas, remaining coconut milk and reserved tempeh. Cover and cook on High for 15 minutes, until peas are tender and tempeh is heated through.

Tips

To sweat eggplant: Place cubed eggplant in a colander, sprinkle liberally with salt, toss well and set aside for 30 minutes to 1 hour. If time is short, blanch the pieces for a minute or two in heavily salted water. In either case, rinse thoroughly in fresh cold water and, using your hands, squeeze out excess moisture. Pat dry with paper towels and it's ready for cooking.

If you are too busy to cook at the end of the day, fry the tofu when you cook the zucchini. Cover and refrigerate. Add to the slow cooker along with the zucchini and cook until heated through.

If you are halving this recipe, be sure to use a small (1½ to 3½ quart) slow cooker.

Tofu Ratatouille

Like any good ratatouille, this one involves quite a bit of preparation. Although it is time-consuming, sautéeing the vegetables individually ensures that their unique flavors aren't lost when the dish is complete. The results are worth the extra effort. Serve this to your most discriminating guests and expect requests for seconds.

● **Large (approx. 5 quart) slow cooker**

Ratatouille

1	large eggplant, peeled, cubed (1-inch/ 2.5 cm) and sweated (see Tips, left)	1
2 tbsp	oil, divided (approx.)	25 mL
8 oz	mushrooms, stems removed, and quartered	250 g
2	small zucchini, thinly sliced	2
1	large onion, finely chopped	1
3	cloves garlic, minced	3
½ tsp	cracked black peppercorns	2 mL
½ tsp	dried thyme	2 mL
½ tsp	ground cinnamon	2 mL
1	can (28 oz/796 mL) tomatoes with juice, coarsely chopped	1
	Salt, to taste	

Tofu

8 oz	firm tofu with fine herbs, cut into 1-inch (2.5 cm) cubes	250 g
	Salt and freshly ground black pepper	
1 tbsp	oil	15 mL

1. *Ratatouille:* In a skillet, heat 1 tbsp (15 mL) of the oil over medium heat. Add mushrooms and cook, stirring, just until they begin to lose their liquid. Using a slotted spoon, transfer to slow cooker stoneware. Return pan to element and add more oil, if needed.

2. Add zucchini, in batches, and cook, stirring, until it softens and begins to brown. Using a slotted spoon, transfer to a bowl. Cover and refrigerate.

3. Add eggplant to pan, in batches, and sauté until lightly browned, adding more oil as needed. Transfer to slow cooker as completed. Add onion to pan and cook, stirring, until softened. Add garlic, peppercorns, thyme and cinnamon and cook, stirring, for 1 minute. Add tomatoes with juice and bring to a boil. Add salt, to taste. Pour over contents of slow cooker. Stir to blend.

4. Cover and cook on Low for 6 hours or High for 3 hours, until hot and bubbly. Add reserved zucchini and cook on High for 15 minutes, until heated through.

5. *Tofu:* Season tofu with salt and pepper, to taste. In a skillet, heat oil over medium heat. Add tofu and cook, stirring, until lightly browned, about 15 minutes. Spread tofu over top of eggplant mixture and serve immediately.

Cajun-Style Tofu with Tomatoes and Okra

Serves 4 to 6

Can Be Halved

Tips

If you're using Italian San Marzano tomatoes, which are very rich, omit the tomato paste.

Okra, a tropical vegetable, has a great flavor but it becomes unpleasantly sticky when overcooked. Choose young okra pods, 2 to 4 inches (5 to 10 cm) long that don't feel sticky to the touch. (If sticky they are too ripe.) Gently scrub the pods and cut off the top and tail before slicing.

Whether you add cayenne depends upon how spicy your Cajun spice mix is and how much you like heat.

Make Ahead

Complete Step 1. Cover and refrigerate for up to 2 days. When you're ready to cook, complete the recipe.

Variation

Cajun-Style Tempeh with Tomatoes and Okra: Substitute 1 lb (500 g) sliced tempeh for the tofu. Omit the flour. Combine Cajun spice and cayenne, if using, and sprinkle over the sliced tempeh. Before starting Step 1, heat the oil in a skillet over medium-high heat. Sauté tempeh, turning once, until browned on both sides, about 7 minutes. Cover and refrigerate. Reduce heat to medium and continue with Step 1, using the oil in the pan to soften the vegetables. Add tempeh to slow cooker along with the okra.

Here's a dish that is Cajun-inspired in its ingredients, yet packs just a hint of heat and yields a great sense of freshness. Deliciously different, served over rice, it makes a great one-pot meal.

● **Medium (approx. 3 quart) slow cooker**

2 tbsp	oil	25 mL
1	onion, finely chopped	1
4	stalks celery, diced	4
4	cloves garlic, minced	4
1 tsp	salt	5 mL
1 tsp	cracked black peppercorns	5 mL
1 tsp	dried thyme	5 mL
2	bay leaves	2
1 tbsp	tomato paste (see Tips, left)	15 mL
1	can (14 oz/398 mL) diced tomatoes with juice	1
2 cups	thinly sliced okra (see Tips, left)	500 mL
1 cup	corn kernels	250 mL
1	red or green bell pepper, seeded and diced	1

Tofu

¼ cup	all-purpose flour	50 mL
1 tbsp	Cajun spice mix	15 mL
¼ tsp	cayenne pepper, optional (see Tips, left)	1 mL
1 lb	firm tofu, cut into 1-inch (2.5 cm) squares	500 g
1 tbsp	oil	15 mL

1. In a skillet, heat oil over medium heat. Add onion and celery and cook, stirring, until softened, about 5 minutes. Add garlic, salt, peppercorns, thyme and bay leaves and cook, stirring, for 1 minute. Stir in tomato paste. Add tomatoes with juice and bring to a boil. Transfer to slow cooker stoneware.

2. Cover and cook on Low for 6 hours or on High for 3 hours. Stir in okra, corn and bell pepper. Cover and cook on High for 20 minutes, until peppers are tender. Discard bay leaves.

3. Meanwhile, on a plate, mix together flour, Cajun spice mix, and cayenne pepper, if using. Roll tofu in mixture until lightly coated. Discard excess flour. In a skillet, heat oil over medium-high heat. Add dredged tofu and sauté, stirring, until nicely browned, about 4 minutes. Spoon tomato mixture into a serving dish. Layer tofu on top and serve.

Serves 6

Vegan Friendly
Entertaining Worthy
Can Be Halved

Tips

If you don't have an oval slow cooker, complete Steps 1 and 2, then transfer the mixture to a shallow ovenproof baking dish before completing Step 3. If you're serving to guests, for a more elegant presentation, transfer cooked vegetables to an ovenproof baking dish before adding the topping.

Without the miso, this dish tastes a lot like a casserole version of leek and potato soup, which I like. If you want to add a little oomph and move it in a slightly different direction, add the miso.

If you are halving this recipe, be sure to use a small (1½ to 3½ quart) slow cooker.

Tofu-Topped Celery and Potato Casserole

This tasty dish is very easy to make yet loaded with nutrition. All you need to add is a tossed salad or some sliced tomatoes to complete the meal.

- **Large (approx. 5 quart) oval slow cooker (see Tips, left)**
- **Food processor**

2	leeks, white part with just a bit of green, cleaned and sliced (see Tips, page 146)	2
6	stalks celery, diced	6
2	cloves garlic, minced	2
2 tbsp	melted butter or olive oil	25 mL
1 tsp	salt	5 mL
½ tsp	cracked black peppercorns	2 mL
2	potatoes, peeled and shredded	2
1 tbsp	white miso, optional (see Tips, left)	15 mL

Topping

8 oz	firm tofu, cut into 2-inch (5 cm) cubes	250 g
½ cup	freshly grated Parmesan or vegan substitute	125 mL
1 tbsp	fresh thyme or ½ tsp (2 mL) dried thyme	15 mL
1 cup	fresh bread crumbs	250 mL

1. In slow cooker stoneware, combine leeks, celery, garlic and melted butter. Stir to coat vegetables thoroughly. Cover and cook on High for 30 minutes to 1 hour, until vegetables are softened. Add salt, peppercorns and potatoes and stir well.

2. Cover and cook on Low for 6 hours or on High for 3 hours, until vegetables are tender. Stir in miso, if using.

3. *Topping:* Preheat broiler. In a food processor, combine tofu, Parmesan and thyme. Process until the texture of fine crumbs. Add bread crumbs and pulse to blend. Sprinkle over vegetables and broil until topping is nicely browned.

Tips

To sweat eggplant: Place cubed eggplant in a colander, sprinkle liberally with salt, toss well and set aside for 30 minutes to 1 hour. If time is short, blanch the pieces for a minute or two in heavily salted water. In either case, rinse thoroughly in fresh cold water and, using your hands, squeeze out excess moisture. Pat dry with paper towels and it's ready for cooking.

For this quantity of chickpeas, use 1 can (14 to 19 oz/398 to 540 mL) drained and rinsed, or 1 cup (250 mL) dried chickpeas (see Basic Beans, page 239).

If you are using a canned or bottled tomato sauce that is a little more or less than the quantity suggested, don't worry. Excellent results have been produced using as little as 2¾ cups (675 mL) to as much as 3¼ cups (800 mL) tomato sauce.

Tofu comes in various textures. Soft or silken tofu works best in sauces, spreads and shakes. Firmer tofu hold its texture in dishes such as stir-fries. Tofu in the mid-range of firmness works best in this topping.

Make Ahead

Complete Steps 1 through 3. Cover and refrigerate for up to 2 days. When you're ready to cook, complete the recipe.

Moussaka with Tofu Topping

This delicious rendition of the classic Greek dish, with an unusual tofu topping, is every bit as good as the original.

- **Large (minimum 5 quart) oval slow cooker (see Tips, page 234)**
- **Food processor or blender**

2	medium eggplants (each about 1 lb/500 g), peeled, cubed (2 inches/5 cm) and sweated (see Tips, left)	2
2 tbsp	oil (approx.)	25 mL
2	onions, finely chopped	2
4	cloves garlic, minced	4
1 tsp	dried oregano	5 mL
1 tsp	ground cumin (see Tips, page 220)	5 mL
½ tsp	salt	2 mL
½ tsp	cracked black peppercorns	2 mL
2 cups	drained cooked chickpeas (see Tips, left)	500 mL
3 cups	tomato sauce (see Tips, left)	750 mL

Topping

1 lb	medium tofu (see Tips, left)	500 g
2	eggs	2
½ cup	freshly grated Parmesan cheese	125 mL
Pinch	ground nutmeg	Pinch
Pinch	ground cinnamon	Pinch

1. In a skillet, heat oil over medium-high heat. Add eggplant, in batches, and cook until browned, adding more oil, if necessary. Set aside.

2. Add onions to pan and cook, stirring, until softened, about 3 minutes. Add garlic, oregano, cumin, salt and peppercorns and cook, stirring, for 1 minute. Add chickpeas and stir well.

3. Spread 1 cup (250 mL) of the tomato sauce evenly over bottom of slow cooker stoneware. Spread one-third of the eggplant over sauce and half of the chickpea mixture over eggplant. Repeat. Finish with remaining eggplant and pour remaining tomato sauce over top.

4. *Topping:* In a food processor or blender, purée tofu, eggs, Parmesan, nutmeg and cinnamon. Spread over eggplant. Place a clean tea towel, folded in half (so you will have two layers), over top of stoneware to absorb moisture. Cover and cook on Low for 6 hours or on High for 3 hours.

Serves 4 to 6

Vegan Friendly

Entertaining Worthy

Can Be Halved

Tip

If halving this recipe, be sure to use a small (approx. 2 quart) slow cooker.

Make Ahead

Complete Step 1. Cover and refrigerate for up to 2 days. When you're ready to cook, complete the recipe.

Tofu in Indian-Spiced Tomato Sauce

This robust dish makes a lively and different meal. I like to serve it with fresh green beans and naan, an Indian bread, to soak up the sauce.

● **Medium (approx. 4 quart) slow cooker**

1 tbsp	oil	15 mL
2	onions, finely chopped	2
2	cloves garlic, minced	2
1/2 tsp	minced gingerroot	2 mL
6	whole cloves	6
4	white or green cardamom pods	4
1	piece (2 inches/5 cm) cinnamon stick	1
1 tsp	caraway seeds	5 mL
1 tsp	salt	5 mL
1/2 tsp	cracked black peppercorns	2 mL
1	can (28 oz/796 mL) tomatoes with juice	1
1	long green chile pepper, seeded and finely chopped	1
Tofu		
1/4 cup	all-purpose flour	50 mL
1 tsp	curry powder	5 mL
1/4 tsp	cayenne pepper	1 mL
8 oz	firm tofu, cut into 1-inch (2.5 cm) cubes	250 g
1 tbsp	vegetable oil	15 mL

1. In a skillet, heat oil over medium heat. Add onions and cook, stirring, until softened, about 3 minutes. Add garlic, ginger, cloves, cardamom, cinnamon stick, caraway seeds, salt and peppercorns and cook, stirring, for 1 minute. Add tomatoes with juice and bring to a boil. Transfer to slow cooker stoneware.

2. Cover and cook on Low for 6 hours or on High for 3 hours, until hot and bubbly. Discard cloves, cardamom and cinnamon stick. Stir in chile pepper.

3. *Tofu:* On a plate, mix together flour, curry powder and cayenne. Roll tofu in mixture until lightly coated. Discard excess flour. In a skillet, heat oil over medium-high heat. Add dredged tofu and sauté, stirring, until nicely browned. Spoon tomato mixture into a serving dish. Lay tofu on top and serve.

Soy-Braised Tofu

Makes about 3 cups (750 mL)

Vegan Friendly

Tips

To drain tofu: Place a layer of paper towels on a plate. Set tofu in the middle. Cover with another layer of paper towel and a heavy plate. Set aside for 30 minutes. Peel off paper and cut into cubes.

I use a fine Microplane grater to purée the gingerroot and garlic for this recipe. It creates tiny particles that are completely integrated into the mixture, enhancing the final flavor of the dish.

It's amazing how tofu soaks up the mouth-watering Asian flavors in this recipe. Use this hot braised tofu as a centerpiece to a meal of vegetarian dishes that might include stir-fried bok choy or wilted greens garnished with toasted sesame seeds. Refrigerate any leftovers for use in other dishes, such as stir-fried mixed vegetables, or salads, such as an Asian-inspired coleslaw. You can also transform this flavorful tofu into a wrap. Place on lettuce leaves, garnish with shredded carrots and fold.

- **Small to medium (1½ to 3½ quart) slow cooker**

1 lb	firm tofu, drained and cut into 1-inch (2.5 cm) cubes (see Tips, left)	500 g
¼ cup	light soy sauce	50 mL
1 tbsp	puréed gingerroot (see Tips, left)	15 mL
1 tbsp	pure maple syrup	15 mL
1 tbsp	toasted sesame oil	15 mL
1 tbsp	freshly squeezed lemon juice	15 mL
1 tsp	puréed garlic	5 mL
½ tsp	cracked black peppercorns	2 mL

1. In slow cooker stoneware, combine soy sauce, ginger, maple syrup, toasted sesame oil, lemon juice, garlic and peppercorns. Add tofu and toss gently until coated on all sides. Cover and refrigerate for 1 hour.

2. Toss well. Cover and cook on Low for 5 hours or on High for 2½ hours, until tofu is hot and has absorbed the flavor.

Tips

To drain tofu: Place a layer of paper towels on a plate. Set tofu in the middle. Cover with another layer of paper towel and a heavy plate. Set aside for 30 minutes. Peel off paper and cut into cubes.

I use a fine Microplane grater to purée the garlic for this recipe. It creates tiny particles that are completely integrated into the mixture, enhancing the final flavor of the dish.

Mediterranean-Style Braised Tofu

This flavorful tofu is very versatile. Serve it as the centerpiece of a vegetarian meal, or use it as the main ingredient in a salad composée. I particularly like it as a substitute for tuna in a Salade Niçoise. If you're tired of eating pasta, serve it topped with warm tomato sauce for a delightfully different dish or, in season, add it to sliced tomatoes vinaigrette. In other words, use your imagination.

● **Small to medium (1½ to 3½ quart) slow cooker**

1 lb	firm tofu, drained and cut into 1-inch (2.5 cm) cubes (see Tips, left)	500 g
¼ cup	extra virgin olive oil	50 mL
1 tbsp	balsamic or red wine vinegar	15 mL
1 tbsp	dried Italian seasoning	15 mL
4	cloves garlic, puréed (see Tips, left)	4
½ tsp	salt	2 mL
½ tsp	cracked black peppercorns	2 mL

1. In slow cooker stoneware, combine olive oil, vinegar, Italian seasoning, garlic, salt and peppercorns. Add tofu and toss gently until coated on all sides. Cover and refrigerate for 1 hour.

2. Toss well. Cover and cook on Low for 5 hours or on High for 2½ hours, until tofu is hot and has absorbed the flavor.

Makes approximately
2 cups (500 mL) cooked
beans (see Tips, below)

Basic Beans

Loaded with nutrition and high in fiber, dried beans are one of our most healthful edibles. The slow cooker excels at turning these unappetizing bullets into potentially sublime fare. It is also extraordinarily convenient — since discovering the slow cooker, I don't cook dried beans any other way. I put presoaked beans into the slow cooker before I go to bed and when I wake up, they are ready for whatever recipe I plan to make.

Vegan Friendly

Tips

This recipe may be doubled or tripled to suit the quantity of beans required for a recipe. Remember to increase the size of your slow cooker accordingly.

Generally, the older beans are (i.e. the longer they have been kept), the longer they will take to cook. If your beans are still tough after a long cooking, they are probably past their prime.

Variation

Dried Lentils: These instructions also work for lentils, with the following changes: Do not presoak them and reduce the cooking time to about 6 hours on Low, 3 hours on High.

- **Small to medium (approx. 2 quart) slow cooker**

1 cup	dried beans or chickpeas	250 mL
3 cups	water	750 mL

1. *Long soak:* In a bowl, combine beans and water. Soak for at least 6 hours or overnight. Drain and rinse thoroughly with cold water. Beans are now ready for cooking.

2. *Quick soak:* In a pot, combine beans and water. Cover and bring to a boil. Boil for 3 minutes. Turn off heat and soak for 1 hour. Drain and rinse thoroughly under cold water. Beans are now ready to cook.

3. *Cooking:* In slow cooker, combine 1 cup (250 mL) presoaked beans and 3 cups (750 mL) fresh cold water. Season with garlic, bay leaves or a bouquet garni made from your favorite herbs tied together in a piece of cheesecloth, if desired. Add salt to taste. Cover and cook on Low for 10 to 12 hours or overnight or on High for 5 to 6 hours, until beans are tender. Drain and rinse. If not using immediately, cover and refrigerate. The beans are now ready for use in your favorite recipe.

Legumes (Dried beans and lentils)

Once cooked, legumes should be covered and stored in the refrigerator, where they will keep for 4 to 5 days. Cooked legumes can also be frozen in an airtight container. They will keep frozen for up to 6 months.

Storing Legumes

Dried beans and lentils should be stored in a dry, airtight container at room temperature. Since they lose their moisture over time, they are best used within a year. You'll know your beans are stale if their skins shrivel up when they are soaked.

Substitutions

Canned beans are a quick and easy substitute for cooked dried beans. Although the sizes of canned beans vary, the differences won't affect the results of most recipes. For 2 cups (500 mL) cooked beans, use a standard can, which usually range in size from 14-oz (398 mL) to 19-oz (540 mL). Rinse well under cold running water before adding to your recipe.

Sides

New Potato Curry

Vegan Friendly

Can Be Halved

Tips

Leave the skins on potatoes, scrub thoroughly and dry on paper towels. Cut in half any that are larger than 1 inch (2.5 cm) in diameter.

If you are halving this recipe, be sure to use a small (1½ to 2 quart) slow cooker.

New Potato Curry

This is an excellent way to cook new potatoes. They cook slowly, almost in their own juices, in a curry-flavored sauce. It's a great side dish, but you can also serve it as a main course along with a bowl of dal and a green vegetable. It also makes a delicious summer meal accompanied by a garden salad.

● **Small to medium (2 to 4 quart) slow cooker**

2 tbsp	clarified butter or vegetable oil	25 mL
1 lb	small new potatoes, about 12 new potatoes (see Tips, left)	500 g
2	onions, finely chopped	2
1	clove garlic, minced	1
½ tsp	salt	2 mL
½ tsp	cracked black peppercorns	2 mL
½ cup	water or vegetable broth	125 mL
1 tsp	curry powder, preferably Madras, dissolved in 2 tbsp (25 mL) freshly squeezed lemon juice	5 mL
¼ cup	finely chopped cilantro	50 mL

1. In a skillet, heat butter over medium-high heat. Add potatoes and cook, stirring, just until they begin to brown. Transfer to slow cooker stoneware.

2. Reduce heat to medium. Add onions and cook, stirring, until softened, about 3 minutes. Add garlic, salt and peppercorns and cook, stirring, for 1 minute. Add water or broth, bring to a boil and pour over potatoes.

3. Cover and cook on Low for 8 hours or on High for 4 hours, until potatoes are tender. Stir in curry powder solution. Cover and cook on High for 10 minutes to meld flavors. Garnish with cilantro.

Vegan Friendly

Can Be Halved

Tips

Leave the skins on potatoes, scrub thoroughly and cut in half lengthwise. Dry thoroughly on paper towels.

If you are halving this recipe, be sure to use a small ($1\frac{1}{2}$ to 2 quart) slow cooker.

Braised Fingerling Potatoes with Garlic

These potatoes are so easy to prepare, yet the results are delicious. Succulent and flavorful, they make a wonderful accompaniment to many dishes.

- **Medium (approx. 4 quart) slow cooker**
- **Large sheet of parchment paper**

12	fingerling potatoes (see Tips, left)	12
4	cloves garlic, minced	4
2 tbsp	extra virgin olive oil	25 mL
	Salt and freshly ground black pepper	

1. In slow cooker stoneware, combine potatoes, garlic and olive oil. Toss well. Place a large piece of parchment over the potatoes, pressing it down to brush the food and extending up the sides of the stoneware so it overlaps the rim.

2. Cover and cook on Low for 6 hours or on High for 3 hours, until potatoes are tender. Lift out the parchment and discard, being careful not to spill the accumulated liquid into the stoneware. Season to taste with salt and pepper and serve.

Kashmiri-Style Slow-Cooked Potatoes

Tips

For the best flavor, toast cumin seeds and grind them yourself. *To toast seeds:* Place in a dry skillet over medium heat and cook, stirring, until fragrant, about 3 minutes. Immediately transfer to a spice grinder or mortar and grind finely.

If halving this recipe, be sure to use a small (approx. 2 quart) slow cooker.

This is an example of dum phukt cooking, which originated in the 16th century and reflects India's Mughal heritage. Basically, it's an Indian form of braising. The food is cooked in a clay pot and sealed with a flour and water paste. The results, which represent the best of slow cooking, are rich and dense. I love the hint of cardamom, which is not a traditional flavor one associates with potatoes.

- **Medium (approx. 4 quart) slow cooker**
- **Large sheet of parchment paper**

4	baking potatoes	4
¼ cup	olive oil	50 mL
2 tsp	ground cumin (see Tips, left)	10 mL
2	onions, thinly sliced on the vertical	2
2	cloves garlic, minced	2
2 tsp	minced gingerroot	10 mL
1 tsp	salt	5 mL
½ tsp	cracked black peppercorns	2 mL
2	cardamom pods, crushed	2
1	piece (2 inches/5 cm) cinnamon stick	1
1	can (14 oz/398 mL) crushed tomatoes with juice	1
½ cup	full-fat plain yogurt	125 mL

1. Peel potatoes and cut in half lengthwise, then cut each half into 4 wedges. Pat dry.

2. In a skillet, heat oil over medium-high heat. Add potatoes, in batches, and cook until they are nicely browned on all sides, about 7 minutes per batch. Using a slotted spoon transfer to slow cooker stoneware. Drain all but 1 tbsp (15 mL) oil from pan.

3. Reduce heat to medium. Add onions and cook, stirring, until softened, about 3 minutes. Add garlic, ginger, salt, peppercorns, cardamom and cinnamon stick and cook, stirring, for 1 minute. Add tomatoes with juice and bring to a boil. Transfer to slow cooker stoneware. Place a large piece of parchment over the potatoes, pressing it down to brush the food and extending up the sides of the stoneware so it overlaps the rim.

4. Cover and cook on Low for 6 hours or on High for 3 hours, until potatoes are tender. Lift out the parchment and discard, being careful not to spill the accumulated liquid into the stoneware. Discard cardamom and cinnamon stick. Stir in yogurt.

Vegan Friendly
Can Be Halved

Tips

If you prefer, use frozen artichokes, thawed, to make this recipe. You'll need 6 artichoke hearts.

If you are halving this recipe, be sure to use a small (1½ to 3½ quart) slow cooker.

I always use Italian flat-leaf parsley because it has much more flavor than the curly leaf variety.

Potatoes and Artichokes

If you like the combination of potatoes and artichokes, you'll love this dish. It's an unusual mixture of crispy potatoes and artichoke hearts in a flavorful gravy.

● **Medium to large (3½ to 5 quart) slow cooker**

3	large potatoes (each about 8 oz/250 g)	3
¼ cup	olive oil	50 mL
4	cloves garlic, minced	4
2 tsp	dried Italian seasoning	10 mL
½ tsp	salt	2 mL
½ tsp	cracked black peppercorns	2 mL
1 tbsp	all-purpose flour	15 mL
¼ cup	dry white wine	50 mL
1 cup	vegetable broth	250 mL
1	can (14 oz/398 mL) artichokes, drained and quartered	1
¼ cup	finely chopped Italian flat-leaf parsley	50 mL

1. Peel potatoes and cut in half lengthwise, then cut each half into 4 wedges. Pat dry.

2. In a skillet, heat oil over medium-high heat. Add potatoes, in batches, and cook until they are nicely browned on all sides, about 7 minutes per batch. Using a slotted spoon, transfer to paper towels to drain. Drain all but 1 tbsp (15 mL) oil from pan.

3. Reduce heat to medium. Add garlic, Italian seasoning, salt and peppercorns to pan and cook, stirring, for 1 minute. Add flour and cook, stirring, for 1 minute. Add wine and broth and cook, stirring, until mixture comes to a boil and thickens, about 3 minutes. Stir in artichokes. Place potatoes in stoneware, add artichoke mixture and gently stir.

4. Cover and cook on Low for 6 hours or on High for 3 hours, until potatoes are tender. Serve immediately, garnished liberally with parsley.

Leek Risotto

Vegan Friendly

Can Be Halved

Tips

To clean leeks: Fill sink full of lukewarm water. Split leeks in half lengthwise and submerge in water, swishing them around to remove all traces of dirt. Transfer to a colander and rinse under cold water.

If you prefer, use an additional 1/2 cup (125 mL) of broth instead of the wine.

If halving this recipe, be sure to use a small (approx. 2 quart) slow cooker.

This dish makes a great side or a course at a multi-dish meal. Accompanied by a tossed green salad, and some crusty rolls, it also makes a light weeknight meal.

● **Medium (approx. 4 quart) slow cooker**

1 tbsp	oil	15 mL
3	leeks, white part with just a bit of green, cleaned and thinly sliced (see Tips, left)	3
2	cloves garlic, minced	2
1/2 tsp	cracked black peppercorns	2 mL
1 cup	Arborio rice	250 mL
1/2 cup	dry white wine (see Tips, left)	125 mL
2 1/2 cups	vegetable broth	625 mL
1/2 cup	freshly grated Parmesan cheese, optional	125 mL
1/4 cup	finely chopped Italian flat-leaf parsley	50 mL

1. In a large skillet, heat oil over medium heat. Add leeks and cook, stirring, until softened, about 5 minutes. Add garlic and peppercorns and cook, stirring, for 1 minute. Add rice and cook, stirring, until coated. Add white wine and broth and stir well. Transfer to slow cooker stoneware.

2. Place a clean tea towel, folded in half (so you will have two layers), over top of stoneware to absorb moisture. Cover and cook on Low for 4 hours or on High for 2 hours, until liquid is absorbed and rice is tender to the bite. Stir in Parmesan, if using, and parsley and serve.

Vegan Friendly

Can Be Halved

Tips

For the best flavor, toast coriander seeds and grind them yourself. *To toast seeds:* Place in a dry skillet over medium heat and cook, stirring, until fragrant, about 3 minutes. Immediately transfer to a spice grinder or mortar and grind finely.

If halving this recipe, be sure to use a small (approx. 2 quart) slow cooker.

Orange-Braised Fennel

If you're looking for something that tastes deliciously different, try this. The flavors of orange and coriander combine intriguingly with the fennel, which is slightly more intensely flavored than usual because it has been browned before braising. Serve this with anything that benefits from a hint of tartness.

- **Small to medium (1½ to 3½ quart) slow cooker**
- **Large sheet of parchment paper**

2 tbsp	olive oil	25 mL
3	bulbs fennel, trimmed, cored and thinly sliced on the vertical	3
2	cloves garlic, minced	2
1 tsp	ground coriander (see Tips, left)	5 mL
½ tsp	salt	2 mL
½ tsp	cracked black peppercorns	2 mL
	Grated zest and juice of 1 orange	

1. In a skillet, heat oil over medium-high heat. Add fennel, in batches, and cook, stirring, just until it begins to brown, about 5 minutes per batch. Transfer to slow cooker stoneware as completed. When last batch of fennel is almost browned, add garlic, coriander, salt, peppercorns and orange zest to pan and cook, stirring, for 1 minute. Transfer to slow cooker stoneware and stir in orange juice.

2. Place a large piece of parchment over the fennel, pressing it down to brush the food and extending up the sides of the stoneware so it overlaps the rim. Cover and cook on Low for 6 hours or on High for 3 hours, until fennel is tender. Lift out the parchment and discard, being careful not to spill the accumulated liquid into the stoneware.

Tips

Onions are high in natural sugars, which long slow simmering brings out, as does the orange juice in this recipe.

If you are halving this recipe, be sure to use a small (1½ to 3½ quart) slow cooker, checking to make sure the whole onions will fit.

New Orleans Braised Onions

I call these New Orleans onions because I was inspired by an old Creole recipe for Spanish onions. In that version, the onions are braised in beef broth enhanced by the addition of liquor such as bourbon or port. After the onions are cooked, the cooking juices are reduced and herbs, such as capers or fresh thyme, may be added to the concentrated sauce. In my opinion, this simplified version is every bit as tasty. If your guests like spice, pass hot pepper sauce at the table.

• **Large (approx. 5 quart) slow cooker**

2 to 3	large Spanish onions	2 to 3
6 to 9	whole cloves	6 to 9
½ tsp	salt	2 mL
½ tsp	cracked black peppercorns	2 mL
Pinch	dried thyme	Pinch
	Grated zest and juice of 1 orange	
½ cup	vegetable broth	125 mL
	Finely chopped fresh parsley, optional	
	Hot pepper sauce, optional	

1. Stud onions with cloves. Place in slow cooker stoneware and sprinkle with salt, peppercorns, thyme and orange zest. Pour orange juice and broth over onions, cover and cook on Low for 8 hours or on High for 4 hours, until onions are tender.

2. Using a slotted spoon, transfer onions to a serving dish and keep warm in a 250°F (120°C) oven. Transfer liquid to a saucepan over medium heat. Cook until reduced by half.

3. When ready to serve, cut onions into quarters. Place on a deep platter and cover with sauce. Sprinkle with parsley, if desired, and pass the hot pepper sauce, if desired.

Tips

Softening these onions in butter, then cooking them in a bit of broth produces a particularly sweet and mild-tasting result.

If you are halving this recipe, be sure to use a small (1½ to 2 quart) slow cooker.

Make Ahead

Complete Step 1. Cover and refrigerate for up to 2 days. When you're ready to cook, continue with the recipe.

Creamy Sweet Onions

These luscious onions are the perfect accompaniment to any meal. They are delicious on their own but if you want to impress your guests, add the tasty topping.

● **Small to medium (2 to 4 quart) slow cooker**

2 tbsp	butter	25 mL
3	sweet onions, such as Spanish, Vidalia or Texas Sweets, peeled and thinly sliced	3
½ tsp	salt	2 mL
½ tsp	cracked black peppercorns	2 mL
2 tbsp	all-purpose flour	25 mL
½ cup	vegetable broth	125 mL
¼ cup	heavy or whipping (35%) cream	50 mL

Crumb Topping, optional

1 cup	dry bread crumbs	250 mL
½ cup	freshly grated Parmesan, optional	125 mL
1 tsp	paprika	5 mL
¼ tsp	salt	1 mL
	Freshly ground black pepper	
2 tbsp	melted butter	25 mL

1. In a large skillet, melt butter over medium heat. Add onions and cook, stirring, until softened, about 5 minutes. Add salt, peppercorns and flour and cook, stirring, for 1 minute. Add broth and bring to a boil. Transfer to slow cooker stoneware.

2. Cover and cook on Low for 6 hours or on High for 3 hours, until onions are tender. Stir in cream.

3. *Crumb Topping:* In a bowl, combine bread crumbs, Parmesan, if using, paprika, salt, and pepper, to taste. Mix well. Add butter and stir to blend. Spread mixture evenly over onions. Cover, leaving lid slightly ajar to prevent accumulated moisture from dripping on the topping, and cook on High for 30 minutes, until cheese is melted and mixture is hot and bubbly.

Vegan Friendly

Can Be Halved

Tips

Use your favorite hot sauce, such as Tabasco, Louisiana Hot Sauce, Piri Piri, or try other more exotic brands to vary the flavors in this recipe.

If you are halving this recipe, be sure to use a small (1½ to 2 quart) slow cooker.

Make Ahead

Complete Step 1. Cover and refrigerate overnight. The next day, complete the recipe.

Peppery Red Onions

I love making this nippy treat in the autumn when the farmers' markets are brimming over with freshly harvested red onions. They are a tasty low-fat alternative to creamed onions. I particularly enjoy them as a topping for polenta or Grits 'n' Cheddar Cheese (page 184).

● **Small to medium (2 to 4 quart) slow cooker**

4	large red onions, quartered	4
1 tbsp	olive oil	15 mL
1 tsp	dried oregano	5 mL
¼ cup	water or vegetable broth	50 mL
	Salt and black pepper	
	Hot pepper sauce (see Tips, left)	

1. In slow cooker stoneware, combine onions, olive oil, oregano, water, and salt and pepper, to taste. Stir thoroughly.

2. Cover and cook on Low for 6 hours or on High for 3 hours, until onions are tender. Add hot sauce, to taste, toss well and serve.

Tips

I always use unsalted butter, not only because I prefer the taste, but also because it allows me more control over the quantity of salt I consume.

I always use Italian flat-leaf parsley because it has much more flavor than the curly leaf variety.

If halving this recipe, be sure to use a small (approx. 2 quart) slow cooker.

Make Ahead

Complete Step 1. Cover and refrigerate for up to 2 days. When you're ready to cook, complete the recipe.

Creamed Onions

Since long, slow cooking is the essence of getting the best out of onions, they have a natural affinity for the slow cooker. This simple, but elegant dish is a favorite with all members of my family. Whether you add cheese is simply a matter of taste. My family likes it equally well, with or without. Serve over polenta for a light main course.

● **Small to medium (2 to 4 quart) slow cooker**

2 tbsp	butter	25 mL
1 tbsp	olive oil	15 mL
4 to 5	onions, quartered, about 2 lbs (1 kg)	4 to 5
2	sprigs fresh thyme or 1 tsp (5 mL) dried thyme	2
½ tsp	salt	2 mL
½ tsp	freshly ground black pepper	2 mL
½ cup	vegetable broth or water	125 mL
½ cup	heavy or whipping (35%) cream	125 mL
¼ cup	freshly grated Parmesan cheese, optional	50 mL
2 tbsp	finely chopped Italian flat-leaf parsley	25 mL

1. In a large skillet, melt butter and oil over medium heat. Add onions and cook, stirring, until they begin to brown. Add thyme, salt and pepper and cook, stirring, for 1 to 2 minutes. Add broth and bring to a boil. Transfer to slow cooker stoneware.

2. Cover and cook on Low for 6 hours or on High for 3 hours, until onions are tender. Stir in cream, and cheese, if using. Cover and cook on High for 15 minutes. Garnish with parsley.

Vegan Friendly

Entertaining Worthy

Can Be Halved

Tips

If using olive oil rather than butter, drizzle it over the onions before adding the parchment.

If you are halving this recipe, be sure to use a small (1½ to 2 quart) slow cooker.

Braised Sweet Onions in Balsamic Butter

Onions are the workhorse of almost every kitchen. They are the base for so many soups, stews and sauces that we take them for granted. But cooked properly, they are a delicious vegetable all on their own. Here, sweet onions, which are available in North America throughout the spring, assume a starring role. They are complemented by sweetly pungent balsamic vinegar to produce a simple, but quite magnificent dish.

- **Small to medium (2 to 4 quart) slow cooker**
- **Large sheet of parchment paper**

4 to 6	sweet onions, such as Vidalia, quartered	4 to 6
2 tbsp	balsamic vinegar	25 mL
1 tbsp	olive oil	15 mL
½ tsp	salt	2 mL
½ tsp	cracked black peppercorns	2 mL
2 tbsp	butter or olive oil (see Tips, left)	25 mL
	Finely chopped fresh parsley, optional	

1. In slow cooker stoneware, combine onions, vinegar, olive oil, salt and peppercorns. Toss to combine. Dot butter over top. Place a large piece of parchment over the mixture, pressing it down to brush the food and extending up the sides of the stoneware so it overlaps the rim.

2. Cover and cook on Low for 6 hours or on High for 3 hours, until onions are tender. Lift off parchment and discard, being careful not to spill any accumulated liquid into the onions. Garnish liberally with parsley, if using.

Vegan Friendly

Can Be Halved

Tips

For the best flavor, toast cumin seeds and grind them yourself. *To toast seeds:* Place in a dry skillet over medium heat and cook, stirring, until fragrant, about 3 minutes. Immediately transfer to a spice grinder or mortar and grind finely.

If you are halving this recipe, be sure to use a small ($1\frac{1}{2}$ to 2 quart) slow cooker.

Make Ahead

Peel and cut parsnips and carrots. Cover and refrigerate overnight.

Parsnip and Carrot Purée with Cumin

The cumin adds a slightly exotic note to this traditional dish, which makes a great accompaniment to many foods.

● **Medium (approx. 4 quart) slow cooker**

4 cups	cubed ($\frac{1}{2}$ inch/1 cm) peeled parsnips (about 8 medium) (see Tip, page 255)	1 L
2 cups	thinly sliced peeled carrots	500 mL
1 tsp	ground cumin (see Tips, left)	5 mL
2 tbsp	butter or vegan butter substitute	25 mL
1 tsp	granulated sugar	5 mL
$\frac{1}{2}$ tsp	salt	2 mL
$\frac{1}{4}$ tsp	freshly ground black pepper	1 mL
$\frac{1}{4}$ cup	water or vegetable broth	50 mL

1. In slow cooker stoneware, combine parsnips, carrots, cumin, butter, sugar, salt, pepper and water. Cover and cook on Low for 6 hours or on High for 3 hours, until vegetables are tender.

2. Using a potato masher or a food processor or blender, mash or purée mixture until smooth. Serve immediately.

Tips

If you are using very large parsnips, discard the woody core. The easiest way to do this is to cut the parsnips into thirds horizontally and place the flat surface on a cutting board. Using a sharp knife, cut around the core. Discard the core and cut the slices into cubes.

If halving this recipe, be sure to use a small (approx. 2 quart) slow cooker.

Make Ahead

Complete Step 1. Cover and refrigerate overnight. When you're ready to cook, complete the recipe.

Creamy Braised Parsnips with Peas

If you're tired of the same old sides, try this. The combination of peas and parsnips is delectable, and a splash of cream adds a very pleasant finish.

- **Small to medium (2 to 4 quart) slow cooker**
- **Large sheet of parchment paper**

1 tbsp	oil	15 mL
1	onion, finely chopped	1
1 tsp	dried thyme	5 mL
$\frac{1}{2}$ tsp	salt	2 mL
	Freshly ground black pepper	
4 cups	cubed ($\frac{1}{2}$ inch/1 cm) peeled parsnips (about 8 medium) (see Tips, left)	1 L
$\frac{1}{4}$ cup	water	50 mL
$1\frac{1}{2}$ cups	sweet green peas, thawed if frozen	375 mL
$\frac{1}{4}$ cup	heavy or whipping (35%) cream or soy creamer	50 mL

1. In a skillet, heat oil over medium heat. Add onion and cook, stirring, until softened, about 3 minutes. Add thyme, salt and pepper to taste and cook, stirring, for 1 minute. Add parsnips and toss until coated. Transfer to slow cooker stoneware. Add water and stir well.

2. Place a large piece of parchment over the mixture, pressing it down to brush the food and extending up the sides of the stoneware so it overlaps the rim.

3. Cover and cook on Low for 6 hours or on High for 3 hours, until parsnips are tender. Lift out parchment and discard, being careful not to spill the accumulated liquid into the vegetables. Stir in peas and cream. Cover and cook on High for 15 minutes, until peas are tender.

Tips

For the best flavor, toast cumin seeds and grind them yourself. *To toast seeds:* Place in a dry skillet over medium heat and cook, stirring, until fragrant, about 3 minutes. Immediately transfer to a spice grinder or mortar and grind finely.

Peeling the beets before they are cooked ensures that all the delicious cooking juices end up on your plate.

Make Ahead

Complete Step 1. Cover and refrigerate for up to 2 days. When you're ready to cook, complete the recipe.

Cumin Beets

I love the simple, but unusual and effective combination of flavors in this dish, which is inspired by Indian cuisine. It's my favorite way of cooking small summer beets fresh from the garden because I don't have to heat up my kitchen with a pot of simmering water on the stovetop. If you prefer a spicy dish, add hot pepper sauce, to taste, after the beets have finished cooking.

● **Small (approx. 2 quart) slow cooker**

1 tbsp	oil	15 mL
1	onion, finely chopped	1
3	cloves garlic, minced	3
1 tsp	ground cumin (see Tips, left)	5 mL
1 tsp	salt	5 mL
½ tsp	freshly ground black pepper	2 mL
2	medium tomatoes, peeled and coarsely chopped	2
1 cup	water	250 mL
1 lb	beets, peeled and used whole, if small, or sliced thinly (see Tips, left)	500 g
	Hot pepper sauce, optional	

1. In a skillet, heat oil over medium heat. Add onion and cook, stirring, until softened, about 3 minutes. Stir in garlic, cumin, salt and pepper and cook, stirring, for 1 minute. Add tomatoes and water and bring to a boil.

2. Place beets in slow cooker stoneware and pour tomato mixture over them. Cover and cook on Low for 8 hours or on High for 4 hours, until beets are tender. Pass hot pepper sauce at the table, if using.

Entertaining Worthy

Can Be Halved

Tips

I always use unsalted butter, not only because I prefer the taste, but also because it allows me more control over the quantity of salt I consume.

If you are halving this recipe, be sure to use a small ($1\frac{1}{2}$ to 2 quart) slow cooker.

Candied Sweet Potatoes

These sweet potatoes are so delicious, I don't need an excuse to make them. My husband always has seconds.

• **Small to medium (2 to 4 quart) slow cooker**

3	sweet potatoes, peeled and cut into $1\frac{1}{2}$-inch (4 cm) thick rounds	3
1 cup	packed brown sugar	250 mL
1 tsp	salt	5 mL
	Freshly ground black pepper	
2 tbsp	butter	25 mL
2 tbsp	orange marmalade	25 mL

1. In slow cooker stoneware, combine potatoes, brown sugar, salt, and black pepper, to taste. Stir well. Dot with butter.

2. Place a clean tea towel, folded in half (so you will have two layers), over top of stoneware to absorb moisture. Cover and cook on Low for 6 hours or on High for 3 hours, until potatoes are tender. Stir in marmalade. Cover and cook on High for 10 minutes, until melted.

Vegan Friendly

Entertaining Worthy

Can Be Halved

Tips

Sweet potatoes are neither potatoes nor yams. They are a tuber (like yams) that is native to the Americas. They are quite perishable and don't like the cold. Don't store them at temperatures that are lower than 50°F (10°C).

If you are halving this recipe, be sure to use a small (1$\frac{1}{2}$ to 2 quart) slow cooker.

Ginger-Spiked Sweet Potatoes with Maple Syrup

Here's a slightly different way of cooking sweet potatoes that is vegan friendly. Simply braised in orange juice, finished with luscious maple syrup and garnish with toasted pecans, they are quite yummy.

- **Small to medium (approx. 2 quart) slow cooker**

4	sweet potatoes, peeled and cut into $\frac{1}{2}$-inch (1 cm) thick rounds (see Tips, left)	4
1 tbsp	finely grated orange zest	15 mL
$\frac{1}{2}$ cup	freshly squeezed orange juice	125 mL
1 tbsp	minced gingerroot	15 mL
$\frac{1}{2}$ tsp	salt	2 mL
$\frac{1}{2}$ tsp	cracked black peppercorns	2 mL
$\frac{1}{4}$ cup	pure maple syrup	50 mL
	Toasted pecans	

1. In slow cooker stoneware, combine sweet potatoes, orange zest and juice, ginger, salt and peppercorns. Cover and cook on Low for 6 hours or on High for 3 hours, until potatoes are tender. Using a potato masher or a large fork, mash potatoes. Stir in maple syrup and garnish with toasted pecans.

Tips

Carrots are high in beta-carotene, an antioxidant that our bodies turn into vitamin A. Cooking actually increases the vegetable's beta-carotene and increases its sweetness.

If you are halving this recipe, be sure to use a small ($1\frac{1}{2}$ to $3\frac{1}{2}$ quart) slow cooker.

Make Ahead

Complete Step 1 and refrigerate overnight. The next day, complete the recipe.

Variation

Braised Carrots with Black Olives: Substitute $\frac{1}{2}$ cup (125 mL) chopped black olives, preferably kalamata, a particularly pungent Greek variety, for the capers

Braised Carrots with Capers

This dish is simplicity itself and yet the results are startlingly fresh.

• **Small to medium (2 to 4 quart) slow cooker**

2 tbsp	extra virgin olive oil	25 mL
12	large carrots, peeled and thinly sliced	12
12	cloves garlic, thinly sliced	12
$\frac{1}{2}$ tsp	salt	2 mL
$\frac{1}{2}$ tsp	freshly ground black pepper	2 mL
$\frac{1}{2}$ cup	drained capers	125 mL

1. In slow cooker stoneware, combine oil, carrots, garlic, salt and pepper. Toss to combine.

2. Cover and cook on Low for 6 hours or on High for 3 hours, until carrots are tender. Add capers and toss to combine. Serve immediately.

Tips

Winter squash, such as butternut, are a great winter vegetable because they keep well without being refrigerated. Slow simmering maximizes the sweetness of this vegetable and creates a creamy texture.

If you are halving this recipe, be sure to use a small (1½ to 2 quart) slow cooker.

Parmesan-Laced Butternut Squash with Toasted Walnuts

If you're preparing a big dinner and want to get at least one dish out of the way, here's a perfect way to cook squash. Basically, it braises in its own juices, producing a beautifully flavored result. The hint of thyme is a perfect complement, the Parmesan adds lovely creaminess, and the toasted walnuts add great texture along with flavor.

- **Small to medium (2 to 4 quart) slow cooker**
- **Large sheet of parchment paper**

6 cups	cubed (½ inch/1 cm) peeled butternut squash (about 1 medium) (see Tips, left)	1.5 L
1 tbsp	melted butter or vegan alternative	15 mL
1 tbsp	brown sugar	15 mL
½ tsp	dried thyme	2 mL
½ tsp	salt	2 mL
½ tsp	cracked black peppercorns	2 mL
¼ cup	water	50 mL
¼ cup	freshly grated Parmesan or vegan alternative	50 mL
2 tbsp	toasted chopped walnuts	25 mL

1. In slow cooker stoneware, combine squash, butter, brown sugar, thyme, salt and peppercorns. Drizzle water over top and toss to combine. Place a large piece of parchment over the squash, pressing it down to brush the food and extending up the sides of the stoneware so it overlaps the rim.

2. Cover and cook on Low for 6 hours or on High for 3 hours, until squash is very tender. Lift out the parchment and discard, being careful not to spill the accumulated liquid into the stoneware. Using a wooden spoon, mash squash until desired consistency is achieved. Stir in Parmesan. Transfer to a serving bowl and garnish with walnuts. Serve hot.

Can Be Halved

Tips

Use 2 cups (500 mL) dried lima beans, cooked and drained (see Basic Beans, page 239) or 4 cups (1 L) rinsed, drained canned lima beans. If you're using frozen lima beans, they do not need to be pre-cooked but they should be thawed before using.

If you are halving this recipe, be sure to use a small ($1\frac{1}{2}$ to $3\frac{1}{2}$ quart) slow cooker.

Cheesy Butterbeans

Serve these tasty beans as part of a multi-course meal or add a salad and enjoy them as a light main course.

- **Small to medium (2 to 4 quart) slow cooker**

4 cups	cooked lima beans (see Tips, left)	1 L
1	can (28 oz/796 mL) diced tomatoes, drained, $\frac{1}{2}$ cup (125 mL) of the juice set aside	1
$\frac{1}{2}$ cup	chopped green onions	125 mL
1 tsp	salt	5 mL
	Freshly ground black pepper	
1	green bell pepper, chopped	1
1 cup	shredded old (aged) Cheddar cheese	250 mL

1. In slow cooker stoneware, combine beans, tomatoes, $\frac{1}{2}$ cup (125 mL) tomato juice, green onions, salt, and black pepper, to taste.

2. Cover and cook on Low for 6 hours or on High for 3 hours, until hot and bubbly. Stir in green pepper and cheese. Cover and cook on High for 20 minutes, until pepper is tender and cheese is melted.

Creamy Mexican Beans

Tips

I recommend making this in a small slow cooker to ensure that there is enough liquid to cover the beans.

Use ½ cup (125 mL) dried lima beans, cooked and drained (see Basic Beans, page 239) or 1 cup (250 mL) rinsed, drained canned lima beans. If you're using frozen lima beans, they do not need to be pre-cooked but they should be thawed before using.

Because there are tomatoes in the sauce, which will toughen beans during cooking, dried lima beans should be cooked before being added to this recipe.

Be sure the cream cheese is very soft before you add it to the slow cooker. Otherwise, it will take too long to melt.

Make Ahead

Complete Step 1. Cover and refrigerate for up to 2 days. When you're ready to cook, complete the recipe.

This rich side dish also does double duty as a main course. Serve it over rice or another grain, with a green salad for a delicious light meal.

- **Small (approx. 2 quart) slow cooker (see Tips, left)**

1 tbsp	oil	15 mL
2	onions, finely chopped	2
4	cloves garlic, minced	4
1 tsp	dried oregano	5 mL
1 tsp	cracked black peppercorns	5 mL
1 tsp	salt	5 mL
1	can (19 oz/540 mL) tomatoes, drained and coarsely chopped	1
1 tbsp	finely chopped drained oil-packed sun-dried tomatoes	15 mL
1 cup	vegetable broth	250 mL
1 cup	cooked lima beans (see Tips, left)	250 mL
4 oz	cream cheese, softened and cut into 1-inch (2.5 cm) squares	125 g
2	jalapeño peppers, seeded and minced	2

1. In a skillet, heat oil over medium heat. Add onions and cook, stirring, until softened, about 3 minutes. Add garlic, oregano, peppercorns and salt and cook, stirring, for 1 minute. Stir in tomatoes, sun-dried tomatoes and broth and bring to a boil. Transfer to slow cooker stoneware.

2. Add beans. Cover and cook on Low for 6 hours or on High for 3 hours. Stir in cream cheese and jalapeño peppers. Cover and cook on High for 15 minutes, until cheese is melted and mixture is hot and bubbly.

Slow-Cooked Sunchokes

Serves 6

Vegan Friendly

Can Be Halved

Tips

Sunchokes vary dramatically in size and shape, and their configuration determines how quickly they will cook. This recipe was tested with particularly large chokes. After cooking for 3 hours on High, they were still a bit chewy, which is how I like them. If your chokes are smaller or if you prefer the final result to be softer, adjust the cooking time accordingly.

If you prefer, peel the chokes before cooking, placing them in a bowl of acidulated water as they are peeled to prevent browning. If you're not peeling them, be sure to scrub them gently under running water before cutting.

If you are halving this recipe, be sure to use a small ($1\frac{1}{2}$ to 2 quart) slow cooker.

Sunchokes, also known as Jerusalem artichokes, are knobby-looking tubers native to North America that begin appearing in farmers' markets in the northeast in the early fall. They are crunchy and sweet-tasting and remind me of water chestnuts, although they are often mashed and served as a replacement for potatoes. In this treatment, they are tossed in olive oil and cooked with a minimum amount of moisture, which retains their wonderful nutty flavor.

- **Small ($1\frac{1}{2}$ to 3 quart) slow cooker**

4 cups	cubed (about 2 inches/5 cm) sunchokes (see Tips, left)	1 L
2 tbsp	extra virgin olive oil	25 mL
	Salt and freshly ground pepper	
	Finely chopped fresh parsley or chives	

1. In slow cooker stoneware, combine sunchokes and olive oil. Toss to coat sunchokes well. Cover and cook on High for 3 hours, until chokes are just tender. Season to taste with salt and pepper and garnish liberally with parsley.

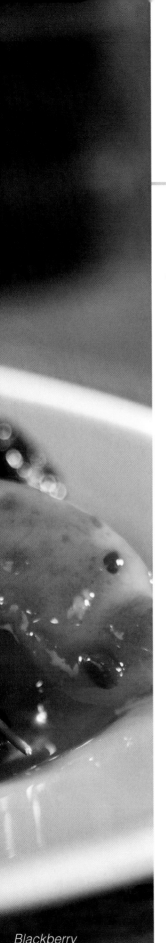

Desserts

*Blackberry
Peach Cobbler*

Tips

If you're making this when fresh fruit is out of season, you can substitute 2 cans (each 14 oz/398 mL) sliced peaches, drained, for the fresh and use an equal quantity of frozen blackberries, thawed.

If you are halving this recipe, be sure to use a small (1½ to 2 quart) slow cooker.

Blackberry Peach Cobbler

This recipe is an adaptation of one that appeared in the now-defunct Gourmet *magazine. It's an absolutely mouth-watering dessert for late summer, when these luscious fruits are at their peak. The advantage of making it in the slow cooker, rather than in the oven, is that you can be doing other things while it cooks to perfection.*

- **Medium (approx 3½ quart) slow cooker**
- **Lightly greased slow cooker stoneware**

4	peaches, peeled and sliced (see Tips, left)	4
3 cups	blackberries (see Tips, left)	750 mL
¾ cup	granulated sugar	175 mL
1 tbsp	cornstarch	15 mL
1 tbsp	freshly squeezed lemon juice	15 mL

Topping

1½ cups	all-purpose flour	375 mL
2 tsp	baking powder	10 mL
1 tsp	grated lemon zest	5 mL
½ tsp	salt	2 mL
½ cup	cold butter, cut into 1-inch (2.5 cm) cubes	125 mL
½ cup	milk	125 mL

1. In prepared stoneware, combine peaches, blackberries, sugar, cornstarch and lemon juice. Stir well. Cover and cook on Low for 4 hours or on High for 2 hours.

2. *Topping:* In a bowl, combine flour, baking powder, lemon zest and salt. Using your fingers or a pastry blender, cut in butter until mixture resembles coarse crumbs. Drizzle with milk and stir with a fork until a batter forms.

3. Drop batter by spoonfuls over hot fruit. Cover and cook on High for 1 hour, until a toothpick inserted in the center comes out clean.

Tips

Mascarpone is an Italian cream cheese. It is decadent and delicious and makes a wonderful treat.

Use sweetened or unsweetened coconut in this recipe, whichever you prefer.

Rhubarb-Mascarpone Crumble with Coconut

If you grow rhubarb in your garden and want to make something other than pie, try this easy-to-make dessert. The combination of coconut in the topping and mascarpone with the fruit adds deep richness to what is fundamentally a very simple dessert. I like to serve small portions and top with a scoop of vanilla ice cream.

- **Medium to large (3½ to 5 quart) slow cooker**
- **Lightly greased slow cooker stoneware**

6 cups	chopped (2 inches/5 cm) rhubarb (about 12 stalks)	1.5 L
²/₃ cup	mascarpone (about 4 oz/125 g) (see Tips, left)	150 mL
¼ cup	granulated sugar	50 mL
	Finely grated zest of 1 orange	
¼ cup	freshly squeezed orange juice	50 mL
1 tbsp	cornstarch	15 mL

Topping

½ cup	rolled oats	125 mL
½ cup	packed brown sugar	125 mL
¼ cup	whole wheat or all-purpose flour	50 mL
¼ cup	flaked coconut (see Tips, left)	50 mL
¼ cup	cold butter, diced	50 mL
	Vanilla ice cream	

1. In a bowl, combine rhubarb, mascarpone, sugar, orange zest, orange juice and cornstarch. Mix well and transfer to prepared stoneware.

2. *Topping:* In a separate bowl, combine rolled oats, brown sugar, flour, coconut and butter. Using two forks or your fingers, combine until crumbly. Spread over rhubarb mixture.

3. Place a clean tea towel, folded in half (so you will have two layers), over top of stoneware to absorb moisture. Cover and cook on High for 3 hours, until hot and bubbly. Serve with ice cream.

Tips

When buying Demerara sugar check the label to make sure you are getting pure raw cane sugar. Some brands are just refined sugar in disguise.

If you are halving this recipe, be sure to use a small ($1\frac{1}{2}$ to 2 quart) slow cooker.

Toffee Apple Crisp

This is simply a slightly decadent version of a classic old-fashioned dessert. Instead of sweetening the apples with mere sugar, they are coddled in a luscious butterscotch sauce. Lovely on its own, divine with a dollop of vanilla ice cream.

- **Medium (approx. 4 quart) slow cooker**
- **Lightly greased slow cooker stoneware**

$\frac{1}{2}$ cup	raw cane sugar, such as Demerara or other evaporated cane juice sugar (see Tips, left)	125 mL
$\frac{1}{4}$ cup	butter	50 mL
$\frac{1}{4}$ cup	water	50 mL
Pinch	salt	Pinch
8	apples, peeled, cored and sliced	8
Topping		
$\frac{3}{4}$ cup	rolled oats	175 mL
$\frac{3}{4}$ cup	all-purpose flour	175 mL
$\frac{1}{2}$ cup	raw cane sugar, such as Demerara or other evaporated cane juice sugar	125 mL
$\frac{1}{4}$ tsp	salt	1 mL
$\frac{1}{4}$ tsp	ground cinnamon	1 mL
$\frac{1}{4}$ cup	butter, diced	50 mL

1. In a saucepan, combine sugar, butter, water and salt. Stir over low heat until sugar dissolves. Increase heat to medium and boil until slightly syrupy, about 1 minute, watching closely to ensure mixture doesn't boil over. Arrange apple slices over bottom of prepared stoneware and cover with syrup.

2. *Topping:* In a bowl, combine rolled oats, flour, sugar, salt and cinnamon. Stir well. Add butter and using two forks or your fingers, combine until crumbly. Spread over apple mixture.

3. Place a clean tea towel, folded in half (so you will have two layers), over top of stoneware. Cover and cook on High for 3 to 4 hours, until topping is nicely caramelized and mixture is hot and bubbly.

Serves 8

Vegan Friendly

Entertaining Worthy

Can Be Halved

Tips

If you are not using firm apples, watch closely to make sure they don't disintegrate into applesauce. Even so, they will taste delicious.

Depending upon the configuration of your slow cooker, you may need to add a bit more wine to ensure the apples are submerged.

If you are halving this recipe, be sure to use a small ($1\frac{1}{2}$ to 2 quart) slow cooker.

Wine-Poached Apples

This is a simple, but elegant dessert. I like to serve it cold with delicate cookies after a substantial meal.

● **Small (maximum 3½ quart) slow cooker**

8	firm apples, peeled, cored and quartered (see Tips, left)	8
2 cups	dry red wine (approx.) (see Tips, left)	500 mL
1 cup	granulated sugar	250 mL
1	piece (2 inches/5 cm) cinnamon stick	1
4	whole cloves	4
	Whipped cream or vegan alternative, optional	

1. Place apples in slow cooker stoneware. Add wine, sugar, cinnamon and cloves. Cover and cook on High for 2 hours, until apples are al dente. Transfer to a serving dish and chill thoroughly. Discard cinnamon and cloves. Serve plain or with whipped cream.

Tips

When buying nuts, be sure to source them from a purveyor with high turnover. Because nuts are high in fat (but healthy fat), they tend to become rancid very quickly. This is especially true of walnuts. In my experience, the vast majority of walnuts sold in supermarkets have already passed their peak. Taste before you buy. If they are not sweet, substitute an equal quantity of pecans.

I like the rich molasses taste and the more favorable nutritional profile of muscovado sugar, but light or dark brown sugar makes an acceptable substitute in this recipe.

If you are halving this recipe, you will need a smaller oval slow cooker (approx. 3 quart) that will comfortably accommodate 4 apples.

The Ultimate Baked Apples

These luscious apples, simple to make yet delicious, are the definitive autumn dessert. I like to serve these with a dollop of whipped cream, but they are equally delicious, and healthier, accompanied by yogurt or on their own.

● **Large (minimum 5 quart) oval slow cooker**

½ cup	chopped toasted walnuts (see Tips, left)	125 mL
½ cup	dried cranberries	125 mL
2 tbsp	packed muscovado or other evaporated cane juice sugar (see Tips, left)	25 mL
1 tsp	grated orange zest	5 mL
8	apples, cored	8
1 cup	cranberry juice	250 mL
	Vanilla-flavored yogurt or whipped cream or vegan alternative, optional	

1. In a bowl, combine walnuts, cranberries, sugar and orange zest. To stuff the apples, hold your hand over the bottom of the apple and, using your fingers, tightly pack core space with filling. One at a time, place filled apples in slow cooker stoneware. Drizzle cranberry juice evenly over tops.

2. Cover and cook on Low for 8 hours or on High for 4 hours, until apples are tender.

3. Transfer apples to a serving dish and spoon cooking juices over them. Serve hot with a dollop of yogurt, if desired.

Vegan Friendly

Entertaining Worthy

Tip

Apple cider differs from apple juice in that it is pressed juice that is unfiltered and has much more flavor. In this recipe, use naturally sweet cider, not the hard cider, which is fermented.

Ginger-Spiked Apple Cider Compote

If you've gone apple picking and are wondering what to do with all that luscious fruit you have on hand, try this deliciously different compote. It's very refreshing and, topped with whipped cream spiked with candied ginger, good enough to serve to guests.

- **Small to medium (2 to 3½ quart) slow cooker**

3 cups	apple cider (see Tip, left)	750 mL
½ cup	raw cane sugar, such as Demerara or other evaporated cane sugar	125 mL
2	slices (¼ inch/0.5 cm) peeled gingerroot	2
6	firm apples, peeled, cored and quartered	6
	Whipped cream or vegan alternative, optional	
	Finely chopped candied ginger, optional	

1. In slow cooker stoneware, combine apple cider, sugar and gingerroot. Add apples and stir well.

2. Cover and cook on High until apples are al dente, about 2 hours. Transfer into a serving dish and chill thoroughly. To serve, ladle into bowls and top with sweetened whipped cream spiked with candied ginger, if using.

Vegan Friendly

Entertaining Worthy

Tips

Because these oranges are unpeeled, I strongly recommend using organic produce.

If you prefer, substitute an equal quantity of any other orange-flavored liqueur, such as Triple Sec or Grand Marnier, for the Cointreau.

Oranges in Cointreau

This delightfully different dessert is so easy to make, yet sumptuous enough to satisfy even the most sophisticated palate. It's delicious topped with whipped cream, but I love to serve it as an oh-so-chic sundae, over vanilla ice cream or a complementary sorbet. Yum!

● **Small (approx. 2 quart) slow cooker**

1 cup	granulated sugar, divided	250 mL
6	oranges (preferably organic, see Tips, left), cut into $\frac{1}{4}$-inch (0.5 cm) slices, seeds removed	6
1	piece (2 inches/5 cm) cinnamon stick	1
2 tbsp	Cointreau (see Tips, left)	25 mL

1. Sprinkle $\frac{1}{4}$ cup (50 mL) of the sugar over the bottom of slow cooker stoneware. Arrange the orange slices on top in overlapping layers, burying the cinnamon stick in the center. Sprinkle the remaining sugar evenly over the oranges. Place a clean tea towel, folded in half (so you will have two layers), over top of stoneware to absorb moisture.

2. Cover and cook on High for 4 hours, until the liquid is syrupy and the fruit is soft. Discard cinnamon stick. Stir in Cointreau.

Tip

Like many fruits, apricots are often picked before they are fully ripe, in which case they tend to be bitter. Taste a small piece of fruit before cooking and if this is the case, adjust the quantity of sugar accordingly. If you are lucky enough to have lovely sweet apricots, use less.

Variation

Braised Peaches with Amaretto: Substitute 4 peaches for the apricots.

Apricots in Amaretto with Toasted Almonds

Serve this over your favorite vanilla or even coconut ice cream — it's the ultimate sundae. Make extra because there will be requests for seconds.

- **Small (approx. 2 quart) slow cooker**
- **Large sheet of parchment paper**

½ cup	granulated sugar (approx.)	125 mL
10	apricots, peeled, halved and pitted	10
1	piece (2 inches/5 cm) cinnamon stick	1
¼ cup	Amaretto liqueur	50 mL
	Ice cream, regular or vegan alternative	
¼ cup	toasted sliced almonds	50 mL

1. Sprinkle 2 tbsp (25 mL) of the sugar over bottom of stoneware. Arrange apricots on top, burying cinnamon stick in the middle. Sprinkle remaining sugar evenly over apricots. Place a large piece of parchment over the mixture, pressing it down to brush the food and extending up the sides of the stoneware so it overlaps the rim.

2. Cover and cook on High for 3 hours, until liquid is syrupy and fruit is tender. Lift out parchment and discard, being careful not to spill the accumulated liquid into the sauce. Add Amaretto and stir gently. Discard cinnamon stick. Serve over ice cream and garnish with almonds.

Vegan Friendly

Tip

In this recipe, fresh bread crumbs are far superior to the ready-made kind, which can be very dry. They are easily made in a food processor by removing the crust, if desired, cutting the bread into manageable chunks and then processing until the appropriate degree of fineness is achieved. Tightly covered, bread crumbs will keep for two or three days in the refrigerator.

Cherry-Spiked Pear Betty

As soon as local pears come into season, I'm chomping at the bit to make this delectable old-fashioned dessert. The cherry jam adds a hint of flavor and welcome color. It's amazing how delicious plain old bread crumbs become after being tossed with butter and cooked with simmering fruit.

- **Small to medium (2 to 3½ quart) slow cooker**
- **Lightly greased slow cooker stoneware**

2 cups	fresh bread crumbs	500 mL
⅓ cup	melted butter or margarine	75 mL
½ tsp	ground cinnamon	2 mL
¾ cup	granulated sugar	175 mL
1 tsp	finely grated lemon zest	5 mL
2 tbsp	freshly squeezed lemon juice	25 mL
3 tbsp	cherry jam	45 mL
1 tbsp	all-purpose flour	15 mL
6	pears, peeled, cored and quartered	6
	Vanilla ice cream, optional	

1. In a bowl, combine bread crumbs, melted butter and cinnamon. Stir well and set aside.

2. In a separate bowl, combine sugar, lemon zest, lemon juice, cherry jam and flour. Mix well. Add pears and gently toss until well coated with mixture.

3. In prepared slow cooker stoneware, layer one-third of bread crumb mixture, then one-half of pear mixture. Repeat layers of bread crumbs and fruit, then finish with a layer of bread crumbs on top. Place a tea towel, folded in half (so you will have two layers), over top of stoneware to absorb moisture. Cover and cook on High for 2½ hours, until bubbly. Serve with a dollop of ice cream, if using.

Vegan Friendly

Tip

For convenience, I don't specify that the pudding should be stirred while it is cooking, but an occasional stir after it has begun to cook will help to distribute the starch and aid thickening. If you prefer a slightly thicker result, after removing the pudding from the slow cooker, chill and stir several times before serving.

Wholesome Rice Pudding

It's hard to believe that this delicious dessert is also very nutritious. Made with milk and brown rice, it is the kind of dish your great grandmother might have made over a wood-burning fire — simple, flavorful, an ultimate comfort food.

- **Small (maximum 3 1/2 quart) slow cooker**
- **Lightly greased slow cooker stoneware**

3/4 cup	short-grain brown rice	175 mL
1/2 cup	raw cane sugar, such as Demerara or other evaporated cane juice sugar	125 mL
1 tsp	ground cinnamon	5 mL
4 cups	whole milk or rice milk	1 L

1. In prepared slow cooker stoneware, combine rice, sugar and cinnamon. Stir well. Add milk and stir again. Cover and cook on High for 4 hours, until rice is tender and pudding is creamy. Stir well and transfer to a serving bowl. Let cool slightly and stir again or cover and refrigerate until ready to serve.

Entertaining Worthy
Can Be Halved

Tips

Long-grain white rice can be successfully used in this recipe, but the pudding will not be as creamy as one made with Arborio rice. You can also produce a creamy result using short-grain brown rice.

Use 1 cup (250 mL) fresh pitted cherries in place of the dried cherries, if desired. Or substitute an equal quantity of dried cranberries, instead.

For a richer pudding, use half milk and half cream.

If you are halving this recipe, be sure to use a small (1½ to 2 quart) slow cooker.

Rice Pudding with Cherries and Almonds

This family favorite is delicious enough to serve at an elegant dinner party. Spoon into crystal goblets and serve warm or cold.

- **Small (approx. 3 quart) slow cooker**
- **Lightly greased slow cooker stoneware**

¾ cup	granulated sugar	175 mL
½ cup	Arborio rice (see Tips, left)	125 mL
¼ cup	dried cherries (see Tips, left)	50 mL
2 tbsp	ground almonds	25 mL
1 tsp	grated lemon zest	5 mL
Pinch	salt	Pinch
4 cups	milk (see Tips, left)	1 L
2	eggs	2
1 tsp	almond extract	5 mL
	Toasted sliced almonds, optional	
	Whipped cream, optional	

1. In prepared slow cooker stoneware, mix together sugar, rice, cherries, almonds, lemon zest and salt. In a large bowl, whisk together milk, eggs and almond extract, and stir into rice mixture.

2. Cover and cook on High for 4 hours, until rice is tender and pudding is set. Serve warm, garnished with toasted almonds and whipped cream, if desired.

Tips

Thai black sticky rice is available in Asian markets. In this recipe do not use Chinese black rice or Italian black Venere rice, neither of which is sticky.

If you are halving this recipe, be sure to use a small (1½ to 2 quart) slow cooker.

Coconut-Laced Black Sticky Rice Pudding

Rice pudding is a dessert I love and this is one of my favorite versions. It's exotic and delicious. You can serve it if you're looking for a Wow! factor but it's so easy to make you can also prepare it for a personal treat.

- **Small (2 to 3½ quart) slow cooker**
- **Lightly greased slow cooker stoneware**

4 cups	water	1 L
1½ cups	Thai black sticky rice (see Tips, left)	375 mL
½ cup	raw cane sugar, such as Demerara or other evaporated cane juice sugar	125 mL
1 tsp	vanilla or almond extract	5 mL
Pinch	salt	Pinch
1	can (14 oz/400 mL) coconut milk	1
	Chopped mangos, peaches or bananas, optional	
	Chopped toasted almonds or toasted shredded coconut, optional	

1. In a small saucepan, bring water and black sticky rice to a vigorous boil over high heat. Boil for 2 minutes. Stir in sugar, vanilla and salt, then transfer to prepared slow cooker stoneware.

2. Cover and cook on Low for 8 hours or overnight or on High for 4 hours. Stir well, then stir in coconut milk. To serve, ladle into bowls and top with chopped fruit and/or toasted almonds, if using.

Vegan Friendly

Entertaining Worthy

Tip

When buying Demerara sugar check the label to make sure you are getting pure raw cane sugar. Some brands are just refined sugar in disguise.

Blueberry Oatmeal Pudding Cake

If you like to feel righteous while enjoying dessert, here's one that fits the bill. Loaded with nutritious whole-grain oatmeal and antioxidant-rich blueberries, this upside down pudding cake is so good you'll want seconds. The next time you're cooking oatmeal, make extra so you'll be able to prepare this dessert.

- **Small to medium (2 to 4 quart) slow cooker**
- **Lightly greased slow cooker stoneware**

2 cups	blueberries, thawed if frozen	500 mL
2 tbsp	raw cane sugar, such as Demerara or other evaporated cane juice sugar	25 mL
2 tbsp	melted butter or margarine	25 mL
1 tbsp	finely grated orange zest (1 orange)	15 mL
1 cup	raw cane sugar, such as Demerara or other evaporated cane juice sugar	250 mL
1/3 cup	butter or margarine, diced	75 mL
1	egg	1
1/4 tsp	salt	1 mL
3/4 cup	all-purpose flour	175 mL
1/3 cup	freshly squeezed orange juice (about 1)	75 mL
1 cup	cooked oatmeal	250 mL
	Vanilla ice cream or vegan alternative, optional	

1. In prepared slow cooker stoneware, combine blueberries, 2 tbsp (25 mL) sugar, melted butter and orange zest. Toss well and set aside.

2. In a bowl, beat 1 cup (250 mL) sugar and diced butter until light and creamy, about 3 minutes. Add egg and beat until incorporated. Mix in salt. Gradually add flour, alternating with orange juice and making two additions and beating until blended. Stir in oatmeal. Spread over blueberries.

3. Place a clean tea towel, folded in half (so you will have two layers), over top of stoneware to absorb moisture. Cover and cook on High for 3 hours or until a tester inserted in center of cake comes out clean. To serve, slice and invert on plate. Top with a scoop of vanilla ice cream, if using.

Vegan Friendly

Entertaining Worthy

Tip

I always use unsalted butter, not only because I prefer the taste, but also because it allows me more control over the quantity of salt I consume.

Ginger-Spiked Apricot and Almond Pudding Cake

This delectable dessert is a wonderful combination of tastes and textures. It is superb served with a dollop of vanilla ice cream.

- **Medium (approx. 4 quart) slow cooker**
- **Lightly greased slow cooker stoneware**

1 cup	all-purpose flour	250 mL
1 tsp	baking powder	5 mL
1/2 tsp	salt	2 mL
2 cups	raw cane sugar, such as Demerara or other evaporated cane juice sugar, divided	500 mL
1/4 cup	butter or margarine, softened	50 mL
1	egg	1
1 tsp	vanilla extract	5 mL
1/2 cup	white chocolate chips	125 mL
1/2 cup	chopped dried apricots	125 mL
1/2 cup	chopped toasted almonds	125 mL
1/4 cup	finely chopped candied ginger	50 mL
1 cup	boiling water	250 mL
	Vanilla ice cream or vegan alternative, optional	

1. In a bowl, mix together flour, baking powder and salt.

2. In a separate bowl, beat 1 cup (250 mL) of the sugar with butter until creamy. Add egg and vanilla and beat until incorporated. Add dry ingredients, mixing just to blend. Stir in chocolate chips, apricots, almonds and ginger. Spread mixture evenly in prepared slow cooker stoneware.

3. In a heatproof measuring cup, combine remaining 1 cup (250 mL) sugar and boiling water. Stir until sugar dissolves. Pour over batter (do not mix). Cover and cook on High for 2 1/2 to 3 hours, until a toothpick inserted in the center of the cake comes out clean. Serve hot topped with a dollop of vanilla ice cream, if using.

Tip

An English pudding basin is actually a simple rimmed bowl, most often white, that comes in various sizes. The rim is an asset because it enables you to make a seal with foil, which can be well secured with string or an elastic or silicone band. A small ovenproof mixing bowl can be substituted.

Sticky Toffee Pudding with Butterscotch Sauce

If you like the flavor of butterscotch, which I do, you'll love this deliciously decadent dessert. It's basically a moist cake studded with bananas and dates and topped with a lip-smackin' sauce. Expect to have seconds.

- **Large (approx. 5 quart) oval slow cooker**
- **6-cup (1.5 L) pudding basin (see Tip, left), baking or soufflé dish, lightly greased**

1½ cups	all-purpose flour	375 mL
2 tsp	baking powder	10 mL
1 tsp	salt	5 mL
½ cup	butter, softened	125 mL
¾ cup	raw cane sugar, such as Demerara or other evaporated can juice sugar	175 mL
2	eggs	2
1 tsp	vanilla extract	5 mL
½ cup	milk	125 mL
1 cup	chopped pitted soft dates, such as medjool (see Tip, opposite)	250 mL
2	bananas, diced	2

Butterscotch Sauce

1 cup	raw cane sugar, such as Demerara or other evaporated cane juice sugar	250 mL
¼ cup	butter	50 mL
½ cup	heavy or whipping (35%) cream	125 mL
2 tbsp	brandy or 1 tsp (5 mL) vanilla extract	25 mL
	Ice cream or whipped cream	

1. In a bowl, mix together flour, baking powder and salt.

2. In another bowl, beat butter and sugar until smooth and creamy. Add eggs and beat until incorporated. Stir in vanilla. Alternately beat in flour mixture and milk in two additions, mixing well after each addition. Stir in dates and banana. Pour batter into prepared dish. Cover basin tightly with foil and secure with a string. Place in slow cooker stoneware and pour in enough boiling water to reach 1 inch (2.5 cm) up the sides of the dish. Cover and cook on High for 3 to 4 hours, until a toothpick inserted in center of pudding comes out clean.

I love the flavor of dates, but they are hard to chop because they are so sticky. Wiping the blade of your knife with a bit of olive oil or spraying it with cooking spray helps with this problem.

3. *Butterscotch Sauce:* Just before the pudding is ready, preheat broiler. In a saucepan, combine sugar, butter and cream. Bring to a boil over medium heat, stirring constantly. Reduce heat and boil gently until sugar dissolves, about 5 minutes. Stir in brandy.

4. Unmold pudding onto an ovenproof platter or baking dish and pour half the sauce over top. Broil until topping is bubbly, about 2 minutes. Serve immediately, with remainder of sauce on the side and topped with ice cream.

Buttermilk Lemon Sponge

Tip

Because you are using the zest of a lemon as well as its juice, I strongly recommend using organic produce.

Here's the perfect dessert: creamy yet light, with just a hint of lemon. As it cooks, the egg whites separate into a "sponge" layer, leaving a velvety version of lemon curd on the bottom. Serve this warm, with a mound of fresh berries on the side. Blueberries, raspberries, strawberries — whatever is in season — make an ideal finish.

- **Large (minimum 5 quart) oval slow cooker**
- **4-cup (1 L) baking dish, greased**

½ cup	granulated sugar	125 mL
2	eggs, separated	2
⅔ cup	buttermilk	150 mL
1 tbsp	finely grated lemon zest	15 mL
3 tbsp	freshly squeezed lemon juice	45 mL
¼ cup	all-purpose flour	50 mL
¼ tsp	salt	1 mL

1. In a bowl, whisk sugar and egg yolks until smooth. Whisk in buttermilk, lemon zest and lemon juice. Whisk in flour and salt until blended.

2. In a separate bowl, beat egg whites until stiff. Gently fold into lemon mixture to make a smooth batter. Spoon into prepared dish. Cover with foil and secure with string.

3. Place dish in slow cooker stoneware and pour in enough boiling water to reach 1 inch (2.5 cm) up the sides of the dish. Cover and cook on High for 2½ hours, until a toothpick inserted in the center of the pudding comes out clean.

Tip

An English pudding basin is actually a simple rimmed bowl, most often white, that comes in various sizes. The rim is an asset because it enables you to make a seal with foil, which can be well secured with string or an elastic or silicone band. A small ovenproof mixing bowl can be substituted.

Double Chocolate Mousse Cake

If you are cooking for chocoholics and looking for something they will appreciate, look no further. This rich dark chocolate cake, which resembles a flourless chocolate cake, is topped by a chocolate sauce. The double hit will send them into raptures.

- **Large (minimum 5 quart) oval slow cooker**
- **6-cup (1.5 L) pudding basin or bowl, greased (see Tip, left)**

4 oz	unsweetened chocolate, chopped	125 g
1 cup	milk	250 mL
¼ cup	butter	50 mL
⅓ cup	granulated sugar	75 mL
2	eggs, separated	2
½ tsp	vanilla extract	2 mL
¼ cup	all-purpose flour	50 mL

Chocolate Sauce

2 tbsp	unsweetened cocoa powder	25 mL
¾ cup	water, divided	175 mL
¼ cup	granulated sugar	50 mL
2 tbsp	cornstarch	25 mL
2 oz	bittersweet chocolate, chopped	60 g
1 tbsp	butter	15 mL
1 tsp	vanilla extract	5 mL

1. In a saucepan, combine unsweetened chocolate and milk. Heat over low heat, stirring gently, until chocolate melts and mixture is smooth. Remove from heat and set aside.

2. In a bowl, beat butter and sugar until creamy. Add egg yolks, beating until incorporated. Beat in vanilla. Alternately beat in flour and chocolate mixture in two additions, beating well after each addition.

3. In a clean bowl, with an electric mixer, beat egg whites until stiff. Gently fold into chocolate mixture. Pour into prepared dish. Cover tightly with foil and secure with string or an elastic band. Place dish in slow cooker stoneware and add boiling water to reach 1 inch (2.5 cm) up the sides of the dish. Cover and cook on High for 2½ hours, until a tester inserted in center of pudding comes out clean.

4. *Chocolate Sauce:* In a saucepan, combine cocoa powder and $\frac{1}{4}$ cup (50 mL) of the water. Stir until smooth. Add remaining water, sugar and cornstarch. Cook over low heat, stirring constantly and making sure mixture does not come to a boil, until thickened, about 10 minutes. Remove from heat. Stir in chocolate, butter and vanilla, until chocolate melts and mixture is blended.

5. To serve, invert pudding onto a round serving plate. Drizzle chocolate sauce over top. Serve immediately.

Tips

Stout is a type of dark beer, the best-known example of which is Guinness.

Be sure to use a large saucepan when heating the stout and molasses. Once you add the baking soda it will foam up and spill over the sides if your pot isn't large enough.

Cocoa powder has a tendency to clump. Sifting ensures more-even blending.

Stout-Laced Chocolate Gingerbread

This is a particularly delicious version of old-fashioned gingerbread. The stout and molasses combine to produce a robustly flavored cake that screams for a dollop of vanilla ice cream. The combination is nirvana.

- **Large (approx. 5 quart) slow cooker**
- **Lightly greased slow cooker stoneware**

1 cup	stout (see Tips, left)	250 mL
1 cup	light (fancy) molasses	250 mL
1 tsp	baking soda	5 mL
2 cups	all-purpose flour	500 mL
¾ cup	unsweetened cocoa powder, sifted	175 mL
2 tsp	ground ginger	10 mL
1 tsp	ground cinnamon	5 mL
1 tsp	baking powder	5 mL
3	eggs	3
1 cup	raw cane sugar, such as Demerara or other evaporated cane juice sugar	250 mL
½ cup	sour cream	125 mL
½ cup	melted butter	125 mL
1 cup	finely chopped crystallized ginger	250 mL
	Vanilla ice cream	

1. In a large saucepan, whisk together stout and molasses. Bring to a boil over medium heat. Remove from heat and whisk in baking soda. Let cool.

2. In a bowl, combine flour, cocoa powder, ground ginger, cinnamon and baking powder. Mix well, and make a well in the center.

3. In a separate bowl, beat eggs. Add sugar, sour cream and melted butter and beat until blended. Stir in crystallized ginger. Add stout mixture and mix well. Pour half of mixture into the well in the dry ingredients and mix well. Add remainder and mix just until blended. Transfer to prepared stoneware.

4. Place two clean tea towels, folded in half (so you will have four layers), over top of stoneware to absorb moisture. Cover and cook on High for 2½ to 3 hours or until a tester inserted in center of cake comes out clean. Serve with vanilla ice cream.

Tip

I make this in a 7-inch (18 cm) square baking dish. The cooking times will vary in a differently proportioned dish.

Variation

Blueberry Custard Cake: Substitute blueberries for the raspberries.

Raspberry Custard Cake

This is a delicious old-fashioned dessert. As it cooks, the batter separates into a light soufflé-like layer on top, with a rich, creamy custard on the bottom. Serve hot or warm, accompanied by a light cookie, with whipped cream on the side, if desired.

- **Large (minimum 5 quart) oval slow cooker**
- **6-cup (1.5 L) baking or soufflé dish, lightly greased**

1 cup	granulated sugar, divided	250 mL
2 tbsp	butter, softened	25 mL
4	eggs, separated	4
	Grated zest and juice of 1 lemon	
Pinch	salt	Pinch
¼ cup	all-purpose flour	50 mL
1 cup	milk	250 mL
1½ cups	raspberries, thawed if frozen	375 mL
	Confectioner's (icing) sugar	

1. In a bowl, beat ¾ cup (175 mL) of the sugar with butter until light and fluffy. Beat in egg yolks until incorporated. Stir in lemon zest and juice. Add salt, then flour and mix until blended. Gradually add milk, beating to make a smooth batter.

2. In a separate bowl, with clean beaters, beat egg whites until soft peaks form. Add remaining ¼ cup (50 mL) of sugar and beat until stiff peaks form. Fold into lemon mixture, then fold in raspberries.

3. Pour mixture into prepared dish. Cover tightly with foil and secure with a string. Place dish in slow cooker stoneware and add boiling water to reach 1 inch (2.5 cm) up the sides. Cover and cook on High for 3 hours, until the cake springs back when touched lightly in the center. Dust lightly with confectioner's sugar and serve.

Tip

An English pudding basin is actually a simple rimmed bowl, most often white, that comes in various sizes. The rim is an asset as it enables you to make a seal with foil, which can be well secured with string or an elastic or silicone band. A small ovenproof mixing bowl can be substituted.

Plum Pudding

Here's a lightened-up version of a traditional holiday favorite. Allow a week for the mixed pudding to soak in the refrigerator. I like to serve this warm, with a simple lemon sauce or store-bought lemon curd, but if you're a traditionalist, hard sauce works well, too. Don't worry about leftovers. It reheats well and, with a steaming cup of tea makes a great snack, taking the chill off even the most blustery winter day.

- **Large (minimum 5 quart) oval slow cooker**
- **6-cup (1.5 L) pudding basin (see Tip, left), baking dish or soufflé dish, lightly greased**

1 cup	seedless raisins	250 mL
½ cup	finely chopped mixed candied fruit	125 mL
2 tbsp	chopped candied orange peel	25 mL
2 tbsp	chopped candied ginger	25 mL
	Finely grated zest of 1 orange	
	Finely grated zest of 1 lemon	
½ cup	brandy or dark rum (approx.)	125 mL
¾ cup	all-purpose flour	175 mL
¾ cup	fine dry white bread crumbs	175 mL
2 tbsp	ground toasted blanched almonds	25 mL
1 tsp	ground cinnamon	5 mL
¾ tsp	baking powder	3 mL
¼ tsp	freshly grated nutmeg	1 mL
¼ tsp	salt	1 mL
¾ cup	packed brown sugar	175 mL
½ cup	butter or margarine, softened	125 mL
2	eggs	2
2 tbsp	light (fancy) molasses	25 mL

1. In a bowl, combine raisins, candied fruit, orange peel, candied ginger and orange and lemon zests. Add brandy and stir well. Set aside for 1 hour.

2. In a separate bowl, mix together flour, bread crumbs, almonds, cinnamon, baking powder, nutmeg and salt. Set aside.

3. In a clean bowl, beat brown sugar and butter until creamy. Beat in eggs and molasses until incorporated. Stir in soaked fruit mixture. Add flour mixture and mix just until blended. Spoon batter into prepared dish. Cover tightly with plastic wrap and let stand in refrigerator for 1 week, spooning additional brandy over the top two or three times in 1-tbsp (15 mL) increments.

4. Remove plastic wrap. Cover tightly with foil and secure with a string. Place dish in slow cooker stoneware and pour in enough boiling water to reach 1 inch (2.5 cm) up the sides of the dish. Cover and cook on High for 4 hours, until a toothpick inserted in the center of the pudding comes out clean. Serve hot.

Tip
You'll need about
12 sandwich cookies to
make this quantity of
crumbs. Place cookies, with
filling, in a food processor
fitted with a metal blade
and process until fine
crumbs are achieved.

Chocolate-Spiked Peanut Butter and Banana Cheesecake

If you're a fan of chocolate and peanut butter, this combination verges on sinful. Start with a small slice. You can always have seconds.

- **Large (minimum 5 quart) oval slow cooker**
- **7-inch (18 cm) well-greased springform pan or 7-inch (18 cm) 6-cup (1.5 L) soufflé dish, lined with greased heavy-duty foil**
- **Food processor**

Crust

1¼ cups	chocolate sandwich cookie crumbs (see Tip, left)	300 mL
3 tbsp	melted butter	45 mL

Cheesecake

1 lb	cream cheese, cubed and softened	500 g
½ cup	packed brown sugar	125 mL
2	eggs	2
½ cup	creamy peanut butter	125 mL
¼ cup	sour cream	50 mL
4 oz	semisweet or bittersweet chocolate, melted	125 g
2	bananas, thinly sliced	2

1. *Crust:* In a bowl, combine cookie crumbs and melted butter. Mix well. Press mixture into the bottom of prepared pan. Place in freezer until ready to use.

2. *Cheesecake:* In a food processor fitted with a metal blade, combine cream cheese and brown sugar. Process until smooth. Add eggs, peanut butter and sour cream and process until combined. Add melted chocolate and pulse until blended.

3. Arrange banana slices evenly over crust. Pour cheesecake mixture over top and cover tightly with foil. Place pan in slow cooker stoneware and pour in enough boiling water to reach 1 inch (2.5 cm) up the sides of the pan. Cover and cook on High for 3 to 4 hours or until edges are set and center is slightly jiggly. Remove from slow cooker and chill thoroughly before serving.

Blueberry White Chocolate Cheesecake with Chocolate Cookie Crust

Deliciously decadent. What more can I say? Serve small slices, but expect that the urge to have seconds will be hard to resist.

- **Large (minimum 5 quart) oval slow cooker**
- **Food processor**

Crust

1¼ cups	chocolate sandwich cookie crumbs (see Tips, left)	300 mL
3 tbsp	melted butter	45 mL

Cheesecake

1 lb	cream cheese, cubed and softened	500 g
½ cup	granulated sugar	125 mL
2	eggs	2
1 tsp	vanilla extract	5 mL
1 tsp	grated lemon zest	5 mL
2 tbsp	freshly squeezed lemon juice	25 mL
6 oz	white chocolate, chopped	175 g
¼ cup	heavy or whipping (35%) cream	50 mL
1 cup	blueberries, thawed if frozen	250 mL

1. *Crust:* In a bowl, combine cookie crumbs and melted butter. Mix well. Press mixture into bottom of prepared pan. Place in freezer until ready to use.

2. *Cheesecake:* In a food processor fitted with a metal blade, combine cream cheese and sugar. Process until smooth. Add eggs, vanilla, lemon zest and lemon juice and process until combined.

3. In a saucepan over low heat, combine white chocolate and cream. Cook, stirring, until melted. Add to cheese mixture and process until smooth.

4. Arrange blueberries evenly over crust. Pour cheesecake mixture over top and cover tightly with foil. Place pan in slow cooker stoneware and pour in enough boiling water to reach 1 inch (2.5 cm) up the sides of the pan. Cover and cook on High for 3 to 4 hours or until edges are set and center is slightly jiggly. Remove from slow cooker and chill thoroughly before serving.

Index

Library and Archives Canada Cataloguing in Publication

Finlayson, Judith
The vegetarian slow cooker : over 200 delicious recipes / Judith Finlayson.

Includes index.
ISBN 978-0-7788-0239-6

1. Vegetarian cookery. 2. Electric cookery, Slow. I. Title.

TX837.F555 2010   641.5'636   C2009-906685-8